THE
SAFETY
TRAP

THE
SAFETY
TRAP

**A Security Expert's
Secrets for Staying Safe
in a Dangerous World**

Spencer Coursen

ST. MARTIN'S PRESS
NEW YORK

First published in the United States by St. Martin's Press,
an imprint of St. Martin's Publishing Group

www.stmartins.com

The Library of Congress Cataloging-in-Publication Data is available upon request.

Book design by Michelle McMillian

ISBN 978-1-250-25814-4 (hardcover)
ISBN 978-1-250-25815-1 (ebook)

Our books may be purchased in bulk for promotional, educational, or business use.
Please contact your local bookseller or the Macmillan Corporate and
Premium Sales Department at 1-800-221-7945, extension 5442, or
by email at MacmillanSpecialMarkets@macmillan.com.

First Edition: 2021

10 9 8 7 6 5 4 3 2 1

To all the helpers, healers, and heroes.
May we always outnumber those who try to do harm.

Contents

[PART III: PUTTING THREAT MANAGEMENT INTO PRACTICE]

[PART IV: PERSONAL THREAT ASSESSMENT CHECKLISTS]

PART I

Getting Started

"The Safety Trap: The false sense of security that occurs when fear has abated, but risk remains."

—*Spencer Coursen, founder, Coursen Security Group. © 2018*

Introduction

Being a protector is a craft I have honed my entire life. It has been part
of a lifelong pursuit. As a big brother to three younger sisters, I helped
to keep my family safe. As a combat veteran, I defended my country. As
a protective agent, I traveled the world keeping dignitaries safe, and as a
private security consultant, I spent many years keeping celebrities, sports
stars, models, and more free from harm. I loved my job. I was well skilled,
and for a while, I could not imagine myself doing anything else.

In 2012, the tragedy at Sandy Hook was a turning point for me. My
own childhood was wrought with fear. I longed for safety and comfort. I
craved the confidence of a strong presence to tell me it would all be over
soon. I'd wished there were someone—or something—I could turn to, to
help me to better protect myself. And all of those emotions came flooding back to me as I watched those children be rushed from their school.
You could see the fear and uncertainty on their faces. Each of them with
their hands up in innocent surrender. My heart cried out for them. I felt
for their parents, the educators too.

Both of my parents were teachers. I have friends and family who still
teach. Some have risen through the ranks to become administrators,
principals, and superintendents. All of them are phenomenal educators
but none of them were professional protectors. I was. And now they were
calling me. All of them afraid. All of them worrying if their school was

next. And with so many others living in fear, I wanted to do everything I could to help.

That was when I made the decision to go into business for myself. I founded Coursen Security Group because I wanted to help others to protect themselves. My global experience had provided me with a finely tuned aperture to help others identify and then eliminate the threats in their everyday lives. I wanted my skill set, which had been predominantly reserved for the top one percent of the population, to be made readily available to the other ninety-nine. Why? Because very few people will ever know the luxury of having their own protective detail, but every single one of us deserves to be protected.

The threats to our everyday lives may evolve with the times, but the risks we are most likely to face have for the most part remained the same. Which means that whenever our world is inundated by chaos and confusion, the single most valuable deliverable is the assurance of well-being. A certainty of safety. More often than not, the best advice is to simply trust your instinct. People already have permission to protect themselves. They simply want to be reminded. They want to know it's okay for them to do what is necessary. When things break bad, everyone wants to begin their return to normalcy. They want to get back to how things were as soon as possible. Even more so, they want to make sure that what happened before won't happen again. Some may seek a second opinion. They want to be reassured. They want whoever is across the table, on the other end of the phone, the author of that email, to be the same guy with the nice suit and easy smile they met at the onset of their concern. The one who didn't judge when they first revealed whatever breach of safety or embarrassing betrayal of trust brought them here in the first place. This is not to say that some concerns do not escalate into crisis. Sometimes additional efforts need to be employed: insights acquired, tradecraft deployed, outcomes ensured.

My firm helps good people make bad things better. One of the ways I help is by assessing the policies, practices, and procedures of an organization to identify the vulnerabilities most likely to be targeted by those who wish to do harm. Over the years, I came to discover that while most of my clients already had what they needed to stay safe, each and every organization faced the same set of consequential concerns. From private families to high-net-worth individuals and from small-town schools to global business enterprises, everyone seemed to be falling into the same kinds of "trappings."

Of course, once these vulnerabilities were brought to light, they all seemed to have the same "aha!" moment of realization that would immediately help them to reduce risk and prevent violence. Happy as they were to have these hazards brought to their attention, they were equally dismayed that had they only known what to look for, their crisis could have been completely avoided. Had they only been more aware, they could have been better prepared.

As my clients would often tell me, they—like so many of their peers—had a completely antiquated view of safety. They viewed safety to almost be something of a guarantee. A provision provided by the powers that be. Then, after finding themselves in the throes of crisis or—even worse—targeted by violence, they realized they didn't have a firm grasp of what safety really was, let alone how it could be achieved.

After helping to return their lives to normal, many clients would often tell me how they would reflect upon my reports as a reference guide. They would often cite key takeaways during their security-related decision-making. My reports had become something of a force multiplier for them. Something they would reread to help them stay safe long after their concern had been resolved. Something they would take home with them and then apply to their everyday lives. The idea for a book came from them. This book is a compilation of my experiences, my outlook, and the protective strategies I have accumulated over a lifetime devoted to keeping some of the world's most influential people protected. I wrote this book to provide some solace of hope to those like my younger self, who prayed each night for a protector to come and save him.

These pages will help to empower, educate, and inform everyone from the second grader to the CEO with the same everyday safeguards that have helped me to succeed. What's more, these insights are tailor-designed to be user-friendly. They can be learned, shared, and applied on the very same day this book is read. And once familiarized, they will stay with you forever.

What Is the Safety Trap?

Safety traps are everywhere. They hide in plain sight, camouflaged by our own willingness to believe that once our fear has been abated, risk is reduced as well. This has become our most misguided behavior, because all too often, when our vigilance goes down, our risk goes up. Do you want to know the one truth that, regardless of circumstance or scenario, has always been proven to be an accurate predictor of risk? Well, here is the simple truth that you may not want to believe, but I promise you is 100 percent factual: *you are the most in danger when you feel the most safe.* Crazy but true! To put it another way—sometimes feeling safe is the most dangerous thing we do. This paradox is what I call the Safety Trap.

The Safety Trap is a phrase I coined to help my clients understand the inherent risks that hide behind our own false sense of security. Anxiety over safety plagues our society, because we tend to treat the symptom of fear without curing the underlying cause for concern. How many times have we seen this play out in our schools? A tragic shooting happens where children are left dead; a community is left in turmoil. Then what happens next? Students march for peace, parents demand action, and politicians promote their plans. A few weeks later: fears die down; the news cycle moves on; everything goes back to how it was. Nothing changes. We simply wait for it to happen again. This is the Safety Trap. Our fears have abated, but the risk remains.

Instead of addressing concerns head-on, ignorance has become our new normal. Which is why I was not at all surprised to read the findings of a national study sponsored by the American Psychiatric Association which revealed Americans are in the middle of an epidemic rise in anxiety. Survey results showed that in 2018, a staggering 40 percent of people reported feeling more anxious than they did a year ago. That's a huge spike, and it follows an already large 36 percent increase in anxiety from 2016 to 2017. Naturally, we are worried about a variety of things— finances, politics, relationships. But do you know what gives us the most anxiety? *Safety.* In fact, 68 percent of survey respondents were most fearful they would not be able to keep themselves or their families safe.

What's perhaps most disheartening about these findings is that this is the safest we've been . . . *ever*. In stark contrast to what our fears and anxiety may belabor us to believe, the truth is, our society gets safer and safer every day. In fact, if you could be born at any time in history, *right now* is the absolute best time to be alive. It's not even a close call. Today's medical advancements are at an all-time high, medicine has never been more effective, transportation has never been safer, technology has never been more advanced, health care has never been more readily available, food has never been more abundant, the crime rate has never been lower, life expectancy has never been higher, even the murder rate is lower than it has ever been. By all relative measures, this is the absolute safest time to be alive. So why is our anxiety over our inability to stay safe at an all-time high?

Here is your first Protective Takeaway: our inability to keep ourselves and our loved ones safe is at an all-time high because our understanding of what safety requires is at an all-time low.

So Why Are We All So Afraid?

Perhaps the most important reason is that while violent crime in America has decreased, the risk of mass violence has increased. According to a mass-shooting database maintained by the *Washington Post,* ever since June 17, 2015, which was when a white supremacist killed nine people at a Bible study in Charleston, South Carolina, four or more people have been killed in a single incident every forty-seven days. As I write this on October 10, 2019, the most recent mass violence occurred just four days ago, October 6, 2019, when four were killed and five were wounded at the Tequila KC Bar in Kansas City—proving once again that, more than at any other time in our history, we are more at risk in those places where we once felt safest. School shootings. Workplace violence. Stadium bombings. Street parade attacks. Bar and restaurant violence. All of them have disrupted our certainty of safety.

Another significant factor is that today's age of social media and the twenty-four-hour news cycle force us to be much more intimate with gruesome realities. Gone are the days of hearing a story about something bad happening just one time on the evening news. Today, more than at any point in our history, we are bombarded by notifications that relay—in gory detail—whatever tragedy du jour has been most recently updated with videos, photos, vantage points, insights, takeaways, and opinions outlining just how violent the world outside your door can be. Talking heads will debate who's to blame, and then with sensational sound bites bait the audience to stay tuned to learn if they might be next . . . right after these commercial messages.

It is no wonder anxieties are so high. Anxiety is literally being crafted and curated, then delivered to us via our phones. But there is something more: these bombardments of concern also serve to remind the overwhelming majority of us just how ill prepared we are—on an individual level—to participate in our own protection.

Another big contributor to why our anxiety is so high is that we—you, me, all of us—have become too comfortable with being comfortable. We expect our safety to be as certain as the water flowing out of the faucet. We respond to safety breaches with the same reaction as when the power goes out: "This isn't supposed to happen!" But then power is restored, and our lives return to normal. After a few moments of discomfort, we simply hope it won't happen again . . . right up until the same cycle repeats.

How Did This Happen?

History has not been kind to the human race. In fact, until a few hundred years ago, it was a bloodbath earmarked by only modest advancements in human control over our environment. For most of our history, we were easily outmatched by brutal environmental conditions and an animal kingdom that considered us easy prey. Our evolutionary successes were humble at best. It wasn't really until the Industrial Revolution that our survival was no longer considered to be under a direct threat by the natural world. Our society has only become safer every day since. Which means that today, despite the news reports of random violence, terror, crime, and catastrophe, it is likelier than ever for us to die of old age, warm in our beds, surrounded by those who love us. But this also means that the number-one risk to our safety is now ourselves. Our reticence regarding risk has allowed us to fall into our own false sense of security, and it is killing us.

Regrettably, the unrealized trade-off of living in a much safer world meant that we would inevitably become weaker. As risks were reduced, we stopped thinking about the things that could harm us. We started avoiding those things that made us feel uncomfortable. We stopped looking for the hazards. We stopped participating in our own protection. Our society has grown too uncomfortable with anything that isn't guaranteed to be comfortable. And as our own recent history has proven, when a society stays comfortable too long, the society becomes weak. And a weak society will always be exploited by the evils of bad men.

This is what scares us most: we have realized, almost too late, that we can no longer afford to live in a world where we simply hope that nothing will happen and then solely rely on the first responders to save us once something does.

We have allowed ourselves to become so effective at responding to crisis that we have all but shunned our responsibilities to prevent these tragedies from arising in the first place. The unforgiving truth is that these incidents are not happening in a vacuum. In almost every single incident of harm, there were observable, recognizable, and preventable pre-incident indicators that were either avoided, discarded, or ignored until the obviousness of what was about to happen was realized too late to do any good.

Our society has come to view safety as a public resource—a commodity—a "guarantee" in the collective agreement. We expect our safety to be an undeniable certainty in our everyday lives. We have police, we have firefighters, first responders, the FBI, and the CIA—all of them out here helping to prop up this big umbrella of protection. We all figure: *I pay my taxes, so I should be protected.* But that's not how the system was meant to work. There was never meant to be an overarching canopy ensuring public safety and personal protection. It can't work that way.

But there we are, going through our lives feeling calm, comfortable, and safe right up until the moment something terrible happens—a bombing, a school shooting, a home invasion—and then we are forced to once again confront the reality of just how vulnerable we really are.

Another part of the problem is the improper framing of safety as a commodity. We have forgotten what it truly means to be safe, and we have no real idea how safety is achieved. And when we need it most, we are dumbstruck to realize that safety is not something you can go out and buy at the store. You can't go to Whole Foods and pick it up from the shelf. You can't buy it in bulk from a wholesaler. You can't put it on layaway to surprise your kids at Christmas. It can't be ordered with overnight delivery by Amazon Prime. Safety in not a deliverable. Safety is a membership. And if you want to reap its rewards, you have got to participate. Safety is a lot like your fitness regimen. You can carry your gym's membership card in your wallet, and you can pay the monthly dues, but that's not going to be enough to keep you physically fit. Some of us may be luckier than others, and some of us may have been blessed with better genes, but if you want to get fit, you're going to have to sweat. Effort is required. Individual results may vary.

All of this only serves to pour fuel on an already big bonfire of anxiety. The truth is most of us are not at all prepared for something like this to happen. Not mentally. Not physically. Not emotionally. So when harm does happen, there's a huge disconnect between our belief that we are safe and the reality that we are not. If you think about it, our assumption that we are safe means that we are very rarely required to—or even think about being required to—participate directly in our own protection.

This is a losing scenario. Safety is a perishable skill, and many of us are out of practice. We have forgotten what it takes to stay safe. We haven't had to do it for so long. This realization only adds to our anxiety—only adds to the strain. And it's not that we have forgotten how to participate. Most of us don't even want to participate. And in those instances where we are forced to do so, it requires coercion to comply.

Think about this: seat belts save lives. There is no debate, but most of us don't wear our seat belts to save our own lives. We wear seat belts to stop the annoying chime from growing louder and more frequent until we finally comply with the requirement of participating in our own protection. Would we wear them without the warning bell? We need to reframe the expectation of what it means to be safe, and we need to relearn how true safety is achieved. Safety is not a destination; it is an ever-expanding journey. And it requires our constant attention.

Why Is Feeling Safe So Dangerous?

I mentioned earlier that feeling safe is actually what puts people in the most danger. To understand why this is true, I need to talk about two related psychological terms: *pattern recognition* and *inattentional blindness*.

Pattern recognition is grounded in the "if this, then that" decision-making process that happens on a near-immediate and often subconscious level. One could argue that the very purpose of intelligence is prediction: the comprehension that a particular sequence of events is likely to lead to the next most logical outcome, and therefore, I'm going to be ready to do X, Y, and Z as a result.

One of the best examples of pattern recognition is what happens when we're driving. Let's say you are cruising down the highway, when all of a sudden, the brake lights on the car one hundred yards ahead begin to illuminate. Then the car fifty yards ahead does the same thing. Then the car thirty, twenty, ten, seven, five—and in less than a second, and without any conscious action telling our body what to do, we realize our own foot has already moved from the accelerator to the brake and is participating in the process of slowing down our own car, helping to keep us safe.

But this wasn't a natural instinct your first time behind the wheel. This practice had to learned. It had to be practiced. For pattern recognition to work, we have to be willing to see and be mindful enough to be aware of the risks around us. We have to have participated in the practice long enough that we feel confident in our ability to prevent tragic outcomes and ensure our own safety. That's right: safety takes practice, and this book is going to show you exactly what you need to do to get back in safety shape.

Inattentional blindness refers to people's inability to detect unexpected objects when they aren't paying attention. The scientists who coined the term did a study where they asked people to pay attention to a cross that appeared on a computer screen. They wanted them to judge which arm of the cross was longer. After a few trials, an unexpected object—like a brightly colored rectangle—would appear on the screen. What the scientists discovered was that the participants, busy paying attention to the cross, very often failed to notice the new object—even when it appeared right in the center of their field of vision. However, when participant attention was not on the cross, the new item on-screen was very readily noticed.

Here's another example: Say you are driving down the road, paying attention to your mirrors, your speed, the other cars. Suddenly, as if from out of nowhere, a family of deer appears on the highway. You slam on your brakes, but it's too late—you can't avoid hitting one of them. How did this happen? Why didn't you notice them in time? The answer comes down to inattentional blindness: quite simply, you didn't see the deer because you didn't expect to see the deer. This is *not* an anomaly. This happens all the time. Even in our own homes when we walk barefoot in the kitchen: we don't stub our toes on the things we notice; we stub our toes on the things we don't.

As you can see, inattentional blindness can lead to a breakdown of our pattern recognition working the way it should. When you don't expect danger, you simply fail to see the signs that something bad is about to happen. But the signs are always there, and staying safe is about training yourself to see them.

Seeing the Patterns of Safety

It's funny how some patterns are so clear yet others elude us. We don't fear the patterns we know well. We don't shy away from being aware of the things we are prepared to handle. But we are tragically fearful of those things we experience the least and are most ill prepared to manage.

Let's describe a scenario where you would be forced to race through an open space in a heavy box with a limited field of view. You would then have to manually maneuver this box from point A to point B while dozens of other boxes zig and zag all around you. This would be a terrifying ordeal for anyone to endure. Imagine if this were your first time: your pulse would rise, your hands would sweat, your vision would narrow, your breathing would be shallow, your fine motor function would deteriorate. You would basically be in a state of complete and total panic. Unless we called it *driving*. Then we would spend our entire childhood waiting for the day we were old enough to get our driver's licenses and finally get out onto the road.

Think about it: there are thousands of automobile accidents every single day, but most of us aren't afraid to drive, because we are aware of the risks we are most likely to face and we are capable and prepared to safeguard against them. We know the pre-incident indicators to look for: the brake lights up ahead, the flashing lights of emergency responders, the orange cones of construction, the yellow lights of yield.

What if I told you that almost everything in your life that could harm you also has the same pre-incident indicators? What if I told you the same signs that warn you of a potential car accident could also warn you of a school or workplace shooting? And what if I also told you that if you chose to not be aware of these warning signs, you would be just as likely to be caught in the cross fire of workplace violence as you would by ignoring your rearview mirror—where an irrationally careless and speeding driver is swerving in and out of lanes and coming up fast behind you.

I hope you're paying attention now, because this is where this book comes in.

Let us use school shootings as an example here, especially since it is something that many parents are worried about these days. The truth of the matter is that while there may be subtle nuances, almost every school shooting is identical to the one before it. Each of these acts has the same ingredients as the others: you have a child who feels ignored, alienated from their parents and rejected by their classmates, who doesn't feel included in anything, who has acted out in the classroom, who has expressed some kind of harmful ideation to themselves or others, or who has expressed thoughts of suicide. Also common is a very recent emotional trigger like a divorce, a bad breakup, the loss of a friend, or a death in the family. Finally, you have a child who, with every online expression and with every interpersonal communication, all but cries out for help but most certainly cries out in pain.

This is why after every incident of such violence, you have those who come forward saying how aware they were that something wasn't right. Who knew or at the very least thought that something was wrong.

These pre-incident indicators are known. Their likelihood of harm is real. And all too often, those warnings were ignored. But society loves nothing more than to shirk responsibility. We want it to be the responsibility of someone else. We don't want to participate. And so the very real consequence of denial enters into the decision-making process. We willingly promote our own inattentional blindness because we don't want to see the problem. And this only bolsters the breakdown in our pattern recognition. The signs were there. We should have seen them. Instead, we did not. Once more ensnared by the Safety Trap—we feel too safe to notice the very real danger around us.

A Framework for Moving Forward

Can you choose to ignore the reality around you and pretend the world is all roses and butterflies? You most certainly can. But why would you choose to sabotage your own safety? Why would you choose to put yourself at more risk? Why would you choose to accept more harm because you don't want to leave your comfort zone? Let me tell you something: safety is achievable; protection is possible. You just have to be willing to take the first step. And if you do, if you take that first step, I promise you will realize something about yourself you may have never otherwise revealed: you are smarter than you think, stronger than you know, and more resilient than you realize.

Is there real fear out there? Yes, there is. Is there a burden of anxiety holding us down? Unfortunately, there is. The good news is, there is a remedy for the fear we are all feeling. There are practical and real-world ways for you to reduce and remove your anxieties. This book will help. After all, no one fears that which they know well. These remaining chapters will help to shine a bright light into those dark corners of chaos and confusion and will illuminate the hazards that hide in plain sight. My strategies for staying safe will soon be yours to behold, and once added to your arsenal of familiarity, will help to ensure the certainty of safety for everyone involved.

PART II

THE SAFETY TRAPS

AVOIDANCE

What Happened

So many of us want to believe that if we just ignore the uncomfortable thing long enough, it will somehow solve itself. The TV star was hoping this same approach would work for her.

When the first email came into her in-box, the TV star thought it was from someone she knew. What she found when she opened the message was nothing like what she was expecting. The video began to play all on its own. She could hear the man pleasuring himself to an array of her videos and photographs that he had opened as individual windows across his oversize computer screen. She couldn't see his face, but she could see the outline of his reflection in the monitor as his arm moved up and down in a violent gesture. She could hear his voice moaning in pleasure. She told me when she heard him first moan out her name, she slammed the laptop closed so hard she was afraid she'd shattered the screen. The next day, another email arrived. Another one the day after that. By the end of the week, she had at least a dozen. She left all of them unopened. She didn't want to see what they were. She didn't want to have to deal with yet another creep who had somehow managed to learn her personal email address. So she just left them unopened—a blue dot next to a bold font causing her more and more anxiety every time she checked her mail. By the middle of the next week, there were at least twenty.

When her assistant came into work the next morning, she asked her to delete them. She also asked her to create a rule so that they would be automatically deleted without her ever having to see them. Her hope was that by simply ignoring them, the issue would somehow resolve itself. So that was what she did. For her, out of sight was out of mind. And she was right. As she would later reveal to me, within a few weeks, she had completely forgotten about the incident in its entirety—for a while, anyway. Six weeks later, the TV star was filming a scene on a downtown city street in Lower Manhattan. There was a man lingering behind the yellow caution tape that separated the film set from the public street. She didn't know what it was about him. Maybe it was the way he was standing there all alone. She felt he was looking at her, and she couldn't be sure, but when their eyes met, she was almost certain he was motioning for her to come over.

Between one of the takes, a production assistant came up to her saying that a man said he knew her and had brought her "that thing that she asked for." The TV star was confused. She'd met so many people in this line of business that she honestly couldn't remember whom she had met and whom she had not. Still, she didn't want to offend anyone. When she asked the production assistant which man she meant, her stomach turned to knots when the PA pointed to the man she had been weirded out by all morning. She made the mistake of looking over at him, because he was definitely looking at her now. He could see the production assistant had just pointed him out. And now he was waving, energetically waving, as if he had something of utmost importance to tell her.

The TV star began to slowly walk over to where the man was standing behind the tape. She could tell that he was pulling something from a messenger bag he had slung over his shoulder. It was an envelope. A large envelope.

When I asked her later why she had decided to walk over to him, she told me it was the envelope. She thought he was a process server, and she thought it better to be done with it here and now rather than having this guy try to track her down for the rest of the day. But as she got closer, she realized she had made a terrible mistake.

I was able to watch the rest of the encounter thanks to the TV star's assistant. Her assistant was used to filming interactions with fans to use as content on the TV star's social media accounts, so when the assistant noticed the TV star walking up toward the crowd, she quickly came up behind her and started filming.

"Oh my god! Oh my god! Oh my god!" the man said as the TV star approached.

"Hi," she said. "So good to see you."

You could see in the video that the TV star's entire demeanor changed as soon as she realized this man was definitely *not* a process server. She literally stopped in her tracks a few feet from the yellow caution tape. She wasn't being sued after all. This was something else entirely—she just didn't know what it was.

"I made this for you." The man was jittery with excitement. Watching the video, you could see he was nervous. His left hand was clutching the envelope, a tight grip more than a light hold. His right hand was up by his chest. He kept wiping it on his sweatshirt. The man let out an exasperated sigh as if he were building up the courage to say what came next. "I knew you would want me to find you here."

The TV star stood there confused. "I'm sorry . . . ?" she said with a bit of exaggeration in her voice. She had clearly misread this entire situation, and her mind was racing to figure out a way to get herself out of this awkward engagement.

The man was now holding out the envelope over the tape for her to take it from him. But as her hand reached out to take it from him, he pulled it back.

"But I don't understand why you've been ignoring me. Why did you stop reading my emails?"

I watched the tape as her face flushed white. She froze. It was at this moment she realized this was the man from the reflection on the computer screen. This was the man who had sent that disgusting video. And then just kept sending . . . and sending.

The man's demeanor had also changed. It had escalated from one of excitement to one of agitation. He was aggressively shaking the envelope at the TV star. "Is it so I would bring you this? Is that what you wanted me to do?"

Her assistant stopped filming and tried to make eye contact with the security guard who was pouring himself a soda at the craft services table. When she was unsuccessful, she keyed her radio and asked for assistance.

But her boss was frozen. Unmoving. And she hadn't been the only one filming. Others in the crowd had been filming this too.

So the PA did the only thing she could think to do.

As the security guard began to make his way over to where they were standing, the assistant walked up and grabbed the envelope from the man's hand, with a very polite "Thank you!" She took her boss by the waist, turned her around, and began walking her back toward the set.

My phone rang a few hours later.

The solution phase began almost immediately. It didn't take long to discover that everything needed to prevent this from happening in the first place had been there all along. The TV star had simply chosen to look the other way. She had hoped that ignoring the problem would make it disappear. Regrettably, she was wrong.

Fortunately, the assistant didn't set up the email filter rule the right way. Instead of the communications being forwarded for deletion, they were sent to a junk mail folder. Which meant that, with her permission, we were able to retrieve and review all the communications she had decided to deny were being sent. Some of them were more of what we expected to find: graphic and explicit. Others were confessional. Some were delusional admissions of personal beliefs.

Equally as expected, each new communication escalated in intensity and ideation. The more recent ones clearly communicated his investment of time, effort, and energy to stage a confrontation. He had purchased new clothes. He had bought a plane ticket. He knew where she was going to be filming, and he very clearly communicated he was making the trip to see her so they could finally move forward with being together.

Was this the TV star's fault? Did she ask for this? Did she want for this to happen? Of course not. No one ever asks for these kinds of things to happen. But could this concern have been de-escalated months earlier? Could this entire interaction have been managed toward a much more favorable outcome that would have all but prevented a one-on-one confrontational encounter? Yes. Unquestionably, yes! Was the crisis involving the TV star able to be resolved? Yes, of course it was. The TV star's entire crisis could have been averted had the initial concern been confronted instead of avoided.

So what is it about our individual proclivity for making things worse? Why is it that we sabotage our own success? Why do we choose these self-defeating strategies? And more importantly, how can we learn to retrain our brains so that we can recognize when we are choosing to avoid our concerns and instead face them head-on?

PROTECTIVE TAKEAWAY

If you choose to ignore today's concerns, you will be forced to confront tomorrow's crisis.

PROTECTIVE AWARENESS

Avoidance Impacts All of Us

Let me be clear: avoiding concerns is not something unique to the rich and famous. Avoidance is employed by all of us. How many of us have seen the blinking light flash on our dashboard warning us that we need an oil change or that our tire pressure is low? How many of us then simply mute the warning and hope it either never comes back or—at the very least—comes back at a "more convenient" time?

Why do we do this? Why is it that we choose to avoid those things that make us uncomfortable? Why is it that we almost always choose to defer present pain for future torment? Part of the reason is that we never learned to be comfortable with being uncomfortable. We never learned how to accept the reality of adverse conditions and then work through them. Part of the problem stems from how we were socialized. Avoidance served us well when we were children. Back when we didn't have the skills or the experience to properly address a concern, when we didn't have the power to change our predicament, we avoided confrontation because we wanted to wait until our parents were there to help. We believed we couldn't do it on our own. And in doing so, we were convinced we required someone bigger, stronger, and smarter than we were to arbitrate on our behalf. Why? Because our life experience had not yet provided us with the confidence to realize that we were smarter than we knew and had more resilience than we realized.

Unfortunately, this practice stayed with us as we got older. In doing so, we trained our brains to believe those things we'd learned to avoid should always be avoided. Then our brains began to believe that we should be afraid of these things. We should avoid them because we feel incapable of confronting them. But this is wrong. This is false. You can confront them. You are capable. Even if you don't have the skills on hand right now, you will be surprised by how quickly you can learn them along the way.

We have a choice! We can cling to the problem-solving strategies that helped to make us feel safe as children, or we can choose to confront the concerns as they come to us. We can wait until someone either makes us contend with our concern or holds our hand as we baby-step our way through the solution phase, or we can choose to confront these concerns on our own terms, when they are first presented and most manageable to resolve.

Avoidance Behaviors

Avoidance behaviors are any actions a person may take to escape difficult thoughts and feelings. Which is not to say that all avoidance is bad. More often than not, I would argue that avoidance is a good thing. If used correctly, avoidance is nothing more than a temporary safeguard that helps us to get past the point of an unwelcome discomfort, shock, or insight, which—if given the choice—we would much rather not be forced to endure. It is only when we use avoidance to deflect dealing with the impact of the real-world influences that we do the most damage to not only ourselves but to those around us as well.

No One Fears That Which They Do Well

It is also important to take note of the difference between having anxiety and feeling anxious. The moments just before a performer takes the stage or an athlete takes the field may have the same initial physiological symptoms of anxiety: elevated heart rate, increased breathing, irritability, sweating—but these are just the mind preparing the body for performance. These are survival stressors that any of us would feel before going in front of any large audience. The very same symptoms are very likely to be felt by any of us just before giving a toast at a wedding or a speech in front of our peers.

The difference between being anxious and having anxiety is that when we are anxious, the symptoms subside once we find our flow, once we realize that we know what we are doing. That we are qualified. That we are prepared. That we are doing it well. That the audience in front of us is accepting of our contribution, and in turn, we feel a certain sense of gratification. We may even feel a sense of satisfaction from applause—the reward we receive by providing the function we have been called on to perform.

The anxiousness subsides because we have accepted the reality before us, and we worked hard to hold on to the power that those fears would have otherwise tried to steal from our grasp. But instead of turning away from the challenge, we turned to stare it down. We made a choice to accept and to act. Choosing instead to cut off the fuel that would have otherwise allowed that anxiousness to grow into anxiety.

Avoidance Behaviors Prevent Us from Learning New Skills

One of the reasons we all love scary movies so much is because we get to experience the rush of adrenaline that comes from feeling fear without any of the consequences of harmful action. When we are in the movie theater, our subconscious minds know that we are safe and turn off the fight-or-flight response. But in doing so, it still allows for our conscious minds to have a physiological response to external stimuli—to what we are seeing on the screen.

This is what I like to refer to as *protective projection*. Protective projections allow our minds to play out how our bodies will perform. It is a safety strategy that the mind does all on its own when it realizes that we may someday find ourselves in a similar circumstance—regardless of how likely that scenario may actually be. The practice is not dissimilar to how sports psychologists train athletes to "visualize the win." When athletes create a mental image of how they want to perform in reality, they can then use this technique to "intend" a desired outcome. Protective projections are very similar. It is the mind mapping out the actions the body will need to perform to ensure our own safety. With each new protective projection we allow our minds to perceive, another safety strategy is added to our problem-solving tool kits. But if we close our eyes, if we look away, if we avoid those very experiences at the very moment we are supposed to be having a lifesaving takeaway, we have just sabotaged our own success for handling a future concern.

You may believe it is perfectly fine to avoid looking at the movie screen when the bad guy enters the house on-screen, because the stakes of doing so are so low. And you may be right. But would it also be fine to avoid the bad guy who had just entered *your* house in the real world, when the stakes are now so high? I'm sure you would say it was not.

What if instead of turning away when the movie got scary, you enjoyed the moment for what it was but also allowed for your mind to learn what to do, and what not to do, based on what the characters did on-screen? What if instead of closing your eyes, you reflected upon what you would do in that situation?

Understand the Difference Between "Gut Instinct" and "Anxiety"

Gut instincts are how we feel *right now*. They are based on our highly evolved survival strategy of pattern recognition, which helps us to predict outcome. Pattern recognition is about interpreting, recognizing, and employing those pre-incident indicators of good, those pre-incident indicators of bad, those pre-incident indicators of concern . . .

Because once you know what to look for, they become impossible to miss.

Think about the pattern of occurrences that happen just after a toddler falls but before they belt out their scream of pain and shame: a little child, just learning how to walk, then hits their head. You hear the thud as they plop down to the ground. Then they go quiet. But then they look up at you. They see your face is concerned as you rush over to them. But before you can get there, their eyes go wide, and their bottom lip begins to quiver. Then their face wrinkles. They raise their fist. They breathe in deeply. Their eyes close. Their head tilts back, and then . . .

Did you hear what came next? Did you hear their scream inside your head? Did you recognize that it was coming? Of course you did. We all did.

But you were not born knowing this. These insights were learned. These recognitions had to be realized. Those pre-incident indicators had to be programmed into your brain. Those safeguards had to be accepted, practiced, and employed in their proper place so often that they became second nature. Just like when we learned to drive a car, where once, we had to consciously tell ourselves there was a stop sign up ahead and move our foot from the accelerator to the brake. Give yourself enough time to slow down. Years later, those same step-by-step practices are realized and implemented as second nature. They happen on a subconscious level. But if you're the passenger in the car, and you see the stop sign up ahead, and the driver isn't taking the necessary precautions, it's very likely you'll have a gut instinct you are going to crash.

The difference between this gut instinct and anxiety would be if every time you saw a stop sign, you had the feeling you were going to crash because of that one time the driver didn't slow down their car on time.

Our "Filtered Forecast"

How many times have we been out and about, then seen something cool and tried to capture a photo? But by the time we reached into our pocket, pulled out our camera, turned it on, opened the app, aimed the camera, and then snapped the picture, the moment was gone.

No one would want their security camera to perform that way.

I have a security camera on my front door that records motion. To do this effectively, the camera is always on; it just doesn't do anything until it notices something worthwhile. But it's always in a constant state of readiness. It's always watching, and then, as soon as there is even the slightest change in a shadow, it begins to record.

It is the only way it can do the job I need it to do. If it performed this function in any other way—if it was always dormant and had to wait for something to happen before it fired up, focused, and only then started to record, the event it was meant to capture may have been missed altogether.

So instead, like our minds, it's always in a passive observation mode. Every sixty seconds, it recycles. Deletes what was never there. Waits another sixty seconds for something to happen.

But like our minds, it knows what patterns to look for. It doesn't look for someone to come into the frame. Instead, it looks for the precursors that forecast someone is likely to be coming into the frame. And like our minds, it is smart enough to know what those forecasts look like. A change in the light. A change in a reflection. A change in the shadows on the floor.

Like our own under-ability to perform with our phones, if the camera had to wait for something to happen before it started to record, it would be too late.

Our Everyday Safety Strategies Are No Different

These everyday patterns of recognition, where our subconscious minds see everything but only focus on what is necessary to help keep us safe from harm, is a process I call our *filtered forecast*—these are the learned and recognizable precursors of attention that click our consciousness into action when moments matter most.

This is an intentional act. It is a learned survival strategy. It is just not a conscious act. It is different from breathing (we don't have to learn how to breathe), but it is a very similar lifesaving and life-ensuring practice of self-preservation that once we learn, we do without thought.

Think about it like this: when we first learn how to drive, we have to tell our foot to move off the accelerator and onto the brake when we want to slow down the car. Watch a new driver do this. They will literally look down at their foot as they tell it what to do. But once we get it down, that motion is ours forever. We never make that conscious decision to do it again. We just do it. In fact, when moments matter most, we do it without ever realizing we have done so.

We do this all the time. In fact, we couldn't unlearn it if we wanted to any more than we could keep ourselves from listening for the thunder after the bright flash of lightning bolts across the sky.

We Have Become Accustomed to Learning What Certain Warning Signs Mean

The sky turns gray. It's probably going to rain.

The sun begins to set. It's going to be dark soon.

Dad slams the door. He's probably upset with Mom.

Mom says, "Everything is fine." She's probably upset with Dad.

The warning signs of harm are no different. It's just that most of us are inattentively blind to what we would otherwise want to look for. But I promise you this. If you could anticipate the screams of that child from before, you can anticipate the precursors of harm. You have to be willing to learn what to look for.

PROTECTIVE PREPAREDNESS

The following are some best practices to keep you from falling into the Safety Trap of Avoidance:

1. **Audit yourself with honesty.** At the end of the next few days, take a few moments and reflect upon the number of times you chose to employ avoidance behaviors instead of contending with the concern head-on. Write them down. What stands out? Think about how you could have handled that situation in a way that puts a period on the end of the ordeal instead of an ellipsis. What could you have done to put an end to that conversation or interaction instead of contributing to its continuance?

2. **Practice mindfulness.** Avoidance is the opposite of acceptance. Mindfulness helps us to be more present and accept our reality. When we practice mindfulness, we allow ourselves to take a big-picture view of our current circumstances, our joys, and our concerns. Once we are able to accept our concern as a reality, we are able to give that concern the recognition it deserves. With that recognition, we are able to give credence to our willingness to work toward having that concern resolved.

3. **Start small. Build strong.** Anyone who has ever opened up a box from IKEA knows the feeling of being overwhelmed by the task at hand. From the moment our eyes dart from hieroglyphic-style instructions to the massive amounts of materials that fall to the floor, we are all but certain there is no way this debris could ever become a dresser. So what do we do? Do we give up? Of course not. We start small. We build strong. One instruction at a time. One piece at a time. Until eventually, the last screw is inserted, the last fastener is tightened, and we are left feeling the sense of accomplishment that the daunting task is not only behind us but that we have renewed our confidence in our ability to overcome. Course correcting our self-sabotaging strategies of avoidance is no different. The key to correcting any avoidance behavior is to baby-step our way right up to whatever we are avoiding until we take back the power that was ours to begin with. Whatever you are avoiding, I promise you it can be resolved in simple, easy-to-manage, easy-to-master steps. You just have to be honest about the reality of the concern, break it down, take a deep breath, choose the easiest step first, and then get yourself started.

4. **Recruit local assets.** No one is saying you have to go down this road alone. Talk to a friend or a family member about what you've been avoiding and how you plan to take back your control. If it's an interpersonal concern, talk over what you want to say. How can you make your point more articulate? How can you make your statement more impactful? How can you ensure that your audience knows that when you are done talking, it is

the end of the conversation and not the beginning of a negoti-ation? Practice your speech. Practice your mannerisms. Practice ignoring whatever comeback they may voice in retaliation. And perhaps, even most importantly, practice how to turn your back and walk away.

5. **Never avoid another chance to become better.** Unfortunately, as we continue to avoid things as we get older, we prevent our-selves from learning the new skills we need to make tomorrow's concerns more manageable. The truth is, with each new life lesson learned, with each new experience embraced, the more power and control we have over our own fates. As a result, we become less afraid, less anxious, and more confident in our abil-ity to make our own bad things better. The only thing standing between you and a safer tomorrow is your willingness to accept and your desire to make a difference.

[2]

FALSE AUTHORITY

What Happened

When One World Trade Center was attacked on the morning of September 11, 2001, workers in Tower Two looked out their windows in sheer terror at the tragedy that had impacted their sister tower. Many instantly remembered the February 26, 1993, attack when a terrorist's truck bomb had detonated in the bowels of the building, and decided to run for their lives. Some made it as far as the stairwell before an announcement came over the loudspeaker, instructing them to stay at their desks. Others made it all the way down to the lobby—in eyesight of safety—only to be instructed by officials of the Port Authority to run back upstairs.

The Port Authority of New York and New Jersey—which built the World Trade Center—was responsible for its day-to-day operations. On that tragic day, more than 99 percent of the 10.4 million square feet controlled by the Port Authority was occupied. But the "authority" of the Port Authority was in being exceptionally skilled, financially secure, and politically neutral enough to handle large-scale and decades-long city-funded project management. They were project management experts, *not* safety and security experts. Their authority was derived from the fact that the Port Authority didn't have to worry about quarterly earnings or political campaigns so long as they kept meeting their deadlines. They were simply doing what they thought they were supposed to do and, in doing so, became directly responsible for the loss of many lives.

For what should have been fifteen lifesaving minutes, the emergency stairwells—whose sole purpose was to help ensure the certainty of safety—became logjammed by opposing instructions. Those listening to their instincts to run were trying to get down, while those who had almost made it out were trying to head back up to their desks. One Morgan Stanley employee told *The New York Times* that he had started down from the sixtieth floor and was told to go back up by a man with a bullhorn. The announcements urging people to go back up were being made by Port Authority officials. For those who worked in offices above the ninety-third floor, once being turned back around, they would have likely returned to their offices only to have the second plane fly into the tower beneath them. As for those who worked on lower floors, they would have been sent directly back into the path of impact. Regardless of where their workplaces were located, once they allowed themselves to be turned back around, they were left with little to no chance for survival.

PROTECTIVE TAKEAWAY

When your life is on the line, *you* are your own authority.

PROTECTIVE AWARENESS

In the Absence of Leadership, Our Nature Is to Gravitate Toward Strength

Staying alive is more important than being wrong. Losing your life is much worse than losing your job. How many of those people who followed the instruction to run back up to their desks and shelter in place cursed themselves for not simply saying "*No!*" to whatever authority figure they presumed to be right? How many of them in their final moments wished they had simply run right past some bullhorn blowhard and lived to tell their story? How many of them would have gladly apologized the next day had they been wrong? Dead people don't get a second chance to make things right. Dead people don't get to say, "I'm sorry. I was scared. I did what I had to do."

So what if you make a mistake? I make at least one dozen mistakes a day. But if my loved ones and I are in a life-threatening situation, I promise you won't ever find me negotiating with some presumptuous figure of authority. If my life is on the line, you had damn well get out of my way.

Those who listened to their initial instinct to *run* had the right idea. They simply allowed themselves to be turned around because someone in a position of authority told them to turn around. To be clear, the Port Authority officials had "authority" over the day-to-day operations of the building. They did not, however, have any authority to interfere with the life-and-death decisions made by the individual employees of the building. Problematically, the employees allowed themselves to be turned around because despite their internal survival signals telling them to run away, they negotiated against themselves for the sake of a much bigger societal fear. In that moment of allowing themselves to be turned around, the employees were more fearful of losing their jobs than they were of losing their lives.

Why? When we are confronted with fear, we are uncertain of our own decision-making. Even if we may think we know what is right, in the absence of leadership, it is in our nature to gravitate toward strength. When confronted by our own uncertainty, we are happy to follow the guidance of others. This is not a desire to shirk responsibility but rather an attempt to preserve our own survival by following the instructions of those who claim to know how to manage a problem better than we could ourselves.

One of the more considerable concerns that arose in the crucial minutes between the first plane hitting Tower One and the second plane hitting Tower Two was that Port Authority officials improperly assumed the role of subject matter experts rather than strictly adhering to their role as an organizational position of authority.

An *expert authority* is when a person is an expert in a particular subject or subject area. These types of authorities tend to specialize only in one area, and that is the reason why the opinions of these people are extremely valuable. An organizational position of authority is very similar to the authority that may be found in a project manager. Their authority is limited to a very specific project, and once that project has been completed, their authority ends as well.

However, some organizations like to ensure that even after a project has been completed, the position of the person is retained. This is precisely what happened at One World Trade Center. Back when the World Trade Center was first planned, the Port Authority was brought in to help steward the construction and project management. But when the project was completed and the doors were first opened in 1973, the Port Authority stayed on.

An Appeal to False Authority

An *appeal to false authority* is commonly understood as a type of fallacy or an argument based on unsound logic. When someone makes an argument using an appeal to authority, they are claiming that something must be true because it is believed by someone said to be an "authority" on the subject. For example: If two people are arguing over which type of bait is best for catching a fish, and one of them makes the argument that their uncle—who runs fishing charters down in Florida—says that the best bait is squid, that would be an appeal to false authority. The uncle may in fact charter boats, but chartering boats does not make the uncle an expert on which bait is best. Whether the uncle is actually an authority or not, the logic is unsound. Instead of presenting actual evidence, the argument just relies on the credibility of the "authority." This is an important distinction: just because someone is an authority in one realm does not make them an authority across all realms of expertise. A *false authority* is an authority figure whose authority is invalid because they have dubious credentials, irrelevant credentials, or no credentials at all.

The false authority with questionable credentials: This false authority is most noticeable in cases where the supposed authority figure does have some sort of relevant credentials, but these credentials are of questionable quality. An example of this kind of authority is in line with those of a "holistic" or "psychic" healer. These are often people who champion their authority despite having no formal medical training and who openly shun more traditional methods and practices in the treatment of ailments. Their bona fides are based mostly in their claim (or a patient's belief) of historic success rather than any documented validation from a governing standard of care.

The false authority with irrelevant credentials: This occurs in cases where the supposed authority figure does have valid credentials in one realm of expertise, but these credentials are irrelevant when the concern is encompassed by an entirely different set of circumstances. You would no more go to the chef of your favorite restaurant for advice on how to fix the squeaky brakes of your car any more than you would go to your trusted mechanic for advice on how to keep your soufflé from collapsing in your oven. Even if during the natural course of conversation, one of them were to offer some free advice, you would likely take that advice with a grain of salt. Why? Because the area in which they were offering advice is *not* their area of expertise.

The false authority with no credentials: This occurs in cases where the supposed authority has no credentials at all. Impersonating a police-like authority to commit a crime is very common. Posing as a police officer enables a bad guy to legitimize the appearance of an illegal act, such as a burglary, making a traffic stop, or making a false arrest. In one such incident, a Texas woman believed she was being legitimately pulled over for a traffic infraction. In reality, the suspect was using a white spotlight mounted on his driver's-side door and a flashing red light attached to his roof. The man ordered the woman to get out of her vehicle and then walked her over to the passenger side of his vehicle—where he sexually assaulted her.

False Authority Is Everywhere

Another ongoing concern with regard to false authority is how often we come across some measure of it in our lives without actually realizing how much of it is impacting and informing our everyday decisions. Seems as though everyone with a microphone and a Wi-Fi connection has a podcast these days. I personally love them and listen to a few different ones every day. A few years ago, I started noticing that podcasts were getting away from the more traditional commercial mode of advertising. Podcast hosts began doing ad reads during the segment breaks of their own shows. Today, these on-mic ad reads are the most effective aspect of podcasts because the host is able to inject their own personality into the ad reads to make them more effective. So effective, in fact, that advertising on podcasts is expected to reach $659 million in 2020, a rather significant increase from the $169 million in 2016.*

But it's not just podcasts; false authorities are ever present in advertising everywhere. Supermodels are hired to sell beauty products, because maybe if you use this product, you can be beautiful just like they are. In reality, the supermodel was already beautiful. She doesn't even need the product. Same for the athlete promoting the new sports car. Does he look great pulling up to the stadium and tossing the valet the keys? He sure does! Does that car do anything to help him win the game? Absolutely not. Does the once-famous TV star really have gold coins as part of their investment portfolio? They very well may, but if they do, I guarantee they aren't overleveraged on that singular investment strategy. Same for the talk show host who's promoting the home loan options. Chances are, they have better lending options available to them than the ones they are selling. And of course, we all roll our eyes each election season when the actors and musicians with varying levels of fame come across our screens to tell us just how passionate they are about a particular project of theirs while spouting off some clearly scripted facts and figures before telling us that this is why they are supporting whomever the candidate du jour may be for elected office.

When It Comes to Safety, Authority Often Has Contradicting Mandates

True authority commands respect. It never *demands* respect. It used to be that the authority figure in charge of security was the person

---

* Erica Sweeny, "The Second Annual Podcast Revenue Study by IAB and PwC: An Analysis of the Largest Players in the Podcasting Industry," MarketingDive.com, June 11, 2018.

who had the most keys. After 9/11, the security industry became flooded with "security experts" promoting whatever mandate had been the standard in practice from wherever they had received their initial training. This does not mean that someone cannot be a subject matter expert within a particular vertical of an overarching spectrum. One of the benefits to my service offerings is that I have experience in the realms of military, government, celebrity, and corporate security. This allows me to tailor my solutions to a client's specific needs. I may consider myself a threat management expert, but I know little to nothing about cybersecurity. I know even less about the vast array of engineering components that encompass technical security. I may know that a technical security countermeasure is a very in-the-know way of saying "bug sweeps," but I am certainly not the guy you would call to see if your car had been tagged with a hidden GPS tracker by a jealous ex-boyfriend. I can certainly point you in the right direction if that's what you're looking for, but those specialties are well outside my personal realm of expertise.

Yet some people still can't believe there is a difference between skill sets. I get asked all the time for advice on how to get into "security" as a career. The first thing I ask them to tell me is what kind of security they're talking about. Are they interested in physical security, personal security, cybersecurity, protective intelligence, threat management, and so on? My favorite is when they ask, "But how do I become a security expert?" They almost seem shocked when I tell them I'm not a security expert. There are no "security experts" any more than there are "medical experts" or "legal experts" or "psychology experts." Today's professional fields are entirely too vast for anyone to have a mastered every aspect of their unique and ever-expanding professional realm.

If you have cancer, are you going to go to any generic medical doctor, or are you going to seek out an expert in the field of cancer? But let's take it a step further. What kind of cancer? Lung cancer? Prostate? Liver? Cervical cancer? See what I mean? Each one is a specialized field of study.

The security profession is no different. Just because a person at a ball game is wearing a yellow windbreaker with block letters spelling

SECURITY across the back doesn't make them a security expert any more than the person making the popcorn is a culinary expert. Being familiar enough with the layout of the stadium to point you in the general direction after they scan your seat ticket does not mean they are qualified to offer instruction on what to do in the event of a mass evacuation. Just because a security guard can tell you which way to the nearest restroom does not mean you should trust the authority of their yellow windbreaker on what to do if an active shooter-situation happens. More than likely, that person working security is doing just that: working security.

The following is an actual job announcement to work game day security at Gillette Stadium. (Note: I am not picking on Gillette Stadium. This announcement is the norm for stadium security across the nation.)

WANT TO WORK NEW ENGLAND PATRIOTS GAMES?
JOIN THE GAME DAY TEAM!
GILLETTE STADIUM EVENT DAY SECURITY

SUMMARY
Conduct entrance screening and inspections according to security requirements, contraband and safety concerns. Politely, professionally, and consistently communicate screening procedures to customers and ensure that restricted items are not permitted into the venue. Assist ticket takers and ushers as needed, verify access into "restricted access" areas. Monitor crowd activities and immediately report any suspicious behavior to the area supervisor or in the event of an emergency the local public safety officials.

QUALIFICATIONS
- High School education or GED required
- Friendly & Customer Service Oriented, relevant experience preferred
- Willingness to work both indoors and outside in variable conditions
- Available to work all full Stadium events that include: nights and weekends

- Ability to take direction, demonstrate flexibility with shifting priorities
- Ability to work for prolonged periods

As one currently employed security guard commented on an indeed .com job board:

A typical day at Gillette stadium is pretty relaxing for the most part. Just answering patrons questions and listening to our supervisors.

Pros: free lunch, you get to watch the events while working.

Cons: long hours, pay is low, weather can get cold, on your feet a lot.

Keep this in mind the next time you are at a public event: taken as a whole, event staff is largely undertrained, is underpaid, and lacks any social accountability. There is almost no incentive for them to do their job particularly well. Why? Because they have a built-in excuse: "I'm a ten-dollar-an-hour staffer. What do I know?" The result is a very diluted focus on safety. Rather than rising to the level of your expectation, they falter to the standard of their training. This means they're more likely to be watching the event (just as you are) while they stand around and simply wait for something to happen.

Truth is, at most schools, office buildings, and organizations of all shapes and sizes, security is almost always an afterthought. It is almost always the last item on a budget, and it is paid the least amount of attention possible. Unless something is legally required, it will more often than not be shunned. By and large, low risk means low priority.

Personal Safety Versus Public Safety

A reactive approach to public safety is easy to prescribe. This is what the police and fire departments do very well. In a standard scenario, a problem is reported, and then they respond in kind. This is also why so much of their funding and training is dedicated toward helping them effectively react and respond to the problems most commonly reported. Local police officers are not in the business of *preventing* active shooters. They are in the business of *responding to* active shooters. The mandate of the police officers is to ensure the public safety by neutralizing the threat as quickly as possible.

This is a completely different methodology from how the Secret Service keeps the president safe. The Presidential Protective Division can't simply stand around and wait for someone to attack the president before they can do their job effectively. By then, it would be much too late. Instead, they employ a preventative approach, which is required for the assurance of personal safety. They identify the threats likeliest to occur, and then they employ safeguards to reduce those risks from ever becoming a reality. This is why they weld manhole covers closed and remove mailboxes along the routes the motorcade will travel. This is why they run background checks of visitors to events where the president will be speaking.

One of the more significant challenges public officials face in the aftermath of a violent incident lies in reframing the public's assumption that both personal and public safety can be achieved at the same time by doing the same thing. But this cannot be achieved any more than the baseball team who has taken the field can score a home run. The team on the field can do everything within their power to keep the team at bat from scoring a run, but no matter how well they play the field, there is no possible way for them to score by playing their positions as prescribed.

Much like a sports team has very specific strategies for playing both offense and defense, protective strategies have specific intent. Methodologies employed to ensure public safety cannot ensure personal protection any more than sunblock can be used to prevent frostbite.

Think about the difference in how safety is defined and ensured at an airport versus that of most concert venues:

At an airport, the TSA screening checkpoint not only ensures that all who pass through their station have the appropriate ticket for the correct day and time, but they also conduct a rather thorough screening for any items that could possibly be used to harm other passengers. They are concerned with your personal safety and have taken the appropriate measures to prevent something from happening.

Now think of a venue where the security team stands at the entrance to make sure everyone has a ticket. Yes, there may be a cursory check of purses and persons, but their overall role as security is to protect against unauthorized entry.

Life and Death Is Not a Game of Hide-and-Seek

The first rule of safety is *not* to hide from risk. The first rule of safety is to get somewhere safe. When an armed assailant comes into your building: *you run out.* If an armed assailant is outside your building: *you run in.* I want to be very clear about something. An active shooter is just as dangerous and unpredictable as a building fire. Would you hide from fire in the hope it would not find you? Of course not. You would run. So why are you choosing to hide from an active shooter? Would you hide under your bed if there was a burglar in your house, or would you do everything you could to get out and run away?

Have you ever played T-ball? Which is harder to hit: the stationary ball sitting on top of the tee or the curveball coming at you from the pitcher's mound? Obviously, the T-ball is much easier to hit. So again, I ask you: If an armed assailant is coming after you, where would you rather be? Cowering in the corner and crying for your life, or running away as fast as you can, putting as much time and distance between you and the threat as possible? It's very easy to run away from a person who's not chasing you, and it's much harder to hit a target that is getting smaller and farther away with every step they take.

You have a choice. You can run and live or you can hide and die. I hope you choose to live.

Evacuation Zones Are Safety Traps

Here's a really important thing to know about evacuations. If your office, school, or workplace is being evacuated, *never* go to the evacuation point. Don't do it. Go to Starbucks. Go see a movie. Go home. But whatever you do, stay as far away as humanly possible from any kind of identifiable evacuation zone.

Why? It's actually pretty simple. Evacuation zones are a *huge* liability.

Think about it like this: schools and office buildings are a matrix of interconnected and compartmentalized areas that offer their own protection in the form of dispersion and separation. Evacuation locations negate this protection by having everyone move from their respectively disjointed locations and instead come together at a single, predesignated position. If someone really wanted to do the most harm, the evacuation point would offer the most "bang for the buck," because almost all evacuation points are outside of the secure perimeter, rehearsed ad nauseam, and easily researched online. Do you want to think like a criminal? Just do a simple #FireDrill search on social media and you'll be able to find thousands of well-documented locations of evacuation points you could target.

So if you're in a situation where you're getting evacuated, go anywhere else. Go home. If the threat to your respective organization is significant enough for them to initiate an evacuation, your day is over. If your building administrators believe it likely enough for the threat to be real, then there are likely bigger issues at play. Take the rest of the day off and let the officials investigate.

I want you to repeat this so you understand: *you always have a choice.*

Accountability Versus Survivability

There is a big difference between accountability and survivability. Don't ever confuse the two. You can run to get counted or you can run for your life. I'll tell you what I'm going to do. I'm going to run. I'm going to run fast. I'm going to run far. I will do my very best to usher as many others as I can to safety, but if you're with me, we're running.

I understand that a great many people reading this may be thinking to themselves, *Are you crazy? There's no way I'm running away from a guy with a gun!* But believe me when I tell you, it's the single most successful strategy available to you. Now I know that we've all been socialized into thinking a certain way. But don't ever negotiate against your basic survival instincts. We are genetically programmed for fight or flight. It's in our DNA. Hiding is not what we are designed to do. Hiding is learned. Hiding is taught. Hiding is socialized. We don't have claws to dig holes to hide in. We are not built to climb trees or scale poles or leap from branch to branch to safety. We have two core choices: fight or flight.

I get it. A lot of you are thinking, *Eh . . . I'm not so sure about this. I'm too weak to fight, and I'm too slow to run. Hiding sounds pretty damn good to me.* If that's what you want to do, that's just fine. If you've been made aware of all the options and that's the decision you choose, fine; you can think that way if you want to. I'm quite sure you won't be the only one. I'm sure many of you are thinking that very thing. But I want you to understand something. I want you to understand that you've pretty much been sold a lie. Do you even know why you were told to hide?

Two reasons. And both of them are heavily grounded in accountability and *not* survivability.

The first reason is that if there is a real active shooter, the police would prefer to keep everyone contained. If the active shooter threat is limited to a very specific geographic area, that means they are fulfilling their obligation to the public's safety. Remember: the primary focus of police activity is public safety, not personal safety.

"Law enforcement agencies and personnel have no duty to protect individuals from the criminal acts of others; instead their duty is to preserve the peace and arrest law breakers for the protection of the general public."*

For this very reason, when writing an emergency response plan, police-aligned authors focus on what would make the job easier if they were a responding officer instead of what would prevent them from being called in the first place. Advocating for your school, your office, or your organization's building to evacuate and for any able-bodied person to run away from danger as fast as they can would be counterproductive to the very outcome they are trying to achieve.

The police don't want everyone to run away. Mostly because they don't want to give the bad guy the chance to escape and "hide in plain sight" as he ran away with all the other inhabitants. That would make their job more difficult. And while this practice is exactly what they

---

* *Lynch v. NC Dept. of Justice*, 376 SE 2nd 247 (NC App. 1989).

would prescribe if they were tasked with ensuring your personal safety, it is the very last thing they want to do when they are first committed to the task of servicing the public's safety first and foremost.

The second reason for these accountability-focused mandates is that the administrators of these plans are more than willing to simply "check the block" in support of whatever overarching emergency response plan is mandated of them to put in place, but only if doing so does not have an adverse impact on the core curriculum of the classroom or the productivity of the office. They are more than willing to ensnare you in the pitfalls of the Safety Trap by placating you with just enough of a participation in your own protection that your fears will be mostly abated, but also shirk the responsibility of doing anything more to ensure your safety because the likelihood of something happening is statistically very low—that is, of course, until it happens to them, and then they'll be the first ones to point fingers at the policy while citing, "But this was all we were required to do."

So sure, if you want to believe that hiding will keep you safe, that's fine. Just like run/hide/fight is fine. Just like hiding under your desk in an air-raid drill is fine. Like stop, drop, and roll is fine.

But maybe you only feel they are fine because they are familiar. You prefer them because they are simple. They are easy to remember—nothing more than mantras that have been dumbed down to the attention span of a tweet-length culture that we have now adapted ourselves to live in. So please, humor me for a moment. Let's look at these socially acceptable practices a little more closely, and let's see if we can't understand just how much of the Safety Trap is built into the very strategies that we were all told were designed to keep us safe.

Because if we want to avoid falling into the Safety Trap, we have to be willing to question with boldness all those things we thought we knew to be true. We can no longer simply placate ourselves with the notion that something is being done. Just because something has always been a certain way does not mean those ways were always prudent, smart, or safe. It may not even be practical for those practices to continue. I want you to understand the overarching framework from which these practices were born. I want you to understand the pattern in practice from which these instructions originated. I want you to be able to see the naked truth for yourself and then decide if you still believe they are, in fact, fine for you to hold so dear.

"Cold War Kids Were Hard to Kill"

There is a Billy Joel song called "Leningrad." And in that song there is the lyric: "Cold War kids were hard to kill / Under their desks in an air-raid drill." Now, other than that line being a good rhyme about a historically accurate act, I don't know what to tell you, other than this: being under your desk in an air-raid drill is *not* going to save you. It was never going to. It was never meant to. It was just something for you to do so you felt like you were participating in your own safety.

In 1951, the Federal Civil Defense Administration (FCDA) was set up to educate and reassure the country that there were ways to survive an atomic attack from the Soviet Union. One of their approaches was to involve schools. In a pilot program in McLean, Virginia, teachers were encouraged to conduct air-raid drills where they would suddenly yell, "Drop!" and the students would then duck and cover by kneeling under their desks while wrapping their arms and hands around their heads and necks. Some schools even distributed metal dog tags, like those worn by World War II soldiers, so that the bodies of students could be identified after an attack.

Thankfully, this reality was never realized. But still, in planning for this realistic risk, the powers that be decided to choose accountability over survivability. Can you imagine? Schools would have been obvious targets, because they can be clearly seen from the air. But when the air-raid alarm sounded, these children were not taught to run, they were not taught to seek safety in a nearby safe haven, or in a nearby bunker, or at the very least, to run home to be with their families in their final moments on earth. No! They were instructed to duck and cover under their desks. So now, after having survived the air raid, when little Jenny doesn't come home, her poor parents are forced to go to the schoolhouse, the only hope for identifying their daughter in the central office of the school, where a dog tag and a body bag are being cross-referenced to the classroom seating chart . . . all because they were told not to run.

Stop, Drop, and Roll

Stop, drop, and roll. We all know it. We grew up with it. If you catch on fire, you stop, you drop to the ground, and you roll on over until all the flames go out. Anyone care to try it? Is it going to save your life? No, not really. You are still feeding the flames with oxygen as you are rolling around on the floor. But here's what it does do: it makes it easier for everyone else to help you. If you're running around the room like a crazy person, it makes it harder for the helpers to cover you with a blanket, spray you down with the fire extinguisher, administer first aid. But if you voluntarily put yourself down on the ground, now you're contained. Less chance for the fire to spread. More likely that others will be able to help save you, and keep the fire from spreading too.

Run/Hide/Fight

Which brings me to today's modern-day disaster of run/hide/fight. The origins of run/hide/fight were born from military application. Pilots and special operators all go through some sort of survival training in case they are ever shot down or caught behind enemy lines. They are taught to escape, evade, and retaliate.

Now let's say you're an American held captive by the enemy, and one night, all the conditions are right for you to mount your escape. You manage to knock out the guard and get out of your cell. Now there's an army of bad guys looking for you. Now tell me . . . do you think their training teaches them to run into another cell to hide, barricade the door, and hope the bad guys don't find them? Hell no!

They are trained to *run*. Run fast and run hard. They are going to do everything they can to put as much time and distance between them and the enemy as possible. And if they get tired, maybe they rest for a moment behind a tree to catch their breath. Or if the enemy is hot on their trail and starts to gain on them, maybe they cover and conceal themselves in some mud and tree limbs until they pass them by. They evade. And when the bad guys pass them by again, they run.

But if something goes wrong and it looks like they might catch you again and take you back to your cell, you strike back. You retaliate. And you fight like your life is on the line. Because you damn well better believe that it is.

But here is where the original intent went from survivability of the military to the accountability of the school administrator. Because after the school tragedies at Columbine, Virginia Tech, and Sandy Hook, there was an outcry from the public to "do something," and within a very short period of time, the now en vogue practice of "preparedness training" began to replicate across a cottage industry of providers. Problem is, none of these applications did anything to make the schools safer. The only thing any of them accomplished was making the recipients of their training more afraid and the next would-be offender more effective.

Almost overnight, the original intent of run/hide/fight had been reduced from "escape, evade, retaliate" to "run to your hiding spot." I audit these run/hide/fight training videos all the time, and every time I finish one, I feel like I need a drink. I watched one recently that had some sort of tactical takeaway that included nine ways to use your belt buckle to block the doorjamb and prevent active entry, but the instructor of the video never once mentions the first-floor window, which is directly behind him as an alternate exit. He never once talks about how the door you've blocked and barricaded to keep you protected is made out of a wood composite that a bullet will travel through with ease. He never once talks about how making all that noise to barricade the door is going to draw more attention to your location.

I don't care what anyone else tells you. I don't care what your corporate policy says. I don't care what your teacher is telling you to do. I don't care if your boss tells you you'll be fired if you run. Only *you* can tell *you* what to do when your life is on the line.

Only you can save yourself. Only you can know if it's smarter to choose flight or fight. You always have a choice. If you want to live . . . *run.*

PROTECTIVE PREPAREDNESS

The following are some best practices to keep you from falling into the Safety Trap of False Authority:

1. **Never negotiate against your instincts.** When your life is on the line, no one is more in charge of your safety than you. If every instinct and intuition in your body is telling you to run, you should *run*. You should run as far and as fast as you can. Do not let anyone stop you. Losing your job should never come before losing your life.

2. **Inspect what you expect.** Just because you want something to be true or believe that something is true doesn't make it true. No matter how seemingly legitimate a position of authority may seem, the onus is on *you* to be sure your assumptions are correct. Have you ever seen a movie where the bank robber dresses up like a cop? It happens all the time. Why? Because it's easier to believe the lie than it is to investigate the truth. So before you decide—especially a decision that may have life-or-death implications—be sure you are working with the best information possible.

3. **Question with boldness.** Question everything, especially the motives behind who is telling you what they are telling you. Do not be placated by being told that everything is being done to keep you safe without actually understanding what those things are, what other options are available, why certain things were chosen over others, and who made those decisions. Most administrators of schools and managers of workplaces are *not* subject matter experts in risk reduction and violence prevention. Most of them are simply doing what is mandated from higher up the ladder.

4. **Feeling vulnerable is not a weakness.** Vulnerability is the key to unlocking our courage. For only when we feel held down can we truly rise up. There can be no courage without risk.

5. **Reframe your expectation of expertise.** Always remember that not all "experts" are created equal. Beware of appeals to false

authority and your own confirmation bias. Just because you may want a person to be an authority on the topic, be careful to not allow this desire to dismiss conflicting information. If you are uncertain, play devil's advocate, and try to punch holes in your own logic—or, even better, have those with a different perspective do it to you. Much like you would seek a second opinion on a current concern impacting your health, wealth, or well-being, so too should you frame your expectation early and often as to those whose "expertise" may be relied upon when moments matter most.

PHYSICAL FITNESS

What Happened

As part of my professional practice, I provide litigation support to law firms that are involved in security-related casework. In one case, I was providing threat management support to a law firm that was involved with a shooting that had taken place at a shopping mall. A big part of my involvement was to determine if there had been any negligence at play. My client wanted to know if the mall's policies regarding safety and security were adequate. To determine this, I conducted a site-security assessment, combed through historical records of security-related incidents the mall kept on file, and reviewed the security footage of the entire incident. Once this was completed, I continued my assessment by interviewing anyone and everyone willing to speak with me. It was important for my report to have as much information as possible. To do this, I wanted to get a feel for what the employees and the patrons involved in that incident felt as they were forced to endure the event.

During one such interview, with a woman who worked at a jewelry store on the second floor, our conversation took a turn away from the security features at the mall and pivoted toward her own experience with feeling unprepared to do what she knew she needed to do to ensure her own safety.

She was in her midforties, a college-educated mother of two, with a youthful smile. She had a ten-year-old son and an eight-year-old daughter. She was one of the co-owners of a high-end boutique jewelry store where she designed custom orders and showcased her own line of jewelry at the store. They had been in business for about five years. I could see why she was successful in her endeavor. She had a creative spark and an engaging personality. Both were essentials for her business.

She recalled to me that when she had first opened her store, there had been some kind of a security scare. There had been a loud noise that sounded like a gunshot, and she had been terrified by the fact she didn't know what to do. So she'd just ducked down behind the counter and waited. But as she hid, she realized there were no screams, there were no alarms, there were no additional indicators of harm. So she poked her head back up and went to investigate what had happened. As it turned out, the "gunshot" she had thought she heard was really just a piece of equipment falling off a truck in the courtyard of the mall one floor below. A maintenance crew had been setting up a holiday display, and one of the large steel frames that was meant to support a backdrop had created a very loud *bang* as it clanged to the floor. She was relieved but still a bit scared by the fact that if that sound had been a real gunshot, she didn't have a plan for what she would have done.

As she looked around her shop, she noticed that right there behind her was a door. On the other side of that door was a hallway. A hundred feet down that hallway was a set of stairs. She knew that route well. She had walked it a few times before. She walked it when she sometimes took the service elevator from her parking spot out back. She remembered that when they had been first setting up the shop, that was the way in which they had brought in all their merchandise for the grand opening. Her mall employee parking spot was even positioned just a few feet away from the service entrance on the ground floor. So that was that, she confided in herself. If she ever had to escape, that would be how she would get out.

During the course of our conversation, the woman had been perfectly calm while explaining to me the event that had initiated her desire to have a plan. She appeared to be quite proud of the fact that she had such a practical plan in place. But what terrified her was that she had never prepared herself for having to put that plan into action. By solely putting a plan in place, she had allowed for her own fear to be abated, but the risk remained. What she unfortunately realized a few years later—when the sound of the gunshot was revealed to be real—was the reality that she was not as prepared to put her plan into action as she'd believed herself to be.

As our conversation shifted to the shooting, she explained to me that she heard the gunshot go off in the mall and did the same thing she had done before. She crouched down behind the counter and waited for confirmation that it was a false alarm. Except this time, it wasn't. This time, she heard multiple gunshots. This time, she heard the panic. This time, she heard the alarms, and the shouting, and the screams. This time, she knew what she had to do. She told me she turned around and looked at the door. The door that was just a few feet away from her. But instead of crawling to the door and making a run for it, she froze. She cried.

"I haven't had to run that far since high school," she told me through choking sobs. "I didn't know if I could make it." Then she continued through both laughter and tears. "Can you imagine—what would they say?" She wiped her eyes as she began to pantomime a mock conversation between two people:

"Did you hear about Jenny?"
"Jewelry Jenny? From the mall?"
"Yeah! Did you hear what happened?"
"No, what happened?"
"She died!"
"In the shooting?"
"Yes."
"How terrible! She was shot?"
"Well . . ."
"Well, what?"
"She didn't get shot . . ."
"What do you mean? I thought you said she died!"

"Well, she did, but not from getting shot. Poor girl had a heart attack in the hallway, running for the door."

I understood right at that very moment why the sobs and the tears came next. In that moment of realization, she wasn't crying out of fear. She wasn't crying because she had been scared. She wasn't crying because she was worried she would die. She wasn't crying because she was worried about not being able to get home to her children, her husband, or her friends. She was crying out of shame. This was her plan. She had been the one to put this strategy into place. She knew what she would need to do, and she had failed herself to meet that expectation. She had never gotten herself into shape. She had never trained. She had never proven to herself that what she needed to be able to do she would confidently be able to perform.

PROTECTIVE TAKEAWAY
Your personal safety, and the safety of your loved ones, depends on your ability to perform under the pressure of stressful conditions.

PROTECTIVE PREPAREDNESS

Fitness Fuels Confidence

Safety and fitness both require an investment of effort. They both require you to be a willing participant in your own improvement. If you want to get fit, you're going to have to sweat. You only get out of it what you are willing to put in. The number-one way to take control of your own confidence is to be proactive. No one can help you to feel confident other than you.

The human body is not designed to be sedentary. We are built to move. We are genetically and biologically hardwired to hunt and gather our food. Our way of life has really begun to do our bodies a disservice. As food, water, and shelter became more prevalent throughout our society, our physical exertion increasingly became more of a lifestyle choice than a necessity for survival.

For more than a millennium, our ability to move was a core function of our survival. And that core function is a crucial part of our genome structure. It is the reason we are more interconnected when we play sports, because sports are really nothing more than rehearsals for combat. Formations. Strategies. Strength. Conditioning. One team against another. All of it is just a modern-day enactment—battlefield drills of war.

There is a reason young children are infatuated with video games where they must hunt and shoot to win. They are drawn to them. Not because they are violent but because they are in our DNA. Historically, that act of going out into the wilderness to hunt, to shoot, and to survive the wild as you track your prey—that was a rite of passage. We have an innate desire to develop these skills because they were what made us a valuable member of our society, our tribe. Our ability to contribute to the success of a hunt gave us purpose. We were appreciated for our ability to provide for and to help protect the tribe. To help ensure the survival of our people.

We had to do these things. We had to participate. We had to play a part. We all had a role to play. Each one of us was an important component in the survival of not only our own lives but in the lives of those who counted on us for protection. We had to do this. It was mandatory because our safety was not a guarantee. Safety was not a certainty. Safety required active participation.

It wasn't very long ago that we were, as a society, never truly safe. The dangers outweighed whatever creature comforts we had been able to acquire. We lived with fear in a different way from how we live with fear today. Fear was not a burden. Fear was a gift. Fear was essential to our everyday core function of survival. We knew we were weaker, slower, and less skilled than the other predators who roamed around us, because we were reminded of this reality every day. We were more vigilant. More on guard. More ready to respond and react whenever the warning signs of harm were first revealed to us.

Today, we live on the other end of the spectrum. Today, we are almost *always* safe. Today, our everyday comforts vastly outweigh the dangers, the risks. And this newfound reality means that most of us find ourselves comfortably able to go about our everyday lives with the relative certainty that nothing is going to happen.

Fitness Improves Survivability

Despite what TV shows and movies may convince you to believe, you will not get superstrong or superfast the moment you get scared. The confidence to act comes from having previously proven to yourself that you have what it takes to push beyond a benchmark of past performance. If you are not constantly pushing yourself to exceed a physical standard, you cannot expect yourself to suddenly push past a terrifying confrontation.

There is a difference between being in shape and being conditioned for a specific sport. The difference is very similar to a professional athlete maintaining their overall level of fitness during the off-season but then ramping back up during their sport's "camp" as they get ready for that season of play. In the real world, a similar reality applies. There are those who are in good enough shape to go all out for an hour on an elliptical machine but who would be completely out of breath if they had to sprint the length of a football field. There are people who can run marathons but who don't know the first thing about doing a dead lift. There are people who can hike ten miles up a mountain on a camping trip but have never run a race in their life.

When it comes to staying safe, your ability to run, jump, push, and pull may very well save your life, but more important than being able to do all these things is the ability to do *any* of these things. There is an underlying commonality that is consistently found among everyone who engages in some kind of physically exerting exercise: people who exercise have a higher degree of comfortableness with being uncomfortable than those who do not. Why is this the case? The very essence of exercise is about getting outside of your comfort zone. Improvement is directly correlated to effort. You get out of it what you put into it. What those who don't exercise don't realize is that when you push yourself past the point of a previously believed point of no return, you don't feel worse . . . you feel better. When we hear a phrase like "It's not the size of the dog in the fight, but the size of the fight in the dog," what is really being discussed is willpower. Willpower is one of those things we all struggle with, but it's also the one thing that is 100 percent under our own control. Have you ever heard the phrase "The good ones work out, but the great ones outwork"? Again, it's all about willpower. How badly you want something and how hard you are willing to work for it all begin with a willingness to improve your willpower. The greater the will-power, the greater the effort, and the greater the effort, the greater the result.

But willpower isn't an overnight fix. Improving our willpower is a de-liberately slow and gradual process. It requires a regimen of discipline and hard work over space and time. It is one of the baby steps to greatness before any bold strides to victory can even be attempted. But with each step taken, we grow stronger, more disciplined, and more comfortable in our own skin. Through this process, we become more informed about the nutritional value of what we eat. We learn to take better care of our bodies. We become more resourceful in our methods and our practices to help us stay on the course to improvement. And when we stumble, fall, or even fail in our attempts to improve, we get better and better about getting back up and trying again. With each passing day of continuous effort, we accept the fact that we cannot change everything all at once. If we want to see real change, we should start small and tackle one long-term goal at a time. That way, when the stressful time comes, we are ready to act, because we know we are prepared to perform.

This is why being physically fit is such an important component not only for staying safe but for reducing your anxiety about not being able to keep yourself safe. Exercising for as little as ten minutes a day will begin to stimulate antianxiety effects. Studies have found that regular exercise can decrease overall levels of tension, elevate and stabilize mood, improve sleep, and improve self-esteem. Our bodies are basically like a battery that requires so much energy to be expended every day. If that energy is not expended during a workout, it only has one place left to go—our anxiety. In one study, researchers found that those who got reg-ular vigorous exercise were 25 percent less likely to develop depression or an anxiety disorder over the next five years.*

Fitness Helps to Alleviate Stress

When we are in a high-stress situation, our heart rates spike, our breaths become more shallow, our peripheral vision constrains, our fine motor

---

* *Exercise for Mood and Anxiety: Proven Strategies for Overcoming Depression and Enhancing Well-Being*, by Michael W. Otto, Ph.D., and Jasper A. J. Smits, Ph.D. (Oxford University Press, 2011).

functions deteriorate, and our abilities to perform everyday body movements become much more cumbersome. This is one of the reasons why in self-defense training they teach people to use big movements like pushing someone away from you and employing more of a "big movements by me against big targets on you" philosophy. They teach this because most people never train beyond a few familiarization classes and then never revisit them again. Which means if they ever find themselves confronted on the street, they will very likely be too physically and emotionally stressed to perform more intricate techniques like wrist-locks or precise punching combinations.

Where physical fitness comes into play is that the more in shape you are, the faster you are able to get yourself back down to a normal operating level. The more athletic you are, the more likely you are to have a lower resting heart rate than other people. A lower heart rate means your body needs fewer heartbeats to deliver the same amount of blood throughout your body. This means when your body is placed under stress, your heart rate is less likely to spike as high, which means your ability to return your heart rate back down to a normal operating level is going to happen much faster. The slower your heart rate, the better you will be able to perform. The better you are able to perform, think clearly, and make more informed decisions, the less likely you are to make fatal errors.

We have all seen the horror movie where the unsuspecting coed in the kitchen gets scared when the bad guy comes through the front door. But instead of running out the back door (which was literally three feet behind her), she'll allow herself to get chased around the entire first floor of the house just so she can run up the stairs to her parents' bedroom and hide under the bed. While she does this, everyone in the audience is thinking, *What is she doing?!* Problem is, in a similar situation, most of us would do the exact same thing. What is important to remember and realize is that when we find ourselves constrained by the confines of fear, we revert back to a basic instinct, and we go with what we know. When it comes to staying safe, there is a common misconception that standards will rise to meet our expectations. In reality, they falter to the lowest level of our accepted practice.

There is a phrase in Ranger School that says, "In combat, a man's brain turns to water and runs out his ears, and he relies on pure instinct alone."* This is why instructors in schools of combat inoculate soldiers against the stressors of war. They engrain and train and methodically prepare you for the eventual reality a soldier will face. So in that moment when combat presents itself, it is the training that becomes second nature; it is the training that becomes instinct. What is true for the troops is true for the rest of us too: the more we prepare today for the realistic challenges we are likely to face, the better positioned we can all be to confront that challenge when it confronts us.

This is what is known as *stress inoculation*. Stress inoculation or stress-inoculation training is what allows for people who operate in high-stress environments to perform under the stressors of their environment. Imagine if you are placed in a race car and told to drive around the track at one hundred miles per hour. If you were hooked up to a blood pressure and a heart rate machine while you did this, before you even put the car into drive, your heart rate and blood pressure would be expected to increase. Halfway around the track and those same vital signs would likely be through the roof. But after your tenth time around the track, they would start to go down. By your one hundredth time around the track, they would be half of what they were. By the time you took lap ten thousand around the track, they would be no different from when you were driving yourself to work.

Movement Is Life

There are three overarching reasons why being fit is so important. The first has everything to do with just keeping the body in working order. When it comes to the human body, the more we move, the better we perform: motion is lotion. When we keep ourselves strong, fit, and healthy, we are less susceptible to injury and more inclined to heal at a faster rate. When we eat well and take good care of ourselves, we are

---

* Author unknown.

less likely to get sick and less likely to infect others. Fitness is health, and health is fitness. The more in tune we are with our bodies and our environments, the less likely we are to fall victim to injury and illness.

The second reason is self-preservation. Our ability to be agile and mobile allows for us to run from our enemy. It gives us the ability to hunt or gather our food, construct shelter to keep us safe from the elements, and if necessary, protect and defend ourselves from confrontation.

The third reason to remain physically fit is to provide for and protect our loved ones. The safety of our loved ones often depends on our ability to perform under the pressure of stressful conditions. The better we are able to move and the more confident we are in our ability to perform in an emotionally disruptive and physically arduous environment, the more certain and less anxious we will be about our ability to ensure our safety. When this is not the case, we often find ourselves much more anxious, and much more at risk to the harmful and sometimes violent intentions of not only our environments but of others as well.

Are You Safety Fit?

Ask any soldier who has ever been in combat to tell you the number-one rule of survival. They'll tell you one thing: *do something*. Shoot and move. You can run or you can fight, but if you want to live, you have to do something. Doing nothing is a deadly option.

Before speaking with the woman from the jewelry store, I had never considered as a realistic possibility that someone could possibly be so insecure, so overwhelmed, and have so improperly framed their own expectation about participating in their own safety that, when push came to shove, they wouldn't even try to save themselves. I have seen videos of people jumping from windows to certain death because they would rather take the chance of surviving the fall than face the certainty of burning alive. I have seen people who couldn't swim to save their lives fall off a boat and then practically run on water to escape the dorsal fin of a distant shark. I had assumed—wrongly—that our own innate sense of self-preservation would take hold over all of us and help us do our best to get to safety. But what I failed to consider was our own willingness to want to live. Some of us would rather just give up. Some of us would rather just sacrifice ourselves not for the greater good but because we were too lazy to give half an effort. This woman had made the decision to risk getting killed by a gunman while cowering in a corner rather than risk being out of breath but otherwise alive after running the hundred feet down the hallway on the other of the door. I mean, seriously, one hundred feet. The average human stride is thirty inches. She was forty paces away from safety, and she was afraid she wouldn't make it because she had never had to run that far. One hundred feet. Forty paces. But since we're having this conversation now, I feel it's kind of important I ask:

When was the last time *you* ran one hundred feet?
When was the last time *you* took the stairs instead of the elevator?
When was the last time *you* chose a workout over wine?
When was the last time *you* chose water over whiskey?
When was the last time *you* pushed yourself outside your zone of comfort?

Now don't get me wrong. I'm not being critical of you, your diet, or your physical composition. I am a far cry from being a specimen of ideal health. It's been a long time since anyone made a joke about being able to do their laundry on my washboard abs. To be honest, I'm at a point in my life where I would rather drink a six-pack than have one. But every morning when I wake up, I see former Navy SEAL David Goggins out there doing a record-breaking number of pull-ups. I see Cameron Hanes running a marathon. Every. Single. Day. I see Jocko waking up at 4 a.m. to claim his first "win" of the day. I see what the Rock is sharing on Instagram, and that's when I remind myself of the Mark Cuban quote about working twenty-four hours a day like someone else is out there working to take it all away from you.

Believe me, I am far from perfect, but I still do my best to maintain. I'm still one to rise up to meet a challenge. I still incorporate an aspect of fitness into my everyday life. I pay my gym tax. I walk. I row. I ride my bike. I do some push-ups every day. If I'm traveling, I'll try to find a local gym. If not, I'll run the stairs in the hotel. I'll do some pull-ups on the crossbeams. Every day, I do something. Some days, it's a lot. Some days, it's a little. But every day, I find my way to doing something that makes me feel alive. I do something to remind myself of the reasons my life has purpose and meaning. That my life is worth fighting for, because my life is worth living.

Now are these sweat sessions all Ranger-inspired workouts like I used to do in my youth? No. Very rarely. Almost never. But do I do enough to keep me functional and capable? Yes! Does doing this small part prevent me from ever feeling the anxiety of not being able to run the hundred feet to an exit? Yes. Does doing so prepare me mentally for what I may never be called upon to do physically? Yes. But what about you? What do you do?

Basic Training for Staying Safe

We all know that staying in shape helps us live healthier lives. Equally important is the knowledge that our fitness levels are a critical component of keeping us safe from harm.

Criminals assess likelihood of success the same way lions stalk prey in the wild. Predators are always on the hunt for those least likely to put up a fight. They don't target the strongest of the herd—they attack the weakest. The positive, protective, and confident posture you promote by being in shape not only serves as a deterrent from potential attackers, but being safety fit will also greatly increase your survivability in a crisis.

Emergencies are a lot like broken elevators; they typically occur when we are least expecting it and most ill prepared. Too many of us have found ourselves winded and sore after having to muster intense physical exertion at an unexpected time.

When your life is on the line, you don't want to be the one wishing you had done your workouts. You want to be the one who is forever grateful you did.

As you go about your day, take a moment to notice your surroundings and the physical obstacles you may encounter if faced with the unexpected.

You can then draw from these observations for inspiration when creating your workout plan. You may find it helpful to imagine what tasks you may need to perform in an emergency and then incorporate an exercise to help you overcome the obstacle in that real-world emergency scenario. Here are a few examples:

Live or work on a top floor? Elevators are one of the first things to stop working. Whenever time permits, take the stairs.

Find progress in push-ups. Push-ups are one of the best body-weight exercises you can do anywhere, anytime. The more total weight you can move, the easier it will be to push fallen objects off you. Chest strength doubles for pushing bad guys away from you—and off you too—providing those precious seconds you need to run away.

Need to hold something up over your head? Need to push something across a floor or hold something closed? Squats and shoulder presses will serve you well in this scenario.

Need to jump up to grab that fire-escape ladder? Box jumps are a great way to strengthen your legs and will help you to jump higher than you otherwise could. Pull-ups are a great way to strengthen your back so you can pull yourself up with less effort than you otherwise would.

Don't forget to do some sprints. In today's urban, school, and workplace environments, a 10K run to safety isn't very likely, but having to hurry down a hallway or scurry across the street is quite realistic. If you are at the gym, newer treadmills have some interval features you can use. Try interval sets: Sprint for fifteen seconds, then drop speed to recover for thirty seconds; repeat five times. Walk for two to three minutes, and then do it all again. If you can find yourself a track, sprint the straightaways, and then jog the curves to recover.

PROTECTIVE PREPAREDNESS

The following are some best practices to keep you from falling into the Safety Trap of Physical Fitness.

Disclaimer: Before beginning any exercise regimen, please consult your physician.

1. **Be patient when starting any new exercise program.** Do not expect immediate results. Real-world results do not appear in the duration of a montage training video. Trust the process, and stay dedicated to eating healthily and working hard. Most sedentary people require four to eight weeks before they will begin to feel coordinated and sufficiently in shape enough to take their fitness regimen to the next level. Remember: Crawl. Walk. Jog. Run. Sprint.

2. **A little bit of exercise every day is better than doing a lot of exercise in one day.** If you are just getting started, the frequency of your workout is more important than the intensity of your workout. Start by setting small, daily goals for yourself. Something is better than nothing, meaning that it is better to walk fifteen to twenty minutes every day than it is to wait until the weekend for a three-hour marathon.

3. **Choose exercises that have practical application to real-life performance.** While doing any type of exercise is preferable to doing no exercise at all, whenever possible, it is best to choose exercises that have real-world (and lifesaving) benefits. Great as it may be for you to complete forty minutes on the elliptical machine, that machine does not have any practical application in a lifesaving scenario. If you are doing the elliptical machine to help increase your cardio-respiratory capability, body-weight exercises like Animal Flow, push-ups, sit-ups, crab crawls, and burpees are great ways to both increase strength and increase your heart rate at the same time.

4. **High-intensity interval training (HIIT) is a key component of survival.** One of the best ways to condition your body for a lifesaving

scenario is to incorporate high-intensity interval training into your fitness regimen. This type of training module alternates short periods of intense anaerobic exercise with less intense recovery periods until too exhausted to continue. One popular type of workout is known as Tabata, which incorporates weight lifting or body-weight exercises at a 2:1 ratio (forty seconds of activity followed by twenty seconds of rest) for a predetermined amount of time of at least ten minutes. The benefit of these exercises is that they help to condition the body for a real-world fight-or-flight scenario. It is unlikely in an emergency situation that you will need to do a five-mile run, but being able to sprint down a hallway, push someone off you, and then run out a door, or some other type of running from safe spot to safe spot, is in fact very realistic.

5. **When you think you're ready, try for an obstacle race.** An obstacle race like the Warrior Race, Spartan Race, or Tough Mudder are not for the weak or fainthearted, but if you really want to put your fitness level to a real-world challenge, there is no better measure for what an amateur athlete can endure. Obstacle-course racing is a sport in which competitors, traveling on foot, must overcome various physical challenges in the form of obstacles like rope climbs, monkey bars, wall climbs, buddy carries, and a variety of other daunting tasks.

Additional Takeaways

- Your workouts should always focus first and foremost on taking better care of your body and loving yourself more.
- Fitness can help you to push past the boundaries of what you thought possible.
- Never compare where you are today to where someone else is today. Instead, compare where *you* are today to where you were yesterday.
- When it comes to your diet, eat more foods that are high in

protein and low in ingredients you can't pronounce, sugar, and preservatives.

- Drink more water.
- In a crisis scenario, technology will likely fail you when you need it most, but the constant readiness of a survival mindset and the physical ability to deal with stress will never let you down.
- Don't be vain. Being fit is more important than looking fit. Plenty of people who look like fitness models have never been outside their comfort zones. When your life is on the line, your body doesn't have to look pretty; it just has to work.

[4]

EXPECTATION

What Happened

It took a few moments for the lawyer to signal to her assistant on the other side of her glass-walled office that something was wrong. The assistant called down to the security guard in the lobby and told him to come up right away. Then she called 911. When the lawyer's husband had come to visit in the past, the assistant always tried to give the two of them as much privacy as the layout of the law firm would allow. She thought it weird the husband was here. She had not seen him in a while, and the lawyer almost always gave her a heads-up when he would be coming. The assistant had known for some time the lawyer and her husband were having problems, but she hadn't heard anything more about him for over a month. Things had clearly not gotten better. The husband was growing more irate. The assistant stood up from her desk and backed away. As she did, others in the surrounding area took note of what was happening and did the same.

The security guard arrived a moment later and cleared everyone out of the office suite. The police arrived shortly thereafter. The husband had locked the door to the office and was now refusing to let the lawyer leave. The police sent for a negotiator. The negotiator had been able to convince the husband that prolonging this encounter any longer was only going to make things worse. The negotiator explained that if the husband surrendered now, this could all be explained as a misunderstanding, but if it continued any longer, this would be considered a hostage situation, and that would be bad for everyone.

An hour later, the entire incident was over. The husband hadn't wanted to hurt anyone. For some reason, he had convinced himself that behaving in such a fashion would be the act of love his wife was waiting for to take him back. Fortunately, the matter had been resolved without violence, and the husband was arrested and taken out of the building in handcuffs.

Of course, in the hour it took to resolve the concern, news of what was happening had spread like wildfire throughout the rest of the building. Out of an abundance of caution, offices had instructed their employees and customers to evacuate. A multitude of police cars and tactical vehicles had already positioned themselves in defensive formation around the building. Fire engines and ladder trucks had arrived, and local news crews had already elevated their telescoping satellite dishes up and out of their news vans as producers interviewed the crowd on background for a story that would be sure to lead the evening news. An already bad situation was made worse as each whisper-down-the-lane commentator added their own embellishments to a narrative they knew nothing about. "I heard he had a gun," one said. "He was threatening to blow up the place," said another. Someone else went on the record saying, "He was threatening to kill himself."

All of which were believable but none of which were true. As imaginations ran wild, so did the flow of false information, the consequence of which was a sudden overflow of uncertainty. As concerns grew, fears began to fester, and the expectation that this was a "safe place to work" became increasingly undermined as the uninformed narratives continued to spread. Business owners who rented space throughout the rest of the building were suddenly inundated with emails and phone calls regarding their staff's safety concerns. Since the business owners were being confronted by questions for which they had no answers, they in turn were reaching out to the property manager.

It didn't take long for the incident to become a corporate crisis for the real estate holding company. If the narrative of what happened grew any more out of hand, they would really have a problem. A crisis of confidence can cripple the value of a corporate holding. The realization of the holding company was sudden: What if the law firm no longer felt safe and wanted to move? What if other tenants no longer felt safe? How had the expectation for the safeguards they provided become so suddenly counter to what the tenants expected them to provide?

When it comes to staying safe, expectation is a double-edged sword. On the one hand, the risk of something happening is so low that no one ever expects for it to happen. As a result of this expectation, the allocation of resources dedicated to security safeguards gets pushed lower and lower in the order of priority. So long as nothing happens, no one ever complains. Everyone agrees that finite budgets are best spent where they will have the most effective impact. Of course, when something does happen, the expectation immediately reverts back to ask why we didn't have the best safeguards in place that money could buy. Unfortunately, that's not how the real world works. If you want to ensure you are protected in a car crash, you have to buckle up your seat belt and pay up your insurance premium before the accident. Deciding you really should employ those precautions after the wreck doesn't really do anyone any good.

PROTECTIVE TAKEAWAY

Your expectation for how you are being protected is rarely in line with the reality of the protections being provided.

PROTECTIVE AWARENESS

Unmet Expectations Occur More Than We Want to Admit

You may ask, How does something like this happen? How could a building with security cameras, a gated garage, card readers, and an armed guard in the lobby have fallen victim to such a predatory act? The honest answer is that it happens all the time. Like most breaches of security, it happened because it was allowed to happen. A false sense of security gave way to complacency. And when complacency sets in, bad things are allowed to happen. Not because we want them to but because we become so accustomed to nothing ever happening that we simply assume that nothing ever will. But then when something does happen, we expect the practice to exceed expectation, when in reality, it falters to the lowest level of historic performance.

Unfortunately, this happens all the time.

In 2015, the families of two women killed by a coworker at a northeast Philadelphia Kraft Foods plant in 2010 were awarded over $8 million in compensatory damages and $38.5 million in punitive damages from a security guard firm. (The punitive damage award was later overturned by a higher court.) At the time, the families' attorney, Shanin Specter, said in a statement that the verdict sent a message that company guards "can't simply run away in the middle of the crisis. They actually have to act like security guards."* (The same thing happened with the school resource officer during the Parkland High School shooting. He decided to hide rather than respond.)

To an untrained eye, it may have seemed like the law firm took their security seriously. In reality, it was simply quite poor. The findings of my assessment were not favorable. They revealed every imaginable flaw.

A False Sense of Security

The security cameras weren't in place to keep the public safe; they were employed to keep property from being stolen. No one ever bothered to look at the camera feeds until after something had gone wrong. They were a reactionary measure, not a preventative protection. The gated garage wasn't to keep the public out—anyone could drive in off the street—it was a for-profit operation. Tenants of the building were given a discount on cost, but the general public could park there for a fee, in accordance with an hourly rate. The card readers on doors were not employed with any eye to safety. They were not put in place to maintain

---

* Associated Press, "Jury Awards $38.5 Million-Plus in Fatal Shooting at Philadelphia Kraft plant," March 30, 2015, www.nydailynews.com/news/national/jury-awards-38-5-million-plus -fatal-shooting-plant-article-1.2167811.

any recognizable framework of access control. They were put in place because they were cheaper. With so many tenants coming and going over the years, and with so many people losing their keys on a daily basis, the changing out of locks and the replacing of keys was not cost effective. A systems administrator could grant or remove access credentials with a few key strokes—all but eliminating the need for a locksmith or a hand-counted inventory of keys. And yes, there was an armed guard in the lobby. But he had been there so long, he was really more of a friendly greeter. And in any case, when a uniformed security guard is being paid minimum wage, it would be ill-advised to expect maximum effort. Especially so when their job description is more in-line with observe and report rather than protective enforcement.

But I really must say that on this particular day in question, of all the things that failed that day, that security officer was really the only one who did anything right. When he got the call from the assistant, he saw what was wrong, and he shepherded everyone to safety. But his call to action is to be considered an exception rather than the rule.

And of course, let us not forget that the disgruntled husband had also been there many times before. He knew what barriers to entry he was likely to face, because he knew there were none. He knew the layout. He knew where to go. He knew how to get there. Weeks earlier, when his ex-wife stopped returning his phone calls, his anger started to flare. But she would still respond to his emails and text messages—not often, but often enough to give him hope of working things out. It wasn't until the next week that she stopped answering him altogether. That was when things really spiraled out of hand.

A High Likelihood of Success

For two nights prior to the confrontation at the law firm, the husband had driven by the lawyer's house. His blood pressure boiled over as he imagined every illicit act she might be involved in each time she wasn't there. That was when he decided to stage the confrontation at the one place he knew he could find her, the one place she would be every day: her work. And with no planning at all, he drove over, parked his car, waved to the guard, took the elevator up to her floor, and walked right in through the propped-open door to her office suite. The soon-to-be-held-hostage wife had no warning at all. She wasn't even aware he was there until she looked up from her computer to see him already in her office, closing and locking her door.

You see, there was no real safety here. There was only an expectation of safety that never really existed. In reality, her office was nothing more than a high-rise of improperly framed expectation. A false sense of security waiting to become unveiled.

Was there any "security" here? There were some safeguards in place for the building. There were cameras. There were fire/life/safety systems. They had a system for distributing badges and granting after-hour access, but there were no real protections for the patrons. But no one seemed to mind, because nothing ever happened. Security had been forsaken for the comfort of convenience. But would you feel safe there? Could you feel safe there? Of course you could. That was the biggest part of the problem. Once the rumor mill died, everything went back to normal. My report is likely lost on a shelf. They'll forget that it's there until the next time it's needed. But that won't be today. Today, everyone's fears remain abated. Except for that poor wife. Her fears will stay for a while.

Assumptions Versus Reality

I have conducted security audits for dozens of clients occupying mixed-use office space. Some of my clients, like this one, own the building itself. Other clients are more in line with the law firm in question—they simply rent out space on an annual lease. Regardless of which side of the coin my clients are on, the safety provisions are almost always the same. The building provides a basic framework of security capability, but if the tenant wants to bolster any provisions beyond what is provided, they are more than happy to do so. In 95 percent of the audits I have conducted, none of them do. The law firm impacted by this incident was no different.

When the building owners provide a basic framework of safety, it is easy for the tenants to assume the burden for ensuring safety is on the shoulders of the building alone. It is easy for them to shirk their own responsibility onto those who make the rules. (This is what abates their fears.) Yet while the turnkey availability of certain basic safety amenities may be offered for the sake of ease of use and insurance, this does nothing to reduce the risk their tenants may face. Most business leaders are aware of the risk associated with bringing their services into the marketplace, but what about those concerns inherent to their actual place of business? However unlikely it may be for a business to be directly targeted, the reality is that too few businesses have taken any proactive measures to effectively reduce their vulnerability. (This is the risk that remains.)

Looking through the historical records I had available to me during my audit of the incident with the lawyer and her husband, I saw that the law firm had never once in the five years they had been there communicated a security concern. Other than installing their own dedicated and secure tele-communications lines, no other upgrades or changes had been made. Every other change was cosmetic. They had spent a ton of money on their own preferred office layout and interior design, but when it came to safety and security, not one dime was spent beyond an internet encryption package.

As a result of this law firm's lapse in judgment, a disgruntled husband had been armed with the ability to enter and hold his estranged wife hostage in her office.

Improperly Framed Expectations

How many times have you found yourself displeased or disappointed because the reality of a situation fell short of your expectations? Think of this in terms of a horror movie that finally shows you the monster at the climax of the film. Ninety-nine percent of the time, your mind had created a visual ten times more horrific than what was revealed on the screen. Would it have been better if they had not shown you the monster at all?

Here's another example. Imagine you are chosen as the employee of the month. As your reward, you are given a gift certificate for a free steak dinner. That weekend, you show up at the restaurant, and you are promptly seated at a great table. You choose your selection from the menu, and then you wait with anxious anticipation for your meal to arrive. Except that when it does, your steak is served on a trash can lid.

The steak is exactly what you ordered—grilled and seasoned to perfection—and it smells delicious. But still, it's not what you were expecting.

The waiter can tell you are displeased. "Is there a problem?" he asks. "Did I not bring you what you ordered?"

Your deep and disappointed sigh is only compounded by the waiter's next remark.

"Don't be so disappointed. It's still a free steak dinner, isn't it?"

Now take this same level of disappointment and compound it with the emotional investment of a client or an employee or a public that has entrusted you with their lives. It doesn't make that bad taste any less bitter now, does it?

Even if, when all is said and done and the experience we encountered was altogether positive, the initial bad taste still lingers—even if only in our minds—of what might have been had we only been better informed of what to expect.

Spin Versus Absolute Disclosure

Spin is a synonym for propaganda—a form of disclosure that is intended to communicate something in its most favorable way possible. In media, sales, and politics, spin is what is referred to as an "artful presentation." In other words, it's bullshit. When the stakes are anything less than life and death, spin is to be expected. But here is something important to keep in mind: when it comes to keeping people safe, there is no other environment where the phrase *perception is reality* carries more weight. Whereas spin is presenting something from the best possible vantage point, absolute and accurate disclosure is just what it sounds like: the truth.

The Use of Spin Is a Slippery Slope

Investigators doing pretext are pretending to be someone else, and they are using deceit as a strategy. Great investigators often have a natural sneakiness that serves them well with investigative subjects, and this skill can bleed over into dealing with associates, clients, and colleagues. The tendency to take something that works well in one area and have it bleed over into other relationships . . . well, it can be a problem.

Nowhere is this more of an issue for us than in the area of expediency—by which I mean those times we give someone a fast answer to address an immediate issue at hand, and then we move on. There is good and bad expediency, and one *never* wants to give the expedient answer to one's leadership. Imagine a strategy you'd use when interacting with the other team in a game of sport—a fake-out, for example.

Rule #4

Robert Rogers was a colonial frontiersman who is recognized as the forefather of the U.S. Army Rangers. When he created his infamous "28 Rules of Ranging," no one else had assembled so many tactics into one comprehensive guide. When it comes to employing absolute disclosure to your teammates, rule #4 still holds true:

> Tell the truth about what you see and what you do. There is an army depending on us for correct information. You can lie all you please when you tell other folks about the Rangers, but don't never lie to another Ranger.

I would be lying if I told you I hadn't used a bit of spin a time or two in my career to cover for a mistake I made or to cover for a mistake one of my men had made while in the field. But while I may have told a client's representative that we took the long way home because there was construction up ahead or we had been alerted by local police to avoid a certain area, if asked, I was damn sure to tell my own teammates, especially my own chain of command, that in reality, we had simply missed the turn.

Expectations Cut Many Ways

1. They are a primary measure of success. In the minds of most people, satisfaction comes from how close you were able to come to meeting

their expectations, *not* how close you came to the wording of an agreement or a contract. It may not even be the actual results or the outcome
itself that is called into question but rather the methods, practices, and
philosophies that were employed along the way.

In one such example, I can remember working with a client on a
threat management project where there was such an immediate concern,
we didn't even have the time to get a service agreement signed or even
have the necessary retainer wired before the project needed to begin.
Given our long-standing history with one another, and the expectation
that there would be a professional service provided at a reasonable rate,
we both felt comfortable moving forward with resolving the concern at
hand first and then addressing the business-related matters at the next
possible opportunity. Which we of course did. But in that moment of
need, our mutual trust and understanding helped to provide the expectation for how the concern in question would most likely be resolved and
also for the methods and practices that would help for that resolution to
be achieved.

2. Expectations are a driving force of decision-making. More often than
not, a decision is made not by the terms of service but by what a person
can be reasonably certain they can expect.

In one such example, a client's representative informed me that they
were so happy with the level of protection my team was able to provide
to a public figure, they had been able to say yes to projects they would
have never been able to agree to before because of security concerns
they had been unable to address. The client had been so concerned
with their overall security situation that their fear had actually been
having a negative impact on their bottom line. But now, with my team
on board helping to ensure the certainty of safety, the public figure
no longer needed to worry about being protected. Our due diligence
in our craft and the attention to detail in our service offering had reframed the public figure's expectation for what he was able to do, and
with this newfound freedom came the opportunity to pursue passion
projects he had never felt free to explore before.

**3. Falling short of an expectation one time will forever taint the cer-
tainty of expectation being met every other time.** Conversely, exceeding

expectation one time will reframe the expectation to be exceeded in equal measure each time moving forward.

Sometimes falling short of an expectation can be a blessing, whereas sometimes exceeding expectation can be a curse. In one instance of falling short of expectation, I was with a client who always insisted on leaving as late as possible for the airport. Sometimes they would fly private, which wasn't a problem since the plane would wait, but whenever we flew commercial, we almost always risked missing the plane. To help make the journey more manageable, we had established a relationship with the gate agents of the various airlines we flew the most often. This allowed us to send one protective agent ahead of the public figure with the luggage and necessary identification so that we could bypass the luggage drop-off and expedite their clearance through airport security once they eventually did arrive. On one such occasion, our airline contact was forced to depart early due to a family emergency, and their replacement was not familiar with our arrangement. After some back-and-forth, we were able to get the bags checked by having our contact put in a call to their coworker, but through no fault of our own, the bags were checked in on the wrong flight, and our client was left luggage-less at our next destination. Fortunately for us, that lack of luggage served as the wake-up call she needed to start getting to the airport earlier so as to avoid future mishaps.

On the other side of that coin, I can remember working with one client who always planned to arrive and depart public events via underground or otherwise nonpublic arrival options, but who would sometimes call an audible and want to mix and mingle with the fans for a bit. While this was never part of our plan and was almost always a whirlwind of activity trying to rearrange and pre-stage our protective agents with sometimes less than ninety seconds prior to our arrival, we were always able to somehow pull it off in a safe and successful fashion. Of course, our ability to do so meant that our celebrity client was then emboldened to call out more changes to our preset plan since, as she would say, we "could handle it."

Philosophies and Practices

The following are some philosophies and practices I have found to prove successful:

Expectations Drive Your Success

A fashion model client was arriving at the venue where she was going to be launching a new online campaign. It was mid-November in Manhattan, and she was wearing a large winter coat over the outfit her style team just spent days putting together. From where the SUV would drop us off, it was only ten feet to the front door, but I also knew the red carpet began as soon as that front door opened, and my advance agent was telling me that the press and paparazzi were already staged and ready to take her picture the moment she walked through the door. That's when I realized that I knew this, but did she? This was when anticipating the needs of others came into play. I needed to know what was going on in her head as much as I needed to know what was going on in mine. Did she remember the plan? Did she remember where we were going? This was our tenth stop that day, and if I was getting confused about which stop was which, I was sure she was too. Did she know that there was an awaiting press pool just inside that door? So I told her as we were pulling around the block and up to the front door. And I was glad I did, because by the time I had disembarked from the passenger seat and opened her passenger door, she had already disrobed from the fur coat and gave me a wink and a "Thanks for that." Then she gave my advance agent a nod and a smile that meant she was ready to walk through that door.

Communicate Early and Often

My team was providing temporary residential coverage for a TV personality and his family. The terms of the agreement stated that our agents would only be at the residence while a member of the family was staying at that particular residence (they had more than one). My assistant team leader and I would communicate as often as possible with the respective family members as to their plan for the week so that we could ensure protective coverage was provided while they were on-site.

We were able to develop a clear channel of communication with all the family members at the outset of this new venture because we outlined clear and precise expectations of what we would and could (and would/ could *not*) provide. By framing the expectations of the family, they knew when we should expect them to be on-site at the residence.

This also helped to encourage and promote a two-way communication flow. After the first few days, family members would contact us directly about changes in their own schedules so that we could facilitate our own agent placement plan accordingly. By establishing realistic expectations, we were able to ensure the safety and success of everyone involved.

Under-Promise and Over-Deliver

Clients love being able to pull their SUVs right up to the side of their private plane, but even for the rich and famous, rules are rules. As a result, there were countless times I had to tell a client it would not be possible to get their motorcade of staff onto the tarmac at an FBO because of security regulations (Teterboro in New Jersey and Landmark in Washington, D.C., come to mind), only to be able to pull some strings at the last minute and get them dropped at the side of their plane. I've even had to tell clients that because an event was a head-of-state function, they would be subject to security screening—only to later have a contact facilitate a bypass. When in doubt, always better to reframe an expectation so that those impacted are pleasantly surprised rather than sorely disappointed.

PROTECTIVE PREPAREDNESS

The following are some best practices to keep you from falling into the Safety Trap of Expectation:

1. **Establish realistic expectations**. This is most commonly achieved via the philosophy of under-promise but over-deliver. When the host at your favorite restaurant tells you it will be a twenty-minute wait, but then finds you five minutes later to tell you your table is ready, your expectations have been exceeded. Conversely,

if they tell you your table will be ready in ten minutes, but thirty minutes later, you're making your second trip to the reception stand, your expectations have been severely mismanaged.

2. **Frame and manage expectation as early and as often as possible.** When anxieties are elevated and fears are on high, there can be an emotional response by a client to "do whatever needs to be done." I have often enough heard responses by clients that sound similar to "I don't care how much it costs, just get it resolved." Which is fine, of course, if that was what they truly meant. Sometimes it's true. Other times, it's what they meant until the first invoice arrives. After which, their fears are quickly abated as they realize their concerns were not quite in line with what their budgets could afford. This is, yet again, another reason for why the framing and managing of expectations as early and as often as possible is so important to communicate. By presenting a suite of options that are in line with a professional cost projection, it puts everyone on the same page for what is to be expected, when, and how often. That way, should something escalate, everyone is on the same page in terms of what is to be expected.

3. **Understand how the expectation was set.** Understanding how the expectation was set is important because, as we all know too well, things tend to change. Just because there is an expectation for what would happen with one service provider does not necessarily mean that the same expectation will be met by another. This concern especially holds true for managed security providers whose contracts, personnel, and even providers are subject to change without notification or warning.

4. **Learn to recognize the difference between spin and absolute disclosure.** As a general rule: those who are more inclined to need something from you, want something from you, are trying to get you to believe something, or are trying to get you to buy something are more likely than not engaged in spin—whereas those who you can honestly admit want nothing from you are more likely to be engaging you via absolute disclosure.

5. **Understand your role in helping to frame or manage the expectation.** Not only should you understand your role in how to help frame and manage an expectation, but you should also strive to understand how you can help to reframe and manage an expectation. As we discussed before, expectations can cut in a multitude of ways. When your life is on the line or your expectation for how others will perform may impact your certainty of safety, it is imperative that you do everything you can to make sure the best, most pragmatic, and most realistic frame is placed around your expectation.

5

RESPONSIBILITY

What Happened

On February 14, 2018, Nikolas Cruz completed his pathway toward violence when he shot and killed seventeen people and injured seventeen more at Marjory Stoneman Douglas High School, in Parkland, Florida—a direct result of multiple people, organizations, and administrations shirking their responsibility. Despite warning signs stretching back over a decade, no one intervened. No one took responsibility. No one took it upon themselves to give this troubled individual the help he needed or to make a bad situation any better. Cruz had been the subject of a few dozen 911 calls and at least two separate tips to the FBI. He also came to the attention of the Florida Department of Children and Families.

Even the school resource officer, the only armed officer stationed at the school when the shooting took place, shirked his responsibility. Instead of confronting Cruz, he chose to take cover outside the school. He waited for backup to arrive rather than executing the duties of his position.

How had this been allowed to happen? Everyone was too eager to look the other way.

In one example, a seasoned deputy who was contacted by a woman with a concern regarding Cruz simply "missed" the fact that deputies had been called to the Cruz residence a dozen times, but since Cruz was believed to have by then moved to Lake Worth, the deputy advised the woman to contact the Lake Worth police.

At the school administrative level, when students went to the assistant principal to inform him they had seen Cruz researching guns on a school computer and remarking that he liked to "see people in pain,"* the students were told they should "Google: Autism" and that Cruz wasn't going to be a problem because he was being expelled.

As for the FBI, when a credible tip was reported about Cruz proclaiming on a YouTube video that he was going to be a school shooter, the agent assigned to the case didn't seem to care much about a local concern at all. After a halfhearted and fruitless attempt to identify who Cruz even was, the case was officially closed after being determined that Cruz was not a matter of national security.†

Think this was a onetime instance of safety being sabotaged by the shirking of responsibility? Think again.

Capital Gazette

In 2011, the *Capital Gazette* wrote a story about a local man named Jarrod Ramos who pled guilty to harassing a former female classmate and received a suspended jail sentence and probation. It was a small story in a local paper, but the internet lives forever. In 2012, Jarrod Ramos sued the paper for defamation, but a judge threw out the suit. Ramos appealed, but the judge in that case dismissed the suit as well, citing it did not "come close"‡ to meeting the alleged burden of proof.

From the time the initial case was dismissed, up and through the final dismissal three years later, Jarrod Ramos began a dedicated and systematic

---

* David Fleshler and Megan O'Matz, "Who Made Key Mistakes in Parkland School Shooting? Nine Months Later, No One Held Accountable," *South Florida Sun Sentinel*, November 17, 2018.

† Jason Hanna and David Shortell, "The FBI Is Overhauling Its Tip Line After Missing Red Flags in the Parkland Shooting," CNN, November 27, 2018.

‡ Lia Eustachewich, "Ex-Publisher Says He Warned Staffers About Alleged Gunman," *New York Post*, June 29, 2018.

pattern of harassment against the publisher of the *Capital Gazette*. His threats were direct and specific. On social media, Ramos posted regularly telling staff to kill themselves, hoping the paper would shut down. He would routinely include the hashtag #CapDeathWatch. He made harassing phone calls. He wrote letters. One communication explicitly spelled out he had the "objective of killing every person present."[*] Some employee names were labeled "High Value Targets."[†] He sent a greeting card, a CD that contained photos of *Capital Gazette* employees, and a surveillance video of the office. Everyone who worked at the *Capital Gazette* knew the name Jarrod Ramos. They knew what he looked like. They knew to be on the lookout for him.

The harassment came to an end when on June 28, 2018, Jarrod Ramos shot and killed five employees with a shotgun. Two others were injured while trying to escape.

When the threats began in 2012, the *Capital Gazette* went to the police, but investigators could not conclude that Ramos would act on his threats. When the threats continued, the *Capital Gazette* considered getting a restraining order but feared that would only make things worse. Years later, when the threats continued to escalate, lawyers for the paper contacted the sheriff's department in Anne Arundel County to investigate, but ultimately, the paper decided not to pursue criminal charges.

So why are five lives lost? How had this been allowed to happen? How is it that such clear, direct, and actionable threats were allowed to go unchallenged? It was allowed to happen because no one wanted to see it through. The police were hoping the paper would press charges; the paper was hoping the police would make an arrest. Both sides shirked their responsibility. Both sides passed the buck like it was a game of hot potato, and five innocent lives paid the price for the inaction of those who should have done more to protect them.

---

[*] Matt Stevens, "Virginia Newsroom Discovers Letter from Annapolis Shooting Suspect, Police Say," *New York Times*, July 5, 2018.

[†] Lynn Bui, Erin Cox, and Paul Dugan, "Jarrod Ramos Admits Killing Five in *Capital Gazette* Newsroom Attack," *Washington Post*, October 28, 2019.

PROTECTIVE TAKEAWAY

Safety is not the sole responsibility of a single individual. Everyday safety requires the participation of everyone.

PROTECTIVE AWARENESS

The Blame Game

Everyone knows when they see something wrong. Everyone can recognize a bad behavior. Everyone can notice when something or someone doesn't belong. We all have the innate "Spidey sense" that makes us do a double take or give a quizzical look. But few of us ever escalate those intuitive takeaways to the next level. Why? Because the new social contract tells us we don't have to. If we see a piece of trash on the ground, we don't have to pick it up. We tell ourselves that's someone else's job. If we see a crime being committed, we don't intervene, because that's the job of the police. If we see a parent punishing their child with physical abuse in the mall, we don't do anything because it's not our business. If we see a civil injustice, we don't do anything because we don't want to get sued.

But the real reason we don't do anything is because we are scared. We are afraid of taking ownership of the problem. We are afraid of being blamed if things don't go as planned. We are afraid of taking responsibility for something that was never supposed to be in our purview in the first place. Do people want to help? Of course they do. But will they? Probably not. The more hypothetical a situation, the more inclined people are to say they would help. Just ask someone to help you move a couch. If you ask them on Wednesday to help you on Saturday, they'll likely say yes. You just gave them a few days' head start to come up with an excuse. Come Saturday morning, they're nowhere to be found. As they say, "Everyone's your brother until the rent comes due."

The number-one reason we are so willing to shirk responsibility is that we do not want to be blamed for a bad outcome. Just like the childhood game of musical chairs, no one wants to be left standing alone when the music stops. Responsibility means taking ownership, and taking ownership often means taking on the burden of hard work. Personal responsibility has become the broken crutch by which we prop up our moral high ground. We say we'll step up when something really matters, but in the back of our minds, we know we won't. Our intentions are often no longer-lasting than the emergency tire after a blowout—only good for the next fifty miles. Nothing more than a quick fix. A Band-Aid over a bullet hole. Perhaps it stops the bloodshed for a moment, but it certainly won't serve as a substitute for surgery. No one wants to risk taking that important first step for fear of failure. So instead, they opt to do nothing. Fooled by the notion they cannot lose if they do not play, but in doing so, seal a forlorn fate.

And why is this? Why don't we perform as we promised ourselves we would? Because when the moment comes for us to do so, we suddenly come face-to-face with that wide divide between our comfort and our conviction. And when our hand is not forced, and retreat is within reach, we mostly choose to stay on this side of comfort. And so our self-doubt grows. Our fragility intensifies. The wide divide deepens.

And yet, with each passing hour, and each passing day, we somehow convince ourselves that next time will be different. Next time . . . we will be prepared to act. But the same cycle simply repeats. The dark and ugly truth is that when mayhem is revealed without warning, when we are reintroduced to the harm of others, or even worse, when we are confronted by harm ourselves, we are once again forced to accept the reality that we, very rarely, are prepared to participate in our own protection.

Would You Help a Stranger?

Think back to the last time you saw something that you knew was out of place. A time when something just wasn't right. Were you alone? Did you give a puzzled look to someone else who was witnessing the same thing? What did you do next?

I was traveling home to Texas after spending a long holiday weekend with my family back east. That morning, a wintry mix grounded and delayed many of the flights that were scheduled to fly out. I had gotten to the airport at 8:00 a.m. for a 10:00 a.m. flight. At 6:00 p.m., I was still there. Everyone at the Philadelphia airport had been stuck wandering around for at least three hours longer than anyone wanted to be. Some people had been there for more than a day. Families with children were sleeping on the floor. It was a bad day for travel.

Happy as I am to complain when paying a premium for bad customer service, these delays weren't the result of a broken bathroom, a mechanical issue, or some kind of catering cart calamity. Today's delay was a force majeure—plain and simple. If anything, the customer service that day was above and beyond. The gate agents for my airline had been especially apologetic, courteous, and helpful to me and the twenty or so people who had been in line in front of me to confirm reservations on the next-best flights. They were even going so far as to offer upgraded seating and bonus miles to their frequent-flier loyalists.

There was one particular gate agent, an elderly woman, who had been there the entire day, always with a smile and a courteous conversational tone, doing her very best to help as many people as she could get home. I had been at the airport for almost ten hours, but every time I walked past my gate after getting yet another coffee from the nearby Dunkin' shop, there she was, still smiling . . . still helping.

Maybe her over-graciousness was the reason I took notice of the overly aggressive passenger who was now taking his frustration out on her with his escalating and profanity-laced tone. As I surveyed the faces of the passengers who were sitting around me, they were all noticing the same thing. The woman behind the counter was alone. There was no one else there to help her. She was doing her best to be nice, but this guy was getting overtly aggressive, and there was no airport security in sight. Noisy as the man was being, it was so loud with the chatter of an overcrowded airport. So unless you had been right where we all were, it was unlikely anyone would even notice.

I went through my standard checklist of "How likely a good fighter is this guy?" If push came to shove, and I felt the need to get involved, I wanted to feel confident I could handle any aggression this guy would redirect toward me. We had already been through the airport security checkpoint, so the likelihood of him having a weapon was low. I guessed him to be in his early forties. He was fat and balding. He looked like a roadie past his prime—dark jeans with an old leather jacket over an ill-fitted T-shirt. He was wearing boots—the black Timberland kind—but they were not properly laced or tied particularly tight. Given his top-heavy frame, he would not be particularly sure-footed. He had a watch on his left wrist, which meant he was most likely right-handed, so if he were going to throw a punch, that would be his go-to hand. But his knuckles weren't bruised, and his hands looked soft. There's always the chance this guy was a grappling or jujitsu guru, but if that were the case, his aggressions would have been expended by rolling around on the mat rather than directed toward this woman behind the desk.

This guy wasn't backing down. The body posture of the woman behind the desk had changed. Her hand started to tremble. Her lip began to quiver. Her tone went from courteous to cautious. Her eyes began to dart around. She was looking for help. But there was no help around her to be found. Problem was, her defensiveness was only empowering this guy's aggressiveness.

I took another look at the crowd. Everyone was watching, a few had taken out their mobile phones and had started recording. This was another factor to consider. If I did have to act, I would now have to do it in such a way that I would be comfortable having it broadcast on the evening news.

As I was calculating this all in my head, the aggressive guy escalated the situation by slamming his fist down hard enough on the counter with a loud enough *thud* that the elderly woman jumped backward. "I hate this fucking airline, and I am never flying you again," he said.

Next thing I knew, I was standing at the counter a few inches away from the guy's face, but I made sure my back was to the increased number of people who would now certainly be recording. I gave him a hard look in the eye and then said as quietly and politely as I could, "Excuse me for a moment." I turned to the woman behind the desk and asked if she was okay. She took a few shallow breaths, but smiled. I then asked her if, while I was talking to this gentleman, she could please call for security to join us. As she picked up her phone to call security, I turned back to the man and calmly informed him that his best bet at that moment was to take his own advice and find another airline to fly, because if he was still standing there when security arrived, his day was going to get much worse instead of better. I then turned my body to the side and with a presentation motion of my arm, offered him the view of everyone who had been filming his outbursts this entire time, and said, "It will be your word against theirs." That unforeseen reality was enough to take the wind out of his sails. He didn't say another word. He just backed up, picked up his carry-on bag, and walked away.

It was another twenty minutes before security arrived. I was already back at my seat. The attention of the crowd had already been redirected. The character of the woman behind the counter had already returned to her previously charitable self. The officers spoke with her for a few moments. She smiled as she spoke with them, and then they were gone. No one came to talk to me, no one questioned the crowd, no one seemingly bothered to do much of anything at all. I saw one of the officers point to one of the overhead security cameras and say something into his radio. They likely had the entire thing on tape and would conduct the investigation from there.

Did I have to get involved? Should I have gotten involved? In that moment, I didn't see how I had a choice. A good person needed help making a bad thing better, and aware as everyone else was, no one else was stepping up. This is a truth we all need to accept: safety is not the sole responsibility of a single individual. Everyday safety requires the participation of everyone. As well as things turned out, could they have also made a turn for the worse? Yes. They absolutely could have. But I would have crossed that bridge when I got to it.

I don't remember the first time I heard the Edward Burke quote "The only thing necessary for the triumph of evil is for good men to do nothing," but it stuck with me. As I have mentioned before, my own childhood was wrought with fear. Every time I was picked on or bullied as a child, I wished there had been someone who would come to save me. Maybe that was why I was so infatuated with superheroes and the tales of those like Batman and Superman who would fly in or swoop down just in time to save the day. Or why I was always so enamored by TV shows like *Kung Fu, The Lone Ranger, The A-Team,* and *Knight Rider,* where the hero would come into town to help right whatever wrong was being unjustly imposed by the bad guy. I never got into the whole vigilante thing; I was never much for the Charles Bronson, *Death Wish*, or revenge story lines, but I was always in awe of the ordinary people who found the courage to be extraordinary when no one else would. I wanted to be like that. I wanted to have the courage to do what was right. I wanted to know that I could handle whatever situation arose. I wanted to know that I had the skill set to best anyone who would ever try to do harm to those I loved or who—in times of crisis—could use a helping hand.

The Bystander Effect

In the aftermath of tragedy, coworkers, friends, family, and even the general public come forth in droves with eyewitness accounts and information about suspicious activities and concerning behaviors that were witnessed leading up to the event. So why didn't they say something beforehand? Just like all the people in the airport watching the disgruntled guy harass the gate agent, most people will just stand by and watch. This phenomenon is what is known as the *bystander effect**—a social psychological claim that individuals are less likely to offer help to a victim when other people are present. In fact, the greater the number of people, the less likely it is that one of them will help.

This phenomenon is one of the reasons why when you take a basic CPR or first aid course, one of the first things they teach you to do after establishing that the scene is secure is to point to someone and tell them to call 911.

Because in that moment, it is of critical importance that first responders be notified and that help arrives. If you just yell out, "Someone call 911!" everyone will assume that someone else will call. But if you point to someone, call them out by description so that everyone knows who they are—"You in the blue hat and white shirt: call 911."—it adds an extra level of social accountability, which helps to ensure success.

---

* J. M. Darley and B. Latane, "Bystander Intervention in Emergencies: Diffusion of Responsibility," *Journal of Personality and Social Psychology* 8, no. 4 (1968): 377–383, https://doi.org/10.1037/h0025589.

Now everyone knows whose job it is to call. And once that individual responsibility is recognized, others are more likely to help. As a result, the immediate community is more likely to come together. The call to 911 is more likely to get made because the surrounding tribe will help to coach them on what to say. They will help to confirm the location, the address, the visual cues for the ambulance, the police, or the fire department to look for.

So you see, it's not that we don't know what we're looking for. It's not that we don't know what to do. It's not that we don't want to help. It's not that we don't have the capacity to do good. To support the team. To be a contributing member of the tribe. It's just that we don't want to be the only one doing so. We don't want to be the one bucking the system, disrupting the flow. We don't want to be the one to be first out of the gate.

The Benefits of Prosocial Behavior

A woman in South Philadelphia exits the subway and begins the three-block walk to her residential town house. Arriving home, she looks up the narrow flight of stairs to see a man wrapped in a tarp in front of her door. Unsure of what to do, she stops. She waits. She looks around for help. A look of unease comes across her face. Most who pass her by pay her no notice. Two or three make the concerted effort to look at her, then at the man sleeping on her steps. They all say nothing. While some contemplate an offer of assistance, their eyes half hope the woman won't engage. When she doesn't speak first, they continue on without ever looking back. The woman is too embarrassed to ask for help, yet too frightened to ascend her steps alone. Twenty minutes and thirty people pass her by, until eventually, a young college girl notices the woman in turmoil, and asks if she's all right.

Prosocial behavior refers to "voluntary actions that are intended to help or benefit another individual."* And while the motivations behind

---

* N. Eisenberg and P. H. Mussen, *The Roots of Prosocial Behavior in Children* (New York: Wiley, 1989).

such acts may be difficult to predict—be they kin selection, the reciprocity norm, or the empathy-altruism hypothesis—one core concept cannot be overlooked: sometimes our willingness to help another is the first step to saving ourselves.

Battlefield commanders can't simply point to the top of a hill and with a boisterous yell of "Charge!" make it so. They must communicate their intent with a clear, direct, and specific set of instructions. Beyond the commander's intent lies each individual soldier and their understanding of the plan. They must know exactly where to go and exactly what to do once they get there. Long before commanders lead their soldiers through a war, they must lead them through training. They must instill in their soldiers the importance of looking out for one another. A soldier will storm the fiery gates of hell if they know they are not alone and that their wounds will be properly tended. No one wants to die cold and alone in the mud. But together, fellow soldiers can and will endure anything for the greater good. A good commander doesn't demand respect; they *command* respect. And a good commander never cuts corners or shirks their responsibility to those under their charge. Ensuring the public safety is no different. We've become so focused on the overarching security policies that we've forgotten to educate the public on how to implement effective strategies into their everyday safety practices. Our leaders have shirked their responsibility to help us help ourselves. In becoming so effective at reaction, they have passed the buck on prevention. In fooling us into believing we were safer, we only became more fearful of our inability to ensure our own safety.

The SuperStore Scuffle

In the late summer of 2018, I was asked, for a national news story, to comment on an incident caught on video that had gone viral on social media. In a video that was captured by store security cameras at a SuperStore store in Cypress, California, a father tackled a man who had been taking upskirt photos of his fifteen-year-old daughter. The father's protective awareness was raised when he noticed a twenty-nine-year-old man switch his phone into camera mode and start trailing his teen daughter as she walked over to the makeup section of the store.*

On the video footage, which was first shared publicly by the local police department, the man crouches in the makeup aisle next to a woman wearing a red dress and appears to snap photos before following her around the store. The man then follows the same young woman as she walks back near another woman at the checkout line, where he again kneels down and appears to capture more footage. At this point in the video, the father is seen kicking the man's phone away.

According to the police report, a brief scuffle spilled out into the store's parking lot, where the father snapped a picture of the man's license plate and then called the police to report the incident.

Perhaps most concerning about this entire ordeal is that this very same store had been warned about this same man doing the same thing earlier in the day, but no action was taken. Furthermore, police reports showed that during the investigation, officers learned the man had also committed the same crime at another nearby SuperStore earlier in the day.

A few weeks later, I was contacted by the same news teams after a video a mother had posted to her own Facebook page had been viewed more than twelve million times. The mom had witnessed and then chased down a man who had targeted her twelve-year-old daughter in a dressing room of a teenage clothing store.

In police reports, the mom, who had left her daughter's dressing room for only a few moments, returned to find the man under the stall, trying to grab her daughter's legs. The video showed the man cowering on the pavement while the mom publicly admonished the man while filming him.

"I'm going to make sure your face gets out so that you're not in any more stalls . . . I'm going to make sure you go viral. You're a sick pervert . . . Do you have kids?" she said with the passion of a mama bear protecting her cubs, adding, "This right here is what a predator looks like . . . I

---

* Elise Solé, "Dad Attacks Man He Suspects of Taking Upskirt Photos of Women: 'You Messed with the Wrong Family,'" Yahoo Lifestyle, August 3, 2018.

caught this guy underneath my daughter's stall while she was changing at a teenage clothier. And I had to chase him all the way down, thankfully I got him. Not today, buddy. Not today!"*

Sad as these two stories are, I'm grateful the mom in the latter and the father in the former had the mindfulness and the awareness to notice that something was wrong. They noticed when something was out of place, and they both had the willingness to act, to not shirk their responsibility but instead do something: protect their children.

PROTECTIVE PREPAREDNESS

The following are some best practices to keep you from falling into the Safety Trap of Responsibility:

1. **Never allow fear to dictate choice.** The best way to conquer fear is to face those fears head-on, with a willingness to step outside your comfort zones. Never expect courage to rise up and help influence your decision to act. Courage comes *after* you have already decided to act. Imagine you are watching a movie about your life. What would you want your character to do? Would you want them to look around and wait for someone else to do something, or would you want you to step up and do something?

2. **Assume responsibility for yourself first.** Before we can assume responsibility for anyone or anything else, we have to be willing to accept responsibility for ourselves first. If we shirk our responsibilities over the small things like returning a phone call, answering an email, or completing that task around the house, we cannot reasonably expect ourselves to accept the responsibility for whatever else life may place in our paths. So how do we begin? We start small. Assume responsibility for one thing every day. Once you have identified it, give it the attention it deserves right away. Imagine your responsibility to be like a baby crying

---

* Elise Solé, "Mom Chases Down Creep Who Spied on Tween Daughter in Dressing Room: 'Not Today, Buddy,'" Yahoo Lifestyle, August 21, 2018.

for food. The longer you avoid the feeding, the louder the cries become, and the heavier your guilt will burden you. Once you identify something in need of your attention, lighten your load and alleviate your anxiety by giving it the time and attention it needs right away.

3. **Don't participate in passivity.** You are smarter than you think and you are stronger than you know, so don't be so quick to shirk responsibility because it is simply something you have never had to contend with before. At a certain point in your life, you had to say or do something for the very first time. And guess what? You're still here! If you are unsure of what to do, you can always ask for help, or you can seek advice or direction. Asking for help is a good first step to assuming responsibility. It shows that you care enough to make a difference. Besides, every time we learn a new skill, or a new way to address a concern, we are adding another skill set to the overall protective strategy that will help to ensure your future safety.

4. **Stop making excuses for yourself.** If you are going to play the role of a lawyer for all the reasons you shirked your own responsibilities, don't be so quick to play the role of a judge for those who did the same. Excuses are not a tool of self-defense. They are a tool of self-sabotage. Every time we make an excuse for our own inaction, we are communicating that we willingly chose to hold ourselves back, remain unchallenged, and settle for less in life.

5. **Choose the hard right over the easy wrong.** It is much easier to shirk our responsibilities than it is to assume our responsibilities. It can be daunting to look at the totality of everything we feel responsible for from an overarching vantage point. Looking at things this way will only set you up for failure.

6

US VERSUS THEM

What Happened

The headquarters for the organization where I was conducting my security assessment in the Washington, D.C., suburb of Falls Church, Virginia, had all the security safeguards an organization could hope for. They had an armed and well-trained security force. They had motion detectors and sound sensors embedded in the well-landscaped grounds that occupied the white space between the high, barbed-wire fence and the well-lit walkways that led up to the entrance doors. The parking lot had floodlights. The security cameras had pan/tilt/zoom and night-vision capability. The cameras all fed into a global operations command center that was monitored 24-7 by a professionally managed security provider. They had the most up-to-date access control program money could buy, complete with biometric and key card dual-authentication capability. The doors themselves even had piggyback notification safeguards built in so one authorized user would be unable to hold the door open for another. From fire/life/safety to a helicopter pad on the rooftop, they had every protective safeguard to protect them against the ill-intentioned efforts of an outside actor that they could possibly want to have on hand.

Which is why I could not for the life of me understand why the CEO of this organization was so hell-bent on ramping up an active-shooter training practicum for his staff to perform. When I began to explain to him how ill-advised such a decision would be, he looked at me as if he thought I was joking. In fairness to him, the Safety Trap of an us-versus-them mentality is something that most business owners and heads of organizations are susceptible to.

If a bad guy with a gun wanted to target this place, they had about as much of a chance at success as someone jumping the White House fence and making a run for the Oval Office. They might get past the fence, but they wouldn't get much farther. But this place had overlooked one significant safeguard. They did not have a single measure in place to prevent against an insider threat. Hard as it would be for someone on the outside to get a weapon anywhere near this place, an employee with an access badge and a functional finger could bring in a gun a day and stockpile them in his office and no one would have been the wiser.

When I asked the CEO about the lack of a protective intelligence framework to reduce the risk of an insider threat, he almost seemed offended. "Why would someone who works here want to harm us? They work for us!" And that right there was the problem. Comfortable as it may have been for him to implement the safeguards that protected his staff from outsiders, it was equally uncomfortable for him to think about just how likely he was to be targeted by those whom he willingly chose to count among those he was trying to protect.

PROTECTIVE TAKEAWAY

Insider threats always pose a greater risk than outside actors.

PROTECTIVE AWARENESS

The Airline Safety Brief

We have all flown on an airplane. We have sat through an airline safety brief after we've boarded the plane, stowed our luggage, and taken our seats. We've sat back and watched the in-flight safety video or watched the airline attendants demonstrate—on a very rudimentary level—the instructions for what to do in case of an emergency. I have sat through, assessed, edited, and proctored more safety briefs than I care to admit in my life, but you know what? The airline safety brief is the best. It is simple, informative, and effective: this is how your seat belt works, these are the exits, follow me if you want to live. Pretty simple, right? Trust the captain. Trust the crew. If push comes to shove, just listen to our instructions and you're all going to be okay. This way, if something does happen, everyone knows whom to trust, where to go, and how to get there. And if push really does come to shove, hopefully you will have a pilot like Captain Sully, who can calmly land his plane on the water with enough confidence that you're comfortable getting right back on another flight a few hours later.

And why are we comfortable with this? Because airlines have been tried and tested. They are awarded this extra level of trust and confidence because ever since 9/11, no one takes their safety more seriously than a flight crew. Which is another reason why the active-shooter training drills are just so damn silly.

Think about this. At no point in our lives have any of us ever boarded a flight only to hear the flight attendants say, "Okay, ladies and gentlemen, today you are in for a very special treat, because today we are doing our bimonthly terrorists-have-hijacked-the-plane drill." Never have we ever been shuffled off the plane and then scurried across the tarmac, then corralled back into some central location inside the terminal only to stand around like a bunch of sheep while some shepherd with a manifest calls out our names to be counted before any of us are allowed back on the plane. Thankfully, this has never happened. And do you know why? Because if there were a bad guy on that plane, now they know exactly what everyone is going to do. They know how everyone is going to react and respond. And you know what? Maybe that bad guy is not going to attack that flight. Maybe he decides to attack the next one. But I promise you this: whatever flight they do decide to target, their attack plan will be much deadlier as a result. Because now the bad guy knows what countermeasures are put in place. They know the plan. They have the inside track. Instead of thwarting the bad guy's objective, they have instead made them more effective. All because some airline wanted to rehearse their hijack response plan.

Pretty dumb, right?

Yet schools, office parks, and organizations around the country have for some reason swarmed around this idea that they need to implement these very same drills into their schools, their workplaces, their homes.

And I am here to tell you: *You. Do. Not.*

Do bad guys do bad things? Yes, of course they do.

But not all bad guys act the same way, and understanding the difference between insider threats and outside actors is a critical component in helping to keep any organization safe.

Outside Actors

An outside actor is someone who targets a populated location for violence because they believe it offers the highest likelihood available to them to remedy their grievance.

If you work at a bank, a movie theater, or some other soft target of congregation like a shopping mall or a concert venue, then yes, you are at a higher risk of being targeted for violence by an outside actor.

A classic example of an outside actor targeting a soft target of congregation occurred in August of 2019, when twenty-two people were killed and another twenty-four injured when an anti-immigrant gunman armed with an AK-47 rifle attacked shoppers at a Walmart in El Paso, Texas. Another example would be the Las Vegas massacre where on the night of October 1, 2017, a gunman opened fire on a crowd of concertgoers at the Route 91 Harvest music festival on the Las Vegas Strip. Fifty-eight people were killed and 413 were wounded, with the ensuing panic bringing the injury total to 851. While sometimes these attacks are motivated by greed or need as in a robbery gone wrong, more often than not when these horrific incidents of violence take place, they are the result of a domestic or international terrorism agenda that is often justified in the mind of the perpetrator as being in line with a political or religious agenda.

But not every venue incurs the same level of risk. While the attacks by outside actors are significant, what causes an even greater impact to the safety and security of an organization is the concern over an insider threat.

Insider Threats

An insider threat is a malicious threat to an organization that originates from people inside the organization itself, such as employees, former employees, contractors, or business associates, who have intimate insight and information concerning the organization's security practices.

If you are one of the millions of businesses operating in the United States, the likelihood of your organization being targeted by an outside actor may be very *low,* but the risk of someone you work with having a grievance is very *high.*

For those who wish to do harm, the single most influential factor of target selection is likelihood of success. This is why insider threats always pose a greater risk of harm than outside actors. Students attack their schools and workers attack their offices because that is often where the initial grievance is born, where the ideation that they can "do something about it" is first nurtured, and where the research and planning for their attack can often be disguised as day-to-day activity.

On December 2, 2015, fourteen people (not including perpetrators) were killed and twenty-two others (not including police) were seriously injured in a terrorist attack when an employee and his wife targeted a San Bernardino County Department of Public Health training event and Christmas party, where the employee had attended and posed for photos hours earlier. It was later revealed that the employee-turned-terrorist had recently taken part in the organization's active-shooter drills.

In times of uncertainty, anxiety is sometimes alleviated by the notion that something is being done. When it comes to workplace safety, that something often leaves much to be desired. As any medical professional will tell you, treating a symptom may offer some temporary relief, but eventually, you'll have to address the core concern. Chicken noodle soup will make you feel better if you get sick, but the flu shot will keep you from falling ill in the first place.

Perhaps the most prominent takeaway from this is the realization (albeit much too late) of just how many violent offenders are actively participating in the very measures meant to thwart their efforts. By taking part in active-shooter drills and everyday security screening measures, these soon-to-be offenders aren't just reading the other team's playbook, they are joining in on their rehearsals.

The reason these active-shooter drills are so effective at driving people into the Safety Trap is that they give employees a false sense of security by having them participate in some scripted plan of protection, but what they are really doing is increasing employee risk, because the would-be offenders are now armed with the actionable intelligence they need to overcome the obstacles they are likely to encounter.

As the takeaway from San Bernardino was able to punctuate so poignantly, the employee-turned-terrorist was intimately familiar with how vulnerable they were. He did those trainings too! He already knew where the exits were, which guards were the weakest, and where his victims were most likely to run and hide.

To help treat this core concern, today's forward-thinking business leaders are learning to proactively embrace crisis management and emergency response plans that can effectively coexist within the framework of their executive protection operations. These overarching vulnerability-reduction programs are no longer viewed as a pain point employed for the benefit of the C-suite few but rather as a cornerstone of productivity that safeguards the quality and capability of corporate growth as a whole.

Practical awareness as part of an overall protective intelligence strategy is not new. For decades, similar techniques have been utilized by financial investors to chart the trends of central banks and monitor market fluctuations. Comparable methodologies are used by the military to identify the geopolitical destabilizers that often precede terror concerns. Today, the digital and technological applications in the workplace allow for the human resource process to effectively identify pre-incident indicators that, when properly managed, reduce risk and prevent violence.

The first steps toward preparing today for a safer tomorrow begin with promoting a positive protective posture, ensuring the policies on paper are the same as what are being put into practice, and by rewarding an awareness to the vulnerabilities that surround you so that those key issues may be effectively addressed. Everyday safety requires the participation of everyone. There is still more work to be done, but a practical approach to the realistic risks we face will help to ensure the certainty of future safety for all involved.

Putting the Puzzle Pieces Together

We know people don't just snap. We know that everyone has their own unique threshold. We know that everyone manages their own stress differently. Yet after every incident of violence that comes across our screen, after every school shooting that terrorizes a community, after every mass shooting that undermines the peace and tranquility of an otherwise noble nation, we always find ourselves asking the same questions time after time: How does that happen? What went wrong? Why can't we stop these things from happening?

These questions become even more poignant in the days that come after, when the investigations reveal just how clear the motives and the warning signs were . . . had only someone taken notice. But hindsight is always twenty-twenty. It's easy to put the puzzle pieces together when you have the picture on the box to use as a reference point. But when those very same puzzle pieces are scattered to the wind, and when too few people are in possession of too few pieces, being able to see that hazard on the horizon is a much more daunting challenge. One cannot thwart a threat if one is not aware a threat exists. One cannot subvert a crisis if one does not realize a concern is in escalation. But ignorance is no excuse. Avoiding the pitfalls of the Safety Trap is about remaining vigilant. About never allowing oneself to feel too safe. To always employ that healthy sense of skepticism that warns that when something is too good to be true, there is very often a camouflaged cost.

Effective threat management is about totality of circumstance. This means the overall focus is prioritized more toward the concerning patterns in practice that occur over the course of space and time. The assessment of a specific incident in the context of a singular occurrence is simply a single piece of an overall jigsaw. When that individual piece is assessed on face value alone, it is easy to see how one would mistake the concern as a false positive: unique and of note but not altogether significant. It is only when that one piece of the puzzle is paired with another piece, then another, and another that a true profile of concern can be properly assessed and managed in an effort to bring an unfavorable intention toward a favorable resolution.

Insider Threats Seek to Promote Themselves— Outside Actors Seek to Promote Their Cause

Perhaps one of the biggest differences between outside actors and insider threats is that more often than not, at least at the onset of their ideation, the insider threats are hoping to be stopped. They want to be noticed. They want their grievances to be realized and addressed and legitimized and remedied. For the insider threat, their escalation into violence is almost always grounded in an emotional ramp-up that has been boiling up inside of them for so long, they are ready to explode. Once violence becomes the only release valve these insider threats identify as an available cure for their angst, turmoil, and pain, the success of their harmful ideation becomes inseparable from their own identity. Their attack plan becomes all consuming. It becomes their purpose.

This is different from an outside actor, who very likely may view their plan of attack as something that is required of them. It is simply a task that has been assigned to them as a crusader of their faith or as a champion of their cause. They have no desire to be stopped. In fact, they will likely stop at nothing to ensure their mission is a success. For the outside actor, their motivation is inspired by something bigger than themselves. This is a completely different narrative from the story the insider threat tells themselves. The insider threat seeks to promote themselves. The outside actor seeks to promote their cause.

Identifying the Warning Signs of Harm

As the history of harm has demonstrated time and time again, targeted violence is the result of an identifiable and observable pattern in practice that when identified, assessed, and managed has been proven to prevent violent outcome.

In their excellent book *Threat Assessment and Management Strategies*—which I must also credit for helping to reframe my own professional career from one of personal protection to one of threat management—Frederick S. Calhoun and Stephen W. Weston discuss the observable behaviors threat assessors need to keep in mind when assessing any inappropriate communication. They refer to this concept as the *path to intended violence*. And while I wholeheartedly agree with many of their insights, my own experiences have found that many violent offenders go beyond the communications they may write or say to others. In fact, their very activity—especially those activities of insider threats—can often be readily identified by the warning signs of harm via the protective intelligence framework most organizations already have on hand. They just need to know where to look. And they need to know what to look for.

As outlined by Calhoun and Weston, the path to intended violence has five steps: grievance, ideation, research and planning, breach, and attack.

Let's talk about these five steps for a moment.

Step #1—Grievance

The first step is a *grievance*. Be it real or imagined, a grievance is any complaint believed to be wrong or unfair. Grievances often begin in the workplace, where the feeling of unfair treatment may give way to an interpersonal dispute. A grievance may also take hold anytime our own sense of value is believed to be undervalued. Maybe we feel slighted or underappreciated. Maybe we were passed over for a promotion or insulted by a bonus. It could be anything.

Maybe it's just Bob. Maybe Bob just doesn't like the fact that he's never invited to hang out with all the cool people in Pete's office.

But everyone knows that Bob and Pete used to be good friends—that is, until they had that falling out a while back. No one is really sure what the reason is for that, but then Bob got that DUI shortly after that relationship went south. Which was also right around the same time Bob got passed over for that promotion he was expecting.

And to make matters worse, that promotion was given to Pete instead. And now, all the cool people at work are hanging out in Pete's office in the morning. Everyone is always going in to hang out with Pete at the end of the day. It is always like happy hour in Pete's office.

But is Bob ever invited? Nope! Not once.

Bob hates the fact that Pete's career is on the up-and-up. Pete has been promoted twice since Bob was first passed over for that promotion. Bob always felt like Pete sacrificed their friendship to take advantage of Bob's misfortune. That never sat well with Bob. Bob never got over that. In fact, it has been a problem ever since.

Step #2—Ideation

The second stage is *ideation*. Ideation is when Bob believes he can do something about his grievance. Bob believes he can make things right, return things to normal, make someone pay . . . like Pete. A subset of ideation is *leakage*—and this is important, because leakage is a warning sign: a pre-incident indicator that something about Bob isn't quite right. Leakage is when Bob allows for his ideation of retaliation to be known. Like when Bob starts to outright tell a coworker in the break room about how much he hates Pete, how Pete is going to be sorry, how Pete isn't as smart as he thinks he is.

Leakage is when Bob starts emailing different people at work a link to that YouTube video with graphic war porn. Leakage is when Bob begins to overshare unsolicited updates about the new gun he bought and how he's been going to the range, becoming a pretty good shot. But mostly, leakage is when Bob does things to seek attention. Leakage is when Bob's behavior—especially in the workplace—becomes noticeably different. Like a two-year-old who feels ignored and throws a tantrum just to get the attention of Mom and Dad, so too is Bob asking for attention. But more than attention, Bob is asking for help—but does so without the emotional intelligence of actually asking.

Help Those Who Are Hurting

This display of self-identifying behavior is an important observation for coworkers to not only beware of but to notice and to report. These behaviors by Bob are your first chance to step up and help get someone the help they need. Chances are, your school, your job, your church, your charity, wherever you are doing whatever you do very likely has a system in place for the anonymous reporting of concerns. Sometimes these concerns relate to the abuses of privilege. Sometimes they may relate to discrimination, racism, or sexual harassment. Whatever system for reporting concerns you have access to using, these interpersonal observations should be reported just the same. Someone might not see everything, but everything is seen by someone. And just like we discussed before: our willingness to help another is often the first step to saving ourselves.

Step #3—Research and Planning

The third step is *research and planning*. I'm serious about saying this: I want you to stop what you are doing right now and take a deep breath. If you are in a rush, bookmark this page and come back later, because this step is critical.

Let me be very clear: as a key leader of your organization—and by *key leader*, I don't care if you are a business owner, the principal of a school, the chairperson of a charity, a human resources manager, the head of an organization, or even if you are simply in some other assigned role where you have an assumed responsibility for the health and safety of those who exist in your organizational community—you need to understand that this is the single most critical step, because not only is this the step where Bob will first start acting outside of his normal operating procedure, this is the stage where you have the most control over the outcome.

This is when Bob starts probing the defenses at work—testing doors and checking locks. This is when Bob starts paying extra attention to the security features. This is when Bob is in the break room looking up at the security camera and waving. He's wondering if anyone will come up to him later and say they saw him wave. He may even ask a colleague while gesturing to the camera, "Do you think we're being watched?" This is when Bob starts coming into work early in the morning, then again late at night. He shows up on weekends and other times he is not scheduled to be there. This is when Bob may start exploring the layout of other parts of the office—places he would have no real reason to be.

While all of this is concerning, this is also when the assets of protective intelligence you likely already have employed will really come into play. Because if your systems and strategies are working as they should. If your cameras are being monitored. If your access control is being audited. If your staff is reporting concerns . . .

This is when the red flag get raised. *This* is when you will be alerted to the fact that Bob has been acting outside of his normal operating procedure. *This* is when you can promote your own protective posture and call Bob in for a meeting. Sit him down for a chat. Ask what's going on. Ask him how he's doing. See if everything is okay.

"Bob, thanks for coming in. Take a seat. I just want to have a quick chat. I've been trying to find a time for us to talk about how everything is going. I know things have been bothering you lately, especially since the promotion, but we've been impressed with your work lately and we have a special project coming up, and I think you might be the perfect match. But I think we should talk about what winning looks like first. What do you say?" Let the conversation begin with the premise of optimism, nonconfrontational, but then, slowly, you work in the questions as to why he's been coming in at odd hours. Why his key card has been trying to access doors he is not authorized to enter. What's with the new fascination with the gun range and the sharing of the YouTube war porn with his colleagues?

Talk to him. Acknowledge him. Ask open-ended questions. Provide the opportunity for him to talk about himself. Doing this has two impact points. The first is that you are letting him know that you care about him as an individual. This is a key step to de-escalating his harmful ideation, because the attention and validation are very likely what he's been desiring all along. Sometimes the simplest safeguard for staying safe is to let those who are hurting know they are recognized, that their contribution is appreciated, that they are a valued member of your tribe. No one wants to intentionally sabotage a potential success, but they will very quickly sabotage a potential failure. ("You can't fire me, because I quit!")

The second important impact point is that by asking Bob about his probing behavior, but by doing so in a way that gives him a way to give it a little bit of face-saving spin, you will ultimately be allowing him to maintain his dignity while still removing his cloak of anonymity. Bob will now know that you will be watching him more closely. He will now realize that whatever likelihood of success he believed his ideation held is now disrupted. His efforts have been realized. His plan is flawed. But you're letting him know all of this under the guise that you care.

If you want to help stop the bad things from happening, you have to be willing to help those who are hurting.

And who knows? Maybe Bob will come clean, ask for help, tell you what's been going on. And *this* is when you can get him the help he needs. Reduce risk. Prevent violence.

Because what happens if you don't do this? What happens if you just don't bother to care? What if you have cameras, but no one ever bothers to look at them until *after* something happens?

What happens when you give someone a key card and access to your building, but then you never audit their profile again? I mean, even your credit card company runs regular audits of your profile. If your credit card gets declined or if your card number gets compromised, don't you get a call? A text? An email? Doesn't your bank reach out and ask, "Hey, was this you? This activity was flagged as suspicious. We just want to be sure your account is protected."

Why aren't you leveraging your access control system the same way?

Why aren't you inspecting what you expect?

Because here's what happens when you don't. Bob begins to double down on his attack plan. Bob becomes even more dedicated to probing your defenses, testing your limits.

Did anyone notice that Bob went somewhere he wasn't supposed to go? What if no one seems to care? Did they notice when Bob did this? Did anyone notice when Bob did that? And with each new breach, Bob begins to believe in himself more and more.

Well, if they don't care about this? What else don't they care about? What else won't they notice?

And now Bob has become empowered. Bob is now beginning to

believe that maybe his plan has potential, that this plan of his might just have a high likelihood of success.

And it's been so long since Bob has been successful at anything . . . now he wants this.

So you know what happens next?

Bob starts preparing.

Step #4—Breach

The breach is when Bob starts smuggling in the tools of his terror: a gun here, a few bullets there. He stashes them in his locker, in hiding places, stockpiling.

And as a key leader of your organization, you have one last chance to do something. This is your last chance to notice. This is your last chance to intervene.

Because the next step will be too late.

Step #5—Attack

The attack is when Bob's violence is initiated.

When the shots finally scream, "Can. You. Hear. Me. Now?"

PROTECTIVE PREPAREDNESS

The following are some best practices to keep you from falling into the Safety Trap of Us Versus Them:

1. **Ask if threat assessments are a required part of the employee termination process.** Corporate responsibility may not always extend to those who were fired, but it certainly is indebted to those still hired. The risk of violence by disgruntled and recently terminated employees is a concern every business should take into consideration.

2. **Ask if there is a crisis management team.** A crisis management team, or CMT, typically includes executive directors, department

heads, staff representatives, threat management, and media advisers. The CMT's job is to ensure the certainty of safety by working together to detect the warning signs of concern, discuss what-if scenarios, and prepare best practices for emergency situations.

3. **Ask about employee safety surveys.** An employee safety survey is a short audit asking employees how they really feel about the safety and security of their workplaces. The answers should provide employers with insights into favorable feedback, procedures in need of improvement, as well as areas of new concern.

4. **Ask about the framework of protective intelligence.** Protective intelligence is the process for collecting and assessing information about persons who have interest, motivation, intention, and practical capability to do harm. While it's true that there is no particular offender profile, observable behaviors, such as the expression of a grievance, acquiring of weapons, research on how to breach security protocols, conducting surveillance, and developing a plan, are all predatory behaviors common among those who intend to initiate a targeted attack.

5. **Ask how you can help.** Everyday safety requires the participation of everyone. The goal is to work together to prevent realistic risks from ever becoming a reality.

7

OVERSHARING

What Happened

I often give presentations to estate managers and advisers to family offices on best practices for reducing vulnerability. One of the key takeaways I try to instill is the importance of not oversharing on social media. Simple as that concept may sound, it is often the most overlooked. Bottom line is this: if you are going to be so cautious as to leave the living room lights and the TV on when you're not at home, don't then go and share on social media that you're away on vacation and won't be back until next week. Even more importantly, don't leave a comment under a "Home Safety Tips" posting by your local police department that you employ this very same practice.

I can't tell you how many people come up to me after each one of these presentations and tell me some version of a story where a family comes home from a date night, a vacation, or a business trip only to find that their home has been burglarized. They almost always seem shocked that this could happen. But then after the investigation takes place, they realize just how much they had overshared on social media—all but daring someone in their network of "friends" to rob them.

In one such incident, a couple came home from a lovely night out only to realize they had been burglarized. The security cameras captured a car pulling up across the street and parking in front of the house. The car sat there with the lights off for a little over thirty minutes. Then the cameras showed a man in a ball cap getting out of the car and walking up to the front door. He rang the doorbell and then quickly returned to his car. When no one answered, the security footage showed him getting back out of the car and walking around to the back of the house. He broke into the home through the back patio door. He made two trips back to his car with bags and backpacks stolen from inside the home and which he had filled with all kinds of valuables.

Unfortunately, the placement of the video cameras and the quality of the image weren't enough to get a clear visual of the man's face, but authorities were able to track the vehicle description to a nearby traffic camera and then again to a nearby gas station. The gas station security cameras were able to get a clear picture of the license plate, which led the police to identifying the suspect. When the police went back to the homeowners with pictures of the suspect, the homeowners recognized him as being an old friend from college—whom they hadn't seen or spoken to in years—but who had connected with them on social media about three months prior. That's when they realized their mistake. On the night they had been robbed, the homeowners had posted that very night about them getting ready for their big date night. It was the first date night they were able to enjoy with each other in quite some time. They had posted the day before about where they were planning to have dinner and the tickets to the play they were going to enjoy after the show. The wife had even posted the date-night itinerary card her husband had sent her earlier in the day with a dozen red roses. Throughout that night, they posted pictures on each other's Instagram stories. They shared stories of their food, the bottle of wine, the program from the play. They posted a cute photo of themselves at intermission.

Happy as they were to celebrate and share with their friends this happy night out in their lives, the suspect too had seen them all. Problem was, he wasn't watching their stories and updates as a caring and supportive friend; he was monitoring them as a countdown clock to ensure his own nefarious success.

PROTECTIVE TAKEAWAY

What you share may not be the reason you are targeted, but everything you share increases the likelihood of success for those who want to target you.

PROTECTIVE AWARENESS

Unintended Consequences

When I was growing up, my parents used to warn me about the perils of getting into cars with strangers. Today, I summon strangers to drive me everywhere I need to go. It used to be that we were warned to never give out our credit cards to an online store. Today, I have a credit card that is financially secured not by a bank but by an online store. It used to be that the internet was mostly intended to be searchable. Today, it is mostly intended to be sociable. Where we once thought it best practice to use a username instead of our real name, today we would immediately shun anyone whose online persona was not one of truthful transparency. More than any time in our online history, ease of use has taken precedence over privacy.

But what if all this freedom to share has the undesired result of making us too comfortable with what we share? One common problem on social media is the concern of oversharing, whereby users disclose too much information that may seem innocent in the moment but which actually increases the risk of unintended consequences.

The Safety Trap of oversharing personal information anywhere online is how easily that information can be shared across multiple platforms. A post you make on Instagram can be easily copied and shared to a forum on Reddit. If you shared one thing for a private audience of close friends, but then that message becomes public, it has the potential to put the user at a serious security risk. When this information is then aggregated across time and space with additional information shared across multiple platforms and then combined with location-based information, the unintended consequences for users can be severe.

Everything you comment, share, and say online is another piece of information that can be leveraged against you. Most people don't realize just how much sensitive data they post over a six-month span.

Just as advertisers and marketing firms are interested in data mining your social media likes, shares, and interests so they can harvest the best insights for products most likely to appeal to you, so too are bad guys using each piece of information to determine their own likelihood of success in targeting you for their own nefarious purposes. Most people just don't realize how much sensitive information they share via the seemingly benign things. And again, it's not just the one post or the one story or the one comment that is overwhelmingly concerning. It's the totality of shares that totaled together begin to paint the picture of an all-encompassing concern. Did you post pictures from your birthday? Now they know your birthday. Did you make a comment underneath the photo of your friend's new Honda describing how your very first car was a Honda too? Now they know the make and model of your first car. Did you post a photo of your childhood home? Now they know the name of the street you grew up on. With just those three pieces of information, a low-level hacker would have a very high likelihood of success in targeting you with a phishing scam or, worse, beating the change-password safeguard questions that often request that same information as part of their verification protocol.

With just a few more pieces of information, a low-level burglary crew may consider you a target of opportunity. Did you just check in at the movie theater? Is your whole family with you? Thanks for the window of opportunity to rob you. Did you post about breaking up with your boyfriend? Now they know you are likely home alone. Do you post vacation photos at the same time every year? Now they know when your home is more vulnerable to exploitation. Have you posted multiple photos from inside your home? Now they know if it's worth their while to break in.

Common Sense Is Key

I came across a thread on Twitter about a woman who was selling a dryer online whose oversharing could have really put her in a whole lot of unintentional risk: "To try to stay safe, I decided to only allow people to pick it up after 5pm when my husband would be home. But a guy who works nights asked if he could come in the AM instead; I said yes as long as you're here before my husband leaves for work."

See what I mean? Not only was this person oversharing her fear, but she was providing the best time of day for that fear to be exploited. She was also communicating this concern to a total stranger—a stranger she was inviting over to her home.

Earlier this year, a reporter I've worked with in the past posted a story that made me immediately reach out to her to think twice. She's an on-air reporter who often covers crime stories. Her husband is a police officer. On any given day, I would have assumed she would have known better. Which was why I found myself surprised to see such an unintended overshare by her on a random Monday morning: "My husband has been working overnights (police shifts are a tough schedule) so I try to keep the kids out of the house all morning so he can sleep. It's a challenge, but it keeps us all sane."

There was no reason to share this information with the public at large. The obvious risk here is now anyone who hates her husband for putting them under arrest or anyone who is obsessively inappropriate with her as a public figure from seeing her on TV now knows several things about the security situation of her residence they would otherwise never have known: she spends her nights alone with a baby, and a young child; the best time to attack the residence is while the wife and kids are out of the house and the husband is in bed sleeping; the best time to stage an abduction is when she has her hands full with the children after they leave the house in the mornings at their regularly scheduled time.

Let me be clear. I am not raising a red flag of concern to incite fear. The likelihood of something happening is very *low,* and her oversharing of this information alone is *not* likely to be the driving motivation behind an inappropriate public figure pursuit. What I am saying is this: should someone have the ideation to plan an attack or stage a confrontation, this information will only serve to increase the likelihood of their success. The oversharing of personal information may not be the reason why it happened, but it will certainly be a key ingredient of the outcome.

Beware of Those Who Love to Share;
Be Careful with Whom You Overshare

Back when I was doing a lot of work on the celebrity circuit, I worked with a lot of other hired professionals, especially hired drivers. A really good driver is one of the best power partners a protector can find. They are few and far between, but if you are lucky enough to find one, they are worth their weight in gold. In government service, driving and other aspects relating to secure transport are always handled by fellow protective agents. We are all trusted and trained to the same standard of professional practice. In the public sector, support staff is always hired on an as-needed basis. What makes a really good hired driver? They know their city, they are familiar with local traffic patterns, they have an excellent sense of timing, they know how to reverse plan, they are polite, and if you're lucky . . . they are friendly. But the most critical component of what makes a really good driver is they don't have to be told what to remember, and they don't have to be told what to forget. In the world of celebrity service, confidentiality is key.

One thing I realized very early when meeting a driver for the first time was the red flags to look for. If upon our initial introduction they told me was how lucky I was to have them because of how many famous people they had driven for, I knew I was in trouble. If they then pulled out their phone to show me all the selfies they had taken with their famous clients while regaling me with all the intimate insights they had learned about each one of them, I immediately knew three things: they were a fanboy/fangirl whose sole purpose in doing this job was to elevate themselves by publicly promoting their proximity to celebrity; they were going to inappropriately ask for and/or take photos of my clients; whatever gossip they were able to ascertain about my client had a high likelihood of being shared with anyone who would listen. One gospel truth of those who work in the world of public figures is this: if they will talk about their last client to you, they will talk about you to their next client.

The best drivers were always the ones who showed up at the time and location where we were supposed to meet and then asked about where we needed to go and when we needed to get there. They asked for a rundown of our schedule to see if there would be any complications. They knew where the good staging areas were for them to keep the vehicle so they could be in position before we came out the doors. They never once talked about any of their other clients, they anticipated our needs, and they were always eager to help, which meant that the next time we were back in town, we made sure they were with us the entire time.

I had a little cheat code that I used with my clients whenever we would travel. If the driver could be trusted, I would introduce them by their name and then provide key pieces of pertinent biographical information. "Ma'am, this is our driver, Charles. He spent twenty years with the police department, and we're lucky to have him with us." Saying that we were lucky to have them with us was my way of letting my client know that we didn't have to worry about him selling our secrets to the local paparazzi or tipping off any of the local stringers who were always on the lookout for a celebrity story they could sell to TMZ.

Discordantly, if I introduced the driver to my client in a manner similar to: "Ma'am, this is Danny. He's been driving celebrities for a very long time, and he is very excited about having us along for the ride while we are in town." Doing this served the purpose of making the driver feel like he was somebody special but also let my client know to not say or do anything in the back of the car that they wouldn't want to read about in an online tabloid the very next day.

The important thing to remember here is that while very few of us will have a protective detail advising us on who can be trusted and who cannot, we all deserve to be protected. Our first step toward reducing our vulnerability begins with our own willingness to protect our own selves first. Just because your barista at Starbucks is nice enough to ask you how your day is going does not mean you need to overshare about the bad date you had with Brad from the gym. What if Brad is a regular at that same Starbucks? The barista now not only knows your coffee preference, but they also just emblazoned your name on the side of your cup, and now you've provided them with another piece of information to make you that much more memorable.

If you're buying a new keyless door lock at Home Depot and the checkout staff tries to make small talk by saying that particular brand is very popular, there is no need to overcommunicate how this will be the first and only security upgrade to your home, when a simple "Great— thanks!" will suffice. Especially if you are a rewards member whose home address is easily accessible by anyone with access to your customer profile.

Just as there is a difference between being friendly and being someone's friend, there is a difference between sharing a personal vulnerability with a trusted confidant and wittingly oversharing a vulnerability to someone who has no business being intimately familiar with your personal business.

There Is No Such Thing as "I Deleted That"

Oversharing on social media can not only put you at risk of harm, it can harm your reputation, impact your future earning potential, and even impact your choices for attending the higher education institution of your choice. When it comes to what you share, always remember that promoting your personal brand is much more important than promoting your personal opinion. If you're not sure about the difference, one quick trip down a social media scroll will make it abundantly clear: Kanye West promotes his personal opinion; Dwayne Johnson promotes his personal brand.

Your "Personal Brand" Is Composed of Three Things: Perception, Image, Exposure

Your brand is the essence of who you are. It is your value, your motivation, and your work ethic all rolled up into one. Your brand and your sacred honor are the two most valuable assets you have under your control. And like your honor, your brand, once tarnished, can never be fully restored. Make no mistake. Each and every one of us is a walking commercial. We are the brand ambassador, the account manager, and the spokesperson of the product called *you*. It doesn't matter if the value you bring to a prospective organization is athletic talent, musical creativity, or intellectual genius. Whatever you do best is what you bring to the table. But simply being good at something is no longer enough. Today's modern marketplace requires you to be the total package, which means that the pitfalls of your personal and professional futures are directly impacted by today's social media. In an age where everything is live-streamed, Snapchat'd, Instagram'd, and geo tagged with a face-tagging finder, privacy has all but gone out the window. One thing is certain: whatever you put on the internet stays there forever, and you are person-ally responsible for all of it.

The one thing I tell all my clients who are making the transition from private citizen to public figure is to delete all their social media histories and begin again with a clean slate. Of course, this is not a surefire strat-egy for success. After all, the internet lives forever. There is no such thing as *I deleted that.* There is no *Well, I can trust him.* There is no *She would never do that to me.* Do you really think that Snapchat you sent is gone forever? Sure, if they took a screenshot, you would be notified, but what if the recipient simply recorded what you sent with another device? And then one day they decided to make that personal share public?

No one is going to risk their reputation, their franchise, or their orga-nization on someone who doesn't have the awareness, the mindfulness, or the willingness to safeguard their own reputation. If you demonstrate a flagrant disregard for the value of your own brand, why would they risk making you the ambassador of a brand infinitely more valuable than their own? Harvard famously rescinded admissions offers to at least ten students after "discovering the students traded sexually explicit memes and messages that sometimes targeted minority groups in a private Face-book group chat."* A teacher in Georgia was asked to resign because of a Facebook photo of her holding wine and a beer. And of course, ev-eryone can remember the unforced error of Justine Sacco's twelve-word,

---

* Hannah Natanson, "Harvard Rescinds Acceptances for at Least Ten Students for Obscene Memes," *Harvard Crimson*, June 5, 2017.

life-altering tweet as she boarded her Heathrow Airport flight to Cape Town, South Africa: "Going to Africa. Hope I don't get AIDS. Just kidding. I'm white!"* When she boarded the flight, none of her 170 followers had even liked her tweet. By the time her plane landed eleven hours later, #HasJustineLandedYet had become a worldwide trend with tens of thousands of angry tweets sent in response to her off-color and poorly crafted "joke." Sacco deleted the tweet soon after landing, but the damage had already been done. Websites had already gone through her entire Twitter history looking for any other off-color tweets they could use as fuel for the fire. She released an apology, but it wasn't enough. She had to cut her vacation short after hotel workers where she had made her reservations threatened to strike if she showed up. She was receiving death threats. She was told no one could guarantee her safety. When she got back home, paparazzi followed her to the gym. She had been fired from her job. Her life as she knew it was over. All because of a desire to share something that didn't need to be shared on social media.

The stakes can be even higher for public figures and prospective athletes. Laremy Tunsil had $7 million in guaranteed money† get taken away after a Twitter video depreciated his brand's value. More recently, Houston Rockets general manager Daryl Morey never expected the Twitter image he shared with "Fight for Freedom, Stand with Hong Kong" to cause an international incident. The image and slogan that had been the rallying cry of the protesters in Hong Kong offended the Chinese, with whom the NBA had significant business deals. The timing could not have been worse, as the NBA was preparing to stage preseason exhibition games in Shanghai and Shenzhen between the Los Angeles Lakers and the Brooklyn Nets in just a few short days. American companies doing business in China have long been warned and have historically been quick to apologize for offending China's geopolitical sensibilities—from labeling Taiwan and Tibet as independent

---

* "Justine Sacco, the PR Exec Who Was Fired from IAC for Her Tweets, Has Landed Back at IAC's Match Group," Vox, January 19, 2018.

† Jason Belzer, "Laremy Tunsil Loses More Than $7 Million in Salary During 2016 NFL Draft Plummet," Forbes, April 28, 2016.

countries on their websites and merchandise, to inaccurately reflecting the status of Chinese-controlled Hong Kong and Macao, to bringing up the atrocities of Tiananmen Square. In an interview at an event in New York, NBA commissioner Adam Silver said Chinese government officials requested that Morey be dismissed for his now-deleted tweet, to which Silver informed the officials there was no chance of that even happening.*

Why Is This a Problem?

I often hear many people argue that those who overshare are really just being authentic. This could not be further from the truth. An authentic person has a belief system that is consistent with their actions, but it is still very possible to be an authentic person and maintain your sense of privacy. Just because it has become more acceptable to share your personal problems in a public setting doesn't mean it's a best practice. In fact, oftentimes it's not. Time and time again, oversharing has caused more problems than it has solved. Part of the problem is the influence of reality TV on today's social culture. When we allow ourselves to be placated by celebrity escapism, it's easy to mistake the entertainment value of what is being presented as the way we should all live our everyday lives. This is an especially fallible notion because too many people believe what they are watching is realistic, when it's not. In fact, most of reality television is curated and scripted. Most people don't realize how many actors are hired, personalities are altered, incidents are rewritten, and how many countless hours of tape are required for a single show to be edited down to a thirty-minute episode.

Another big part of oversharing is a breakdown in self-regulation. In the days of the drunk dial, an ill-advised phone call existed only in the span of time the call took place and was only shared by the two people engaged in the call. Answering machines made that practice last a little longer, text messaging made them live on longer still, but social

---

* Sopan Deb, "N.B.A. Commissioner: China Asked Us to Fire Daryl Morey," *New York Times*, October 17, 2019.

media has made these ill-advised expressions of love, lust, hate, and scorn live on in infamy.

One of the problems with oversharing is that we all want to feel connected, and we all want to be liked, and it is therefore very easy for us to cross the threshold of a boundary we may consciously know to be bad but subconsciously feel is okay in the current context. An example of this may be that your boss tells you he's going through a bad divorce, but instead of saying you're sorry to hear that, you tell him that you're having problems in your relationship too.

We allow this to happen because our emotional energy is often more powerful than mental energy, which makes it much more difficult for us to censor ourselves in real time. We may realize after the fact that we have overshared, but once we're down that rabbit hole, it's hard to climb back out. This is especially the case when we are overstimulated with excitement, nervousness, and even fear.

We also care too much about what other people think. A lot of oversharing is fueled by our insecurities. We all have the need to overcompensate for the deficiencies we perceive in ourselves. When we worry about what others think, we desperately try to make ourselves look good, giving away far more information than we know we should. At least when we are oversharing in person, we can rely on the social cues of our audience to let us know we need to stop. The problem with oversharing online is that those same social cues just aren't there.

PROTECTIVE PREPAREDNESS

The following are some best practices to keep you from falling into the Safety Trap of Oversharing:

1. **Protect your privacy.** It is important to keep in mind that our social networks and all our interactions with them are easier to find than ever before. Everything we share online is indexed and searchable. It is not just our personal relationships that suffer from oversharing but our opportunities too. It has become a common practice for employers and universities to review a candidate's online history before making a decision regarding

employment or acceptance. Reporters search online profiles before writing a story, and criminals peruse them when looking for targets of opportunity. Today's online history is even a consideration when you go through a background check for a security clearance or an entertainment audition, so do yourself a favor and make it a habit to only share private and sensitive information face-to-face or by phone.

2. **Social media is not your daily diary.** Your social media feed should not be a day-in-the-life accounting of the entire history of you. Some people try to emulate the celebrity and influencer sharing schedule without realizing that what those people are posting is curated content and not personal promotion.

3. **Don't hide behind the courage of your keyboard.** Never post something you wouldn't say to someone's face. And if you really have that much courage, pick up the phone and call them. If you feel you need to speak up or respond to a friend's post you found offensive, reply via private message—or even better— pick up the phone and call them. Better still, have an in-person conversation. Taking your grievance public should be your last resort, not your first. Directly sorting out conflicts is the best approach. Reducing your discussion to just those involved in the original conflict reduces the chances of pulling the masses into the mix, which can make matters worse.

4. **Prepare yourself for negative responses.** Think twice before engaging in a public discourse. Ask yourself, *Am I prepared to receive a barrage of negative responses?* If you think what you are about to post is worth you becoming a national news story or the feedback and comments will make you feel upset or angry, hold off on posting. Instead, consider calling or texting a friend to talk through your feelings. Do not put anything in a text or an email or post anything online that you would not want the person you love the most to read on the front page of the *Washington Post*.

5. **Don't post when you're feeling overemotional.** If you are only posting for the sole purpose of attention or some other variable

of validation, don't do it. Do anything else instead: practice mindfulness, call a friend, get in a workout. If you really feel like it has to be written, text it to yourself, email it to yourself, write it down on a piece of paper and mail it to yourself. Whatever you do, don't post it. Emotional oversharing may not be the cause of your concern this time, but at some point in the future, it most certainly will.

8

OVERPROTECTING CHILDREN

What Happened

I spent a few years as the detail leader for a public figure and his family in New York City. The family had two young children, and we would often attend events that were being hosted in Central Park. After one such occasion, my team and I were escorting the family through the park as the family was walking back to their apartment. My assistant team leader (ATL) was walking point when he was approached by a frantic and near-hysterical woman. "Are you police? I can't find my daughter." I immediately scanned the surrounding area to make sure this wasn't a distraction intended to take our attention away from an oncoming threat, but seeing none and noticing the visible signs of terror on the woman's face, I considered her concern to be credible.

As any mother would be, my client's wife was immediately engaged and asked if there was anything we could do to help. The woman told us that they had been visiting the nearby Central Park Zoo. She had been talking to a friend on her phone while her daughter walked beside her, and then—just like that—she was gone. Given the high profile of my client, we had a good working relationship with the NYPD, and they often provided us with the contact information for the mobile command center that would be overseeing the safety of the event we would be attending.

We had only just left the event about twenty minutes prior, so I knew the mobile command center would still be in position. I called the command center to initiate an Amber Alert while my ATL interviewed the woman to retrieve whatever relevant information would help the police in their efforts. Fortunately, the mother had taken some photos of her daughter while they were at the zoo, so we had an excellent physical description of her daughter and the outfit she was wearing to share with the command center. The NYPD command center immediately put out a BOLO (Be On the Look Out) to their officers.

Most missing children are found very quickly after they go missing. A child who goes missing in a grocery store is often found in the candy aisle a few rows over. A child who goes missing at a theme park will often be found wandering over by whatever attraction they find most enticing. Unfortunately, there are other times when the outcome is far less fortunate. Given the emotional investment by my client's wife and the uncertainty of how this particular concern would be resolved, the family decided that my client and the two children would continue home with my ATL and another one of our team members, while I stayed behind with his wife to offer whatever support we would be able to provide to the mother.

The family said their goodbyes, and since the Central Park Zoo was an easily recognizable and equally likely point of return for the daughter, we decided to retrace the mother's steps back in that direction. Twenty minutes later, we were back at the zoo and there was no sign of the daughter. The mother was growing more and more frantic. I can't imagine what was going through her head, but the expression on her face was that of gut-wrenching terror.

To help quell the mother's nervous energy, we decided to circle the zoo. When we were halfway around, my phone rang. It was the police. They had found her daughter sitting on a bench on the other side of the park. She was scared but safe. The police put the daughter on the phone as I handed the mother mine. She was half sobbing and half trying to choke back her own tears as we walked toward where her daughter had been found.

I have seen a lot of reunions in my day, but that one was especially emotional. The daughter burst into tears as she jumped into her mother's arms. I thanked the police for their help. We shook hands. The mother was hugging everyone while the daughter monkey hugged her mother for dear life. She wouldn't be letting go for a while.

While the mother had been on the phone, the daughter had simply wandered off. She thought she knew the way home, but then when she realized that her mother was nowhere to be found and nothing looked familiar, she tried to find her way back until she realized she was lost. She walked until she found a safe place to sit down, and then she just sat there. When her mother asked her why she didn't ask anyone for help, the daughter gave the most self-defeating answer her mother could hear: "I wanted to, but you told me to never talk to strangers." Then she started to cry again. Through her tears, she sobbed, "Everyone was a stranger."

As I walked my client's wife back to her home, we talked about how much of her life was spent in support of keeping her children safe. She was asking me for my advice. She had been shaken by the child's response to the mother. The daughter's response had terrified her into thinking that while she was instilling in her children the same safety strategies she had learned as a child, she may actually be putting her own children more at risk. She was not alone in this concern. Child safety is the cornerstone conversation I have with every family I advise. No matter how at risk a public figure may be, their number-one concern is *always* their children.

How to best protect a child from harm is a challenge every parent will confront. At its most fundamental level, it is a question of overprotectiveness versus overexposure. How do you protect your child without being a helicopter parent while at the same time not make them fearful while trying to explain something before it happens? Truth is, there is no magic answer. Despite the best efforts to keep a child protected, they will inevitably be exposed to crime, chaos, and tragedy well before any of us ever wish they would. But also true is that an aware child is a safe child, and a prepared child will always be far less anxious and much more empowered to influence their own outcome, rather than fearful of whatever unnamed adversity may await.

PROTECTIVE TAKEAWAY

It is better to empower children with simple strategies they can use to keep themselves safe than it is to shield them from the realities of real-world risk.

PROTECTIVE AWARENESS

Stranger Danger Is a One-Way Street

Children have a difficult time understanding the concept of nuance. *Stranger danger* is one of those catchy rhymes that both sounds good and is easy to remember, but it really does more harm than good. If your child is separated from you but requires immediate help, they need to know they have the right to participate in their own protection. What we should really be saying is, "Stranger danger is a one-way street." While it is wildly inappropriate for an adult to ask a child for help, it is perfectly acceptable for a child to ask an adult for help. The world is full of good, decent, hard-working people who will do almost anything to help a young child in obvious need. Now, if a man in a van says that he has lost his puppy and needs help to find him, that is *not* okay. But if your child is alone and afraid, they should know that it is okay to get help from strangers. What you do not want is for your child to have an emergency where no one they know is around to help and they don't know what to do. How can children know which adults are okay to ask for help and which adults are not okay?

The Three *F*s of Family, Food, and Flags are good reminders for where children can go to get help:

FAMILIES: Any adult with a child or young children is okay to ask for help.

FOOD: Anywhere food is being served or sold is a good place to ask for help. If a child is lost in the park and they see someone selling ice cream, that adult is okay to ask for help. Those selling food are checked and inspected prior to being given a permit. If your child is ever in trouble and they don't know where to go, run to a restaurant.

FLAGS: Flags are friendly. Anyone with a flag on their uniform is okay to ask for help. The same goes for any building that has a flag in the front yard—like a post office, a library, school, or firehouse. These are all places which can be trusted, and your child should know that it is okay for them to ask for help if they are alone and scared.

Baby Steps to Safety

From the moment a child is placed in their arms, parents devote themselves to not just ensuring the emotional well-being of their child, but they also dedicate themselves to protecting their child from harm. The reality every parent soon realizes is that while the warm embrace of a mother's hug may make a child feel safe, love alone is not enough to protect their child from the world that surrounds them. Of similar concern, a child tucked safely in their bed at night may be physically secure but may not feel emotionally safe if they believe there is a monster hiding in the closet.

As much as you may want to shield your child from the realities of the world for as long as you can, at some point, they will be confronted by cruel truths of life. When this happens, they will very likely have questions—even if they don't quite know how to ask them.

Instead of avoiding these tough-to-talk-about times, choose to use them as an opportunity to replace any anxieties your child may have with empowering lessons they can carry with them for the rest of their lives. It may be best to frame these conversations with your child into three different topics of discussion: what they know, what they think they know, and what they want to know. This will help you to separate the facts from whatever fictions are fueling their fears. You can then use this information to frame your conversation in the most age-appropriate manner possible and, in doing so, instill within them the certainty of their future safety.

There Are No Foolish Fears

Most childhood fears are the result of backfilling unknown facts with fantasy. Children have active imaginations and will sometimes envision a course of action that may not be rational or realistic. This is especially true of younger children who are afraid that something bad will happen to their families. It is very important that children not be made to feel like their fears are foolish. Instead, do your best to replace their fears with facts. A colleague of mine has a daughter who suddenly one night was afraid to go back into her room. Instead of dismissing her fear as a ploy to stay up later, he asked her to identify *why* she was afraid. After some coddling, she revealed there was a wolf in her closet. He took her by the hand, and the two of them turned on the lights and went looking to see what she could have possibly meant. The "wolf" in question turned out to be the reflective tape on her backpack that was glowing in the shape of "ears" from inside her closet. Once he was able to show his daughter the source of her fears and put her mind at ease, she was much more willing to go back to sleep. But instead of my colleague dismissing his daughter's fears as childish, he explained how they lived in an area where there were no wolves. He brought in his laptop and showed his daughter where wolves did live. He showed her on the map how far they would have to travel. And besides, he explained to her, they lived on the fifty-fourth floor of a downtown high-rise. How on earth would a wolf have gotten here? He then explained all the safety precautions that a wolf would have had to bypass before it could have gotten all the way up to their apartment and into her closet: through the heavy front doors, past the doorman, into the elevator, up to their floor, past the security camera, then somehow unlock the door and sneak into the apartment, finally finding comfort in her closet. By the time he was done, she had offered up the response he had hoped for: "Daddy, that's just silly."

The Magic of Mr. Rogers

Other times, a child's fears may be a side effect of uncertainty. In these moments, children are looking for reassurance. When these fears arise, it is perfectly acceptable to provide whatever reassurance they need. If they are older and frightened by something more tragic, it is perfectly acceptable to explain to them that though horrible, these types of attacks are very rare. Even when they do happen, the outpouring of goodwill always outweigh the ill will of those who are bad.

When I was a boy, and I would see scary things in the news, my mother would say to me:

> "Look for the helpers. You will always find people who are helping."
> —Fred Rogers

This is an effective message to share with children of all ages: focus on the good. Look not at the destruction but at first responders who rushed to help, the police who stopped the offenders, the people who opened their homes to strangers.

This is also a perfectly appropriate time to remind your children about the precautions you take to protect yourself, as well as the everyday safety precautions taken to keep them safe at home and school. Try to realign the outlook of their fears toward a more positive framework of understanding by assuring your child just how much they are safe, loved, and protected.

Children Need a Trusted Source of Information

Parents should not feel burdened to "know everything." If your child asks you a question and you are unsure of how to respond, "I don't know, but I'm going to find out right now" is a perfectly acceptable answer. So is "That's a really important question, and I want us to take time to discuss this. How about tonight at dinner?" This placeholder of an answer will both demonstrate how seriously you are taking their concern while also buying yourself the time you need to seek out the best advice for how to answer your child's specific questions. *This response also serves two important purposes:* it establishes the parent as a trusted source of information in their child's life; and it removes the fear factor some children have of not asking their parents questions for fear they can't help. Empowering your child with the comfort and confidence to come to you with any questions they may have will help lay the foundation for them to feel safe in coming to you in the future—with much more challenging subject-matter conversations.

Practice Makes Perfect

Teaching your child what to do if there is an emergency is just as important as doing your very best to protect them from harm. When talking
to children about safety, try to do so calmly without raising their level
of anxiety. Provide your child with simple solutions to problems they
can solve themselves. Ideally, you want to have them be engaged in their
own decision-making process. You want to encourage them to utilize
their own problem-solving skills and then practice those skills in a safe
learning environment.

While protecting your child is a core principle of parenting, so is empowering them with lessons they will have with them for the rest of their
lives. Teaching your child what to do if there is an emergency is just as
important as doing your very best to prevent an emergency from arising.
If you take your child's hand on a crowded street to prevent them from
getting lost, take one moment more to ask them what they would do
if they couldn't find you. Just like you would play I Spy or some other
street game, it may help to alleviate your child's anxiety by framing these
safety strategies more like a game than an expectation of reality: Let's
play, "What would you do if . . ."

It is important to keep in mind that talking to children about safety or
just telling them what to do is not enough. Children learn best through
active participation. When talking to children about danger, we want to
do so without raising their levels of anxiety. We want to provide them
with simple solutions to problems they can solve themselves. We want to
have them be engaged in their own decision-making processes, to utilize
their own problem-solving skills, and then practice those skills in a safe
learning environment.

Emphasize Practical Preparations

Everyone knows to call 911 in an emergency, but how many have ever
practiced doing it or rehearsed what to say? The next time you are having
family time, put your phone in airplane mode and have them practice
calling 911. You can even role-play the operator on the other end: "911

operator, what is your emergency?" In addition to having your child dial the numbers, have them rehearse what to say, and then have them practice the importance of staying on the phone. Let them know that it's okay if they can't remember the address or if they are too afraid to talk. So long as they can dial and stay on the line, 911 will be able to trace the call. Note: not all phones and carrier companies have the same location identification capabilities. Double-check your own phone first in order to set your child up for success.

When in doubt, keep things simple. You can even have what to say printed on a piece of paper you keep on the fridge: "I need help. Please send police and ambulance." This simple sentence is all that is needed to have help come running. Again, keep things simple. A child's voice saying *police and ambulance* is enough of a head start to help resolve any crisis. Let the professionals on the scene evaluate the severity of a concern. There is no need to put that burden on your child.

Do you have a fire extinguisher in the house? Have you ever practiced using one? Fire extinguishers are one of the most effective devices available for stopping a fire in its tracks. They come in all different weights and sizes, from heavy and industrial to tiny and lightweight. They are both inexpensive and easy to use. If your child can manage using a garden hose in the backyard, they can manage to use a fire extinguisher. So why not empower them with a very practical, real-world, lifesaving skill and spend a few dollars at Home Depot on a Family Safety Day?

Whatever scenarios you think are most realistic, talk to your kids about what to do, and then have them practice what is expected. Personal safety skills increase a child's confidence and competence in an emergency.

Family Reunification

When I was a kid, my sister got lost while we all were playing mini-golf. After that, whenever we went anywhere, my mom would always pick out a spot for us to return to should we ever get separated. "Okay, if we get separated, we'll meet back here near the ice cream stand." To which we would all respond with an eye roll and an in-unison monotone response of "Yes, Mom." But my mom was smarter than we realized. She intuitively knew to pick locations that were easy to identify and easy to remember. We may not have known much else, but we all knew where to beg for ice cream before we left wherever we were for the day.

These are great lessons to instill in your children, because they have a very real and lasting impact on ensuring their future safety. Years from now when your daughter is in college, she'll remember what you said to her at the zoo. When she and her group of friends walk into a new bar for the first time, they'll say to each other, "Okay, if we get separated, we'll meet back here near the entrance of the bar so we can all go home together."

Simple as this scenario may sound, family reunification is one of those key strategies that often goes overlooked. It's easy to think that reunification may be something that is dictated by others, but the reality is it will almost be entirely up to you. Yes, if there is an incident at your child's school, the administration may communicate to parents the update where and when you can expect to pick up your child. But these scenarios will only take place so long as the situation is manageable. Should something more significant take place, these ad hoc policies and procedures will most certainly be the first safeguards to fail.

For this reason above all others, your children *must* be empowered to participate in their own protection. They must know that they have your permission to save themselves should they feel in fear of their life, and they *must* know that they have your permission to not fall fateful victim to a plea of false authority. (For more on this, see chapter 2, "False Authority.")

Safe Havens

A safe haven is anywhere you can go to be protected. For most of us, the best safe haven is our home, but what if we just can't get there? The more we educate and instill in our children the importance of identifying those locations outside the home where they know they can go to be safe, the better prepared we will be when a crisis strikes. As you go about your everyday life, work with your child to emphasize the importance of situational awareness. Take the time to point out where the hospitals are and where the police stations are located. Schedule some time to take them on a tour of the neighborhood firehouse. Should something happen along their everyday journey between home and school or home and their other daily activities, it is important they have these safe havens identified as early and as often as possible. The earlier these locations are predetermined, the more prepared they will be should something happen.

Much like reunification plans, the identification of safe havens is another one of those protective strategies that will stay with them for the rest of their lives. Like a seat belt in a car crash, it is a safeguard that will often prove unnecessary, but when they need it most, they will be forever grateful they have it in place.

After the bombings in Boston, I was asked to give some interviews. One of the questions asked most often from viewers all over the country was, "What should I do if something like that happens to me?" My answer was always the same: "Run away from the danger and get somewhere safe. Have a plan, know where to go, and know how to get there."

After the first few interviews, this question was repeatedly coming up. I soon realized that most families may have had a reunification plan for regrouping when they were confined to an area of operation like a shopping mall or a stadium, but for those who had been at the Boston Marathon, that area of operation was vastly more expansive. There was no distinguishable perimeter. The area of operation was the entire city of Boston. The other key observation was that while families may have taken the proactive steps with their children to identify the safe havens that were close to their homes, almost no one had thought to take this same strategy with them when they traveled *away* from home.

For those who lived in Boston, when the explosive device was set off, many locals had a good working knowledge of their immediate area. They may not have had a plan for what to do, but they at least knew where they were. For all those families who had traveled in for the race, they immediately found themselves at a significant disadvantage for ensuring their safety.

Which was why my previous answer was falling on deaf ears. When people are scared, they don't want to hear general guidelines. They want actionable intelligence and direct instruction. They want to be told where to go. They want to be told what to do once they get there. In a crisis scenario, people may want specific answers to their concerns, but the reality is, once the concern has been realized, it's mostly too late to do anything effective. Our mindset needs to be preventative, not reactionary.

So I'll tell you this now so that should this ever happen to you, you'll already have a plan for what to do:

Run to a Restaurant

Anytime you or your children find yourselves too far away to run home, pick out an easily identifiable restaurant and tell everyone to go there. If you are out on a vacation, you may not remember the street of your hotel, but you will likely remember where you just had lunch. Go there!

Restaurants make great safe havens. Why? Because you can pretty much guarantee they:

- will have the ability to accommodate large crowds of people
- will have food and water
- will have at least the basics of a first aid kit and restrooms
- will have knives and other equipment that can be used for hasty weaponry
- will have hard-line internet and phones, so if the phone towers shut down, you'll still be able to let loved ones know you're okay

The Children Are Our Future

Today's children are the first generation to live their entire lives in a post-9/11 threat matrix. This can be a challenge for those parents who came of age in a time before the modern era of terror warnings and social media concerns. They know the anxieties, concerns, and fears impacting their children are not the way things used to be.

But for children, this is normal. They have always had to take off their shoes at the airport. They have never known a school to not have active-shooter drills. We grew up with stop, drop, and roll; they grow up with run/hide/fight. We had to deal with the issues of asbestos and faulty wiring burning a school down. Today, their concern is the faulty wiring of our society. It is important to remember that today's children have no frame of reference to a time before any of this chaos. My concern as a threat management expert is that this means fear and anxiety have become a normal part of their daily lives. A scared society doesn't advance forward. It breaks contact. It retreats backward.

It is important to me that we make a conscious effort to not pass down to younger generations these often irrational fears and anxieties but rather instill into them that small piece of vigilance that will help all of us to ensure safety—not just today and tomorrow but for the rest of our collective lives.

The protective lessons we teach them today will be lessons they can remember and employ and utilize long after they leave the protective confines of home. By teaching them the rules of safety now, we can cut down on unnecessary anxiety later and help children to avoid an entire generation of people falling into all these safety traps.

Remember: the more educated your child becomes about the realities of the world around them, the less likely they will be to succumb to the fantasies of their fears. Cultivating an open, honest, and conversational relationship with your child will help to reduce the possibility of emotional difficulties and will promote the resiliency your child needs to live a safe, secure, and successful life. We can no longer teach our children only about the good in the world. We need to frame their expectations to the bad as well. Not to be afraid but to be aware. They need to understand the duality of there being both good and evil in all of us. Because sometimes bad things have to happen so that the good in us can grow stronger. For only when we embrace the good can our souls grow bigger, our minds think clearer, and our hearts love deeper. Remind them with every chance you get that each and every day is followed by night. But even the darkest nights have stars in the sky—and that's how we know that the light is winning.

PROTECTIVE PREPAREDNESS

The following are some best practices to keep you from falling into the Safety Trap of Overprotecting Children:

1. **It is always better to have the safety talk too soon rather than too late.** It doesn't matter if the concern is about inappropriate touching or safe sex, as soon as something is a believable reality for your child to recognize, it's time to have the talk. Too many parents believe their own anxieties are irrational and that their child "couldn't possibly be that old already." Trust your instincts. If the risk is high enough to give you anxiety, it's early enough to make your child aware of that real-world risk.

2. **Encourage an open and honest discussion about their fears.** Never downplay or deny the emotional reality of a child's fear or phobia. Children crave certainty and structure. Every moment of their lives, they are exposed to new realizations about the world around them. Encourage them to ask questions. Explore their concerns with practical and realistic feedback. Explain to them the reasons why things happen. If they have questions about homeless people, it may not be enough to say that they are too poor to have a home. What they may really be asking about is *why* are they too poor to have a home. Despite all of the other factors of income inequality, access to affordable housing, veterans with PTSD, drug addiction, and domestic violence (to only name a few), maybe you will realize that this is a good opportunity to discuss mental health. By helping them to understand that some people can be sick in the mind just like they can be sick in the tummy may help ease their fears of becoming poor or homeless themselves. This may also be a good time to explain to your child that just because you don't give the beggar on the street money doesn't mean that you are a bad person or that you don't care about the person in need but that you need to spend your money wisely. This might be an appropriate time to explain to your child that you donate to an organization that helps all the homeless people instead of just the one person who asks.

3. **Don't make safety scary—make safety fun.** The more you are able to encourage your child to participate in effective and practical strategies that will help to keep them safe, the more second nature those strategies will be when they need them the most. If

you are visiting an amusement park, the zoo, or even a shopping mall, have your child pick out a place that is easy to recognize and easy to remember. Since they identified this landmark, they will be more likely to remember it should they get lost—which in turn makes it an ideal place for them to return to (and you to find them) should the two of you get separated. If you are playing the license plate game, help them to not only identify the state where the plate is from but also a phonetically fun way for them to remember the license plate number. TZM-459 could be "The zebra is mine, four fifty-nine." If you are able to turn the license plate game into a jingle, they might even be more likely to remember. This is one of those protective strategies they may not need to employ in the immediate future. But once they have this technique in their bag of safety tricks, they will have it with them for the rest of their lives. If your child is interested in nature shows, this may be a good time to point out the reason all the animals move together in a herd, because it makes them less likely to be targeted by the lions. This is a perfect opportunity to explain to them why it is so important that they never walk alone.

4. **Board games offer a treasure trove of everyday safety strategy.** While board games are a great way to spend quality time together as a family, they also offer the opportunity to engage your children in conversations about what is going on in their lives. No matter what game you are playing, there will be multiple opportunities to initiate a dialogue about a vast variety of subjects and topics. Perhaps more than any other topic, board games offer a parent the perfect springboard to talk about safety. Why? So much of the success in winning a board game is based on strategy. Strategy is grounded in the mindset and the outlook of being able to read your opponent's tells and intentions. Strategy also encompasses tactical decision-making. As much as games like checkers will teach a child how to think quickly and transactionally, and chess will teach a child how to think slowly and methodically, a board game like Monopoly

will offer the opportunity to teach your child about financial literacy—perhaps the most practical skill for remaining financially secure. A board game like Memory will help to teach them how to recall key details about what they had previously seen before—which may help them to recall the identifying details about the strange man who made them feel uneasy in the park. Even for children who may not be able to read and write yet, a board game like Clue will help them to understand the concept of cause and effect—and we know all too well how much of an influence that has on our lives.

5. **Most importantly: listen more than you talk.** The more you listen to your child, the more connected the two of you will become, and the safer they will feel—not just emotionally safe but secure in their comfort to come to you with their concerns too. Ask questions that will spark their interest, and respond with as many open-ended questions as possible. If you are ever unsure of what one of their questions may mean or the intention behind such a question, one effective technique may be to boomerang the question back onto them: "Mommy, what does *bravery* mean?" could be easily responded with, "Well, what does *bravery* mean to you?" Or help them to answer their own question themselves: "Hmmm, well, let's think about this together. Which character in *The Lion King* do you feel was the bravest?" By encouraging your child to take part in the answering of their own questions, you not only encourage them to participate in their own learning process, but you will reconfirm the bond that you will have with your child as a shepherd of safety—not just in learning but in life.

9

ALARM FATIGUE

What Happened

On January 13, 2018, a sunny Saturday morning in Hawaii escalated from fearless to fateful when a ballistic missile alert was issued via the emergency alert system and incited panic throughout the population of the popular island paradise.

EMERGENCY ALERT:
BALLISTIC MISSILE THREAT INBOUND TO HAWAII.
SEEK IMMEDIATE SHELTER.
THIS IS NOT A DRILL.

For a full thirty-eight minutes, people lived in absolute terror. An entire population accepted their fate. They called loved ones, said their goodbyes to their families, and held each other close as they waited for the explosive sounds that would likely mean the end. Some people prayed for forgiveness, while others ran as far as they could away from what they believed would be the likely targets of attack: military installations, government buildings, airports, and landing docks. Then the next slew of text messages, phone calls, emails, and social media updates gave the entire state a deep sigh of relief: it was a false alarm.

What had made the alert so alarming was how legitimate everyone believed the threat to be. No one had ever seen this before. It was new. It was authentic. It appeared to be legitimate. And most concerning, it was believable. For months, news reports and political reporting had commented on the ballistic capability of North Korea, and Hawaii was commonly recognized as the primary target within their missile-striking range.

So when the alert came across their phones, everyone panicked. They thought they had more time. They thought there would be more warning. They did not know what to do. They did not know where to go. They did not have a plan.

Relieved as everyone now was, there was still a lot of fear and panic embodied in the realization that this could happen again. And the next time, it may even be for real. If nothing else, the prevailing opinion was that maybe this was exactly what needed to happen to scare everyone straight. After this, the public officials would surely have a plan to educate the public on the best practices and the most effective safeguards to keep them and their loved ones safe, right? Not exactly. As is often the case, the authorities were much more interested in facilitating a return to normal much more than they were of implementing any real safeguards of safety. They needed a blood sacrifice to take the blame. They needed to reduce the public fear and reestablish the public trust. They needed to instill everyone with the confidence they required to believe that this kind of catastrophe would never happen again. How did they do this? Tom Travis, administrator of the Hawaii Emergency Management Agency, told Hawaii News Now that first and foremost, the person who had mistakenly pressed the button that sent out the alert had been fired and that "all the ballistic missile alarms have been shelved."

Why did they do this? The real-world risk of an actual North Korea attack was considered possible, but not likely. On the other side of that coin, the risk of a similar notification inciting even more panic and thereby diluting the public trust was forecast to be much more likely. This meant they had two choices: put proper safeguards in place to protect the public from a real-world crisis, or cancel everything. Officials in Hawaii chose the latter. It was simply easier for them to prevent the good people of Hawaii from becoming more afraid than it was to empower those same good people on how to protect themselves.

PROTECTIVE TAKEAWAY

The more we are alarmed by concerns without consequence, the less we consider those future alarms to be worthy of concern.

PROTECTIVE AWARENESS

Crying Wolf

We all remember the Aesop fable, "The Boy Who Cried Wolf," where a young villager took joy in watching his elders come running to help whenever he would cry out that a wolf was attacking the sheep. The youngster cried "Wolf" so many times that inevitably, when there really was a wolf, his elders assumed it was just another false alarm and ignored the boy completely—thus condemning the fate of the sheep.

The original takeaway of the fable was intended to be a cautionary tale for children to understand the importance of always telling the truth. After all, truth and trustworthiness are the cornerstones of believability and legitimacy. If others have no faith that what you are telling them is true, then how can anyone ever believe you?

As I am often fond of saying: Awareness + Preparation = Safety. Awareness of the realistic risks we are mostly likely to face allows for us to fine-tune our aperture to those warning signs of harm that provide the necessary framework for us to be able to act in a preventative and precautionary fashion. But there is such a thing as over-awareness. There is such a thing as too much information. Today's crying wolf is what is known as *alarm fatigue,* and this overexposure to all the warning signs is having the opposite effect of what they were intended to provide. It is no longer a source of actionable intelligence that helps to promote our protective awareness. Instead, it has become the leading cause for unintentional consequence. Why? Because the more we are made aware of concerns without consequence, the less we consider any concern to be consequential.

What Is Alarm Fatigue?

Alarm fatigue, also more commonly referred to as *alert fatigue,* occurs when one is exposed to a large number of frequent alarms so often that one eventually becomes numb to their noise. This desensitization can lead to longer response times or, worse, a complete disregard for the alarms altogether. This conditioned response to ignoring what is not relevant to our task at hand happens all the time in our everyday lives. When was the last time you heard your neighbor's burglar alarm go off and had even the slightest inclination to see if they were okay? After all, they more than likely tripped the alarm themselves, right? When was the last time you paid a car alarm any attention? I would be willing to bet it has been more than twenty years since anyone's first thought was anything more than *Someone hit the wrong button while unlocking their car.* Believe it or not, there actually was once a time when if people heard a car alarm, they actually cared enough to see if everything was okay. Today, it's a completely different story. Now no one gives them a second thought.

A Notification for Every Occasion

We have alerts on our phones for everything. Many of us triage these notifications by prioritizing them with our own personal selection of beeps, chirps, and tones distinguishing the push notifications of emails, phone calls, text messages, social media updates, sports scores, and breaking news. We do this because we want to know what is most important to us at a particular time. Establishing these parameters allows us to allocate our limited attention to what is most important to us right now. If we are waiting for an important phone call, that tone is subconsciously elevated to the front of our minds. If hoping for a text back from a significant other about details for our upcoming date that weekend, we listen for those. If our favorite team is on the field during a playoff game but we are unable to watch the game live, we may listen more intently for notifications alerting us to a score update. These are all under our control. They are tailored to our specific needs. Those that are most critical are elevated to the top; those notifications of less immediate importance are often muted or otherwise ignored altogether. Which is not to say that we don't want them—we very much do. We just don't want them right now. We just want them moved to the back burner until we have the appropriate amount of time to sort through them.

After all, these are our personal devices and therefore should be tailored to our personal preferences. The only time the control over our personal devices is outside of our own control is when our phones emit that intentionally hideous and ear-piercing sound that brings our immediate attention to our phones with the intention of alerting us to something of immediate relevance. These notifications began as Amber Alerts—alerting those of us in a specific geo-location that a child had been abducted and to be on the lookout for a child of a certain age, wearing a certain type of clothing, who may have been last seen getting into the vehicle of a very specific description.

In October 2019, California launched the first statewide earthquake early warning system in the nation, thirty years after the devastating Loma Prieta earthquake that killed sixty-three people in the San Francisco Bay area. The system is expected to provide between two to ten seconds of advance warning for citizens to "Drop, Cover, and Hold On." The system will reach people in two ways: through an earthquake app called MyShake and through the same existing wireless emergency alerts that sound an alarm on cell phones for flood warnings and missing children.

Sometimes our phones will even break through to us with an ear-splitting screech, but the one alert most of us have almost no control over unless we have our phones turned all the way off are the impossible-to-ignore authority-sanctioned, emergency notifications.

EMERGENCY ALERT:
WANTED: AHMAD RAHAMI, 28-YR-OLD-MALE.
SEE MEDIA FOR PIC. CALL 911 IF SEEN.

Similar mass-text notifications have certainly been effective in bringing Amber Alerts to a quick resolution. That said, it's a slippery slope. When used sparingly—when there is a clear and present threat to the life of a known victim—they can serve as a Bat Signal for the public at large to be engaged in the see-something-say-something safety strategy. But they have to be timely and directly targeted to be effective. What we don't want is for them to become the everyday car alarm blaring from a random city street, heard but then discarded as just another push notification that is seen but too easily deemed irrelevant. Ultimately, actionable intelligence is about quality and not quantity. Crying wolf only works if the threat is real the first time it is called. Those who hear your warning need to see an imminent threat, because if they don't, the next warning cry will most certainly fall on deaf ears.

Today's security alerts are suffering the same fate. Our overeagerness to remain informed with up-to-the-second notifications combined with our fear of missing out have displaced our awareness of actionable intelligence with the fatefulness of alarm fatigue. When it comes to staying safe, one of the biggest security challenges has always been that what is convenient is rarely secure and what is secure is rarely convenient. I am both old enough to remember when car alarms were a sought-after feature for a new car but young enough to live in an age where the over-notifications from my phone, my laptop, and my social media accounts have become so redundant they don't even warrant my attention. In fact, more often than not, many of our phones are left on a permanent mute, meaning the notifications become less about urgency and more about triaging what warrants our attention later.

Outside of our personal practice, alert fatigue has real-world consequences. In the cybersecurity world, a survey by the Cloud Security Alliance recently found that among IT security professionals, "40.4% say that the alerts they receive lack actionable intelligence to investigate and another 31.9% report that they ignore alerts because so many are false positives."[*] In the Target breach of 2013, which cost the company $252 million and led to the resignation of its CIO and CEO, one of the com-

---

[*] Jon-Michael C. Brook, "Avoiding Cyber Fatigue in Four Easy Steps," Cloud Security Alliance, July 12, 2018.

pany's security products correctly detected the breach. However, due to the high volume of notifications and the frequency of false positives, the company's IT security team ignored the alert.

In hospitals, it is even worse. Patient deaths have actually been directly attributed to alarm fatigue, where research found that "72% to 99% of clinical alarms are false."[*] As a result of these excessive alarms, which can result in desensitization to alarms and missed alarms, patient safety and regulatory agencies have focused on the issue of alarm fatigue, and it is a 2014 Joint Commission National Patient Safety Goal. Quality improvement projects have demonstrated that such strategies as daily electrocardiogram electrode changes, proper skin preparation, education, and customization of alarm parameters have been able to decrease the number of false alarms.

We Are What We Consume

Do you feel healthier after eating a grilled salmon with salad or after eating a supersize pizza with fries? Please keep in mind that I'm not asking which one makes you feel better *while* you are eating, I'm asking how you feel *after* you eat. I love pizza and fries as much as anyone, but what I equally hate as much as anyone is the feeling of overfullness and tiredness, as well as the decoupling of my typically motivated self to do anything more than take a nap so I can avoid thinking about my poor life decision.

Our minds operate in a very similar fashion. Just as your calorie count is determined by adding up the totals from all the food and drink you consume in a day, your "media diet" is the sum of all information. Your media diet includes everything from conversations with friends and family to interactions and presentations at work. It includes everything from social media to podcasts, books to movies, and TV to radio. Any and all information consumed in a day is counted toward your media diet.

---

[*] Sue Sendelbach and Marjorie Funk, "Alarm Fatigue: A Patient Safety Concern," *AACN Advance Critical Care* 24, no. 4 (2013): 378–386.

According to a new study, Americans now spend most of their waking hours—eleven hours a day on average—watching TV, listening to music, spending time on social media, interacting with apps, listening to podcasts, watching YouTube clips, or consuming general media.* (The study did not include print formats like books or magazines, which would have raised the total to twelve hours or more per day on average.)

What you may not realize is just how much of this information is impacting your outlook. In fact, the more fear-based content you watch, the more likely you are to believe that you are unsafe, that crime rates are rising, that you are more likely to be a victim, and that the world is getting worse.

The Sky Is Falling

In previous decades, the journalistic mission was to report the news as it actually happened, with fairness, balance, and integrity. However, capitalistic motives associated with journalism have forced much of today's television news to look to the spectacular, the stirring, and the controversial as news stories. It's no longer a race to break the story first or get the facts right. Instead, it's to acquire good ratings to get advertisers so that profits soar.

While American anxiety over our ability to stay safe is at an all-time high, our willingness to engage with tragedy is paradoxically even higher. Part of our human condition is that we are most fascinated by what we see the most but experience the least. This fascination is the driving factor behind an entire cottage industry of celebrity culture. The red carpets. The runways. Reality TV shows. But for all the attention we will pay to the glitz and glamour of celebrities and their high-end couture, we are exponentially more drawn to content that offers something more lurid: tragedy.

Before the introduction of the internet and social media to the world at large, the nightly news was our only real gateway of exposure to the

---

* Ashley Rodriguez, "Americans Are Now Spending 11 hours Each Day Consuming Media," Quartz, July 31, 2018.

world outside our doors. And for a while, the nightly news held to a certain standard of civility that was all but agreed upon by the national broadcast companies located in New York.

Not long after America had a television in every home, the smaller markets of local news stations began to populate the vast range of Americana. But like all public-facing media, television—and especially television news—was not immune to innovation. As TV stations leaned into the profit center of their nightly news hour, more and more organizations routinely and willingly employed an engagement strategy to attract as much of the audience market share as possible.

"If it bleeds, it leads" is a well-known tenet in news media. If a story involves something gruesome like a brutal death or injury, or if there is a story with some inherent risk like a rescue that could go wrong or if there was some real-world drama that could be beamed "live via satellite" right into your living room (think a child trapped in a well or miners caught in a cave), it was likely to get higher ratings.

But when these tactics had been used in the past, they were typically for fledgling programs where a shock-jock program director would help boost the viewership of a flailing small-market news program by teasing the audience with a fear-based story. They didn't care about the newsworthiness of their content. They only cared about how quickly they could parlay an increase in viewership to an increase in ad buys. But it wasn't long until this became the standard pattern in practice for every content provider with a public-facing outlet.

As the news media learned, and the future of social media would soon realize, anger and fear are much more profitable than peace and joy. What was once a measure for educating the masses is now a commercial enterprise of entertainment whose sole purpose is profit. Very few of the people speaking to you on TV have any real control over editorial content. For a vast number of hosts, those decisions are made by the producers in the control room whose very existence is tied to the ratings of the program and the number of dollars those programs can generate for each new commercial between the intro block and the lead-in to the next show.

More money can be made by fanning the flames of fear than by promoting the value of peace. Never forget to remember just how much money can be made by fanning the flames of fear. Have you ever wondered why the first banner back from a commercial break is always a bright and bold BREAKING NEWS? It's because that is what the advertising dollars demand.

Careers are directly linked to engagement. They want eyeballs. They need viewership. They want to trend. Even someone with an entire career built upon a legitimate dedication to journalistic integrity, such as the venerated MSNBC host Andrea Mitchell, is not immune from her control room directing her to interrupt former congresswoman Jane Harman (D-CA) to report the "breaking news" of an arrest of Justin Bieber. Why? Because Bieber has millions of social media followers. Congresswoman Harman does not.

Control rooms will run the same five-second clip on a loop just to give the graphics team time to come up with some kind of "deadly" themed graphic while they scrum for commentators to come scurrying into the studio to discuss whatever is scaring America today. And don't get me wrong, I have been one of them. I have myself been one of the "experts" called in to be asked about the rash of violence that was at the forefront of that day's tragedy. I was asked to discuss what happened. To identify who was to blame. To explain why we couldn't stop this from happening. To answer where we go from there. At least that's what they tell you to get you to agree to come in. What they really want is for you to debate whomever else was invited to the set with their own framework of beliefs. And I get it. It's not about "the news." It's not about informing the public. These on-air debates only have one purpose: entertainment.

The best way to get invited back to a TV show is to give a hot take—to say something so outlandish or a clapback with a counterpoint so hard that it spikes the audience engagement. Makes for a quotable meme. Gives the producers of whatever shows are coming up next a clip they can replay over and over as part of the curated "package" that will run in the sidebar of the next broadcast. They'll post it to their respective social media pages.

They want you to be divisive. If you come on and say, "We're all going to be okay," you'll get no play. If you come on and say, "We're all gonna die!" they'll keep you around in the greenroom to double down in the next segment block.

Exposure Informs Outlook, Outlook Informs
Insights, Insights Inform Fears

Have you ever noticed how as soon as you buy a new car, you start seeing the same-model car or at least something very similar everywhere you go? This happens because you are now more aware of the inherent details specific to your car. You have been exposed to something new, and now this focus has filtered your outlook. The problem is our outlook is not filtered by only those things we find favorable. On both a conscious and subconscious level, our minds will most often focus on what they've received the most exposure to.

> Today, the most influential filter of our focus, is our phones. [The] emergence of social media may be removing many of the controls news media had in place with instantaneous, supposedly unbiased, unfiltered information. Social media may also be exacerbating the effects of news media by providing many different accounts and opinions on a current topic, altering the perception of crime in society more profoundly than news media alone. Several decades of research proves a correlation exists between news media and fear of crime.[*]

Our exposure to today's twenty-four-hour news cycle combined with our ever-present and constantly updating social media feeds means we are now more likely than ever to have those same tragic stories repeated numerous times throughout any given day. This only serves to make the issue of crime and violence appear more prolific in our society. And when a misrepresentation of reality is not as easily discernible from the real-world truth, the optics of outlook are easily adopted as fact.

At no other point in our history have violent crime stories become the norm across all media platforms. We are routinely bombarded with divisive and conflict-driven narratives by content providers who care more

---

[*] Jamie E. Hildreth, "Fear in the world of Social Media," The University of Texas at Arlington, May 2015, https://rc.library.uta.edu/uta-ir/bitstream/handle/10106/25080/Hildreth_uta_2502M_13132.pdf?sequence=1&isAllowed=y.

about clicks and engagement than they do about the quality of content. When these fears and phobias are continuously filtered into the forefront of our minds, it is nearly impossible for us to remove them from informing our outlook, manipulating our thoughts, and promoting our fears.

Anticipation of Fear Is Worse Than Fear Itself

The success of fear-based news is heavily influenced by its ability to instigate anxiety. This is accomplished by replacing evidence with anecdotes that depict an isolated incident as an emerging trend: "A mother was carjacked downtown today with her baby in the back seat. Are carjackers now targeting moms with small children?" They depict categories of people as dangerous: "An illegal immigrant was arrested in connection with a gangland-style shooting today. Are illegal immigrants the cause for the rising crime in our area?" They replace optimism with fatalism: "What used to be a bright and vibrant part of this small town's history is now overrun with an unsolvable opioid epidemic. Our continuing coverage on the decline of small-town America tonight after the game."

Sensationalism is key—just because they report the same news doesn't mean they report the same stories. What's the difference? What's new is limited by the size and scope of the event. The story, however, is limited only by the size of imaginations. In a twenty-four-hour news cycle, the sky is always falling.

Come for the News, Stay for the Story

The twenty-four-hour news channels and the meme makers who can't survive without their content don't just sensationalize the news; they sensationalize opinion. Political debates were once a long-form discussion on important public policy. Today, they are a sound-bite game of *Survivor*. Primary debates are not intended to inform; they are intended to entertain. It's not public discourse. It's a game show.

We need to remind ourselves of the fact that most of our decisions, beliefs, and values are based on what we know for a fact, our assumptions,

THE SAFETY TRAP   151

and our own experiences. There is a difference between doing research to learn about an issue and being provided with information about an issue. Remember this: to understand any issue completely, one must be able to passionately argue both sides equally. This can be an especially challenging and often unrealistic responsibility given the limited amount of disposable time we have throughout our day.

Most of us do not consume our news in a vacuum. For many of us, "news" is a peripheral input provided to us while we conduct other tasks. This is one of the reasons podcasts and audiobooks have become so mainstream in today's society. They allow for us to be both entertained and informed while also being productive. We can listen while we do laundry, make dinner, and drive to work. We can listen on our daily walks. We can listen while we are at the gym. We are no longer required to sit down in front of the television at a predetermined time or a prescribed "news hour." Today, news is on demand with a second-by-second accounting with a vast spectrum of insights and opinions.

Our media diet has a direct impact on our outlook. Today more than ever, our identities are bonded to our value systems.

The Safety Traps of Social Media

Social media is doing more harm than good. Sure, in the beginning, it was great to connect. It helped bring new people together. Some were even savvy enough to leverage the new medium into a lucrative career. For everyone else, social media has become more like the methadone helping the heroin addict. It doesn't get us high; it just helps to curtail the craving, and we hate ourselves for not admitting our own addiction.

Another component worthy of discussion is how much social media has completely changed our relationships with tragedy. While traditional news may have once offered a nuanced and professionally produced overview of the day's events, social media provides those who are in the middle of a newsworthy circumstance with the ability to portray their experience in a raw, sometimes live, and often graphic display.

Anytime there is a shooting at a school, there will be endless feeds of students filming themselves barricaded inside the classroom. If there is an attack at a movie theater, patrons will live-stream videos of SWAT team officers storming through the doors. All of it streamed in a harsh and unfiltered fashion, right into the palm of your handheld device: gunshots, screams, dead bodies, bloodshed, horror. Crimes are being committed by offenders who broadcast their crimes live. Unfavorable interactions with police are recorded and then shared, which, while holding the bad actors accountable, also erodes the public trust by painting the noble pursuits of the 99 percent of first responders with the same bad brush.

These posts, photos, and videos will go viral in a matter of minutes. And many of these engagements will be shared, liked, retweeted, re-posted, hashtagged, and commented upon by those very same people who answered honestly in the American Psychiatric Association survey* about their anxiety. Those very same people who are so anxious about their inability to keep themselves or their families safe are the very same people who willingly engage with these social media promotions of trag-edy while also allowing themselves to sink deeper into the Safety Trap mindset of "It can't happen to me."

And they can justify this action to themselves because, once again, they were right. This tragedy did *not* impact them—at least not directly, and the fact that it didn't may be making their anxiety even worse.

PROTECTIVE PREPAREDNESS

The following are some best practices to keep you from falling into the Safety Trap of Alarm Fatigue:

1. **Prioritize your notifications: less is more.** Start by turning off all your notifications, and then limit the alerts to the ones you really need the most—*not* the ones you want—but really try to limit them to the ones you need. The fewer, the better. You can also set some noncritical emails and apps to fetch rather than push notifications, which will allow you more control over your personal devices.

---

* www.psychiatry.org/newsroom/apa-public-opinion-poll-annual-meeting-2019.

2. **Put the "Do Not Disturb" option to good use.** Predetermine a time during your day to be designated as disruption- and notification-free. Even if these hours are just one hour before bed through the time you are scheduled to wake up, this will help to reframe the expectation of your mind to one of peace and tranquility without the emotional bombardment of news and media.

3. **Change up your media diet.** Read more books. Watch less reality television. Seek out legitimate sources of information that may challenge your confirmation bias. Consider print media over visual media, as this will reduce yours. While it may seem convenient to have news and opinions broadcast to you, it's actually doing more harm than good. If you want to learn about a particular issue, it's best to find this information outside of a Facebook or Twitter search box. Research more traditional news stories and scholarly journals. Explore both sides of an issue to build your own framework of understanding and opinion.

4. **Limit exposure to media.** Give yourself a set time once or twice a day to check in on local and global happenings. Most phones and personal devices like iPads and laptops will allow you to predetermine your usage rate for screen time and mobile applications. Take full advantage of this feature. If you notice you are constantly having to grant yourself additional access, try to instill more discipline into your daily routine. Even just limiting yourself by one additional minute each day will greatly improve your emotional well-being.

5. **Establish electronics-free days.** Consider having an electronics-free day and enjoy the simple pleasures of being present and mindful in those moments that would otherwise be consumed by your screen. Not only will you find your sleep improving, but this fast from your phone will also allow for your body to reset the false dependence we have on staying connected for fear of missing out. After a few resets, you will soon realize you weren't missing out on anything important at all.

10

EFFECTIVE RESPONSE

What Happened

I do product testing for a company that designs solar-power solutions for electronic devices. They have an entire suite of solar-powered generators that can provide power for anyone working in a remote location where a resupply of fuel for a generator may not be available but sunlight is abundant. Some of their more recent devices have a home power-outage capability that can help to keep a refrigerator running or a space heater functional should the power go out during a winter storm. They are great devices for helping to make a bad situation—like a power outage—more tolerable. But simply having these devices readily available will do nothing to keep the power from going out.

Which is why it is so frustrating to see the principle role of prevention be so deliberately discarded in favor of a more reactive approach. Does the fire department respond well to putting out fires? Yes, of course they do. Will giving a fire department faster engines and bigger hoses help them to extinguish fires in a more effective fashion? Yes! Will any of these provisions help to prevent whatever started those fires in the first place? Absolutely not.

Same goes for the police. Will equipping our first responders with military-grade weaponry, tactical body armor, and armored personal carriers make them more effective at confronting whatever violent encounter they may be called on to subdue? Absolutely! But will these tactical advantages do anything to prevent those same violent encounters from rising up in the first place? Absolutely not.

It seems as though every time there is an issue of national attention, whether it be the bombing in Boston or the tragedy at Sandy Hook, the two big buzz phrases you'll hear most often echoed in the media will always have to do with regulation—typically something to do with gun control or illegal immigration. The second buzz phrase will almost always have to do with some kind of emerging security technology like security, surveillance, and cameras.

While both offer their own pros and cons, both are inherently, and most definitely, a reactive approach rather than preventative measure. Let's look at guns, for example. While proponents for gun regulation may argue for one side or the other, when it comes to safety, the presence of an armed contingency only provides a determination for where the initiation of violence will first take place. To the committed offender, an armed response is not a deterrent, beyond one more factor to consider in their attack plan. We have seen this many times over: committed offenders have attacked the president of the United States while he was protected by the most well-trained, well-armed, and best-financed protective entity the world has ever seen. Committed offenders have robbed banks with armed security, robbed armored trucks, and attacked well-fortified and well-armed structures throughout time. Even in schools, the presence of an armed security officer has almost zero impact on preventing a student from escalating their harmful ideation to violent acts.

From there, we go to the allocation of resources. Where can the money better be spent so that safety can be ensured? Were there cameras in place? Were they the right cameras? Can we get better cameras? What about other security features? What else can we get to help secure our schools, our businesses, and our soft targets of congregation? The problem with all these technological advantages is that they work in much the same way. While many may have the capability to provide some kind of protective intelligence framework, they are almost always employed as a reactive measure. The other concern with these camera decisions being made by those who have no real understanding about what security is or how safety can be achieved is that cameras were never intended to be used by themselves. To work effectively as a preventative recourse, cameras are intended to be used in conjunction with other security features like motion sensors, pressure sensors, and approach beams, where they can be used to confirm the suspicious activity the early warning systems detected.

What are the implications of all of this for regular folks? Don't let the presence of reactive tools—a helmet, a generator, a security camera, even a gun—take the place of the truly preventative measures you need to ensure your own safety.

PROTECTIVE TAKEAWAY
Never let your competence in reacting to a crisis lead to your incompetence in preventing that very same concern.

PROTECTIVE AWARENESS

Being Prepared for a Crisis Does Not Mean You Can Prevent a Crisis

When we head out to spend a day at the beach, we make sure we have a lot of sunblock on hand. We reapply it liberally during those hours we are exposed to the sun. What we would not do is forsake sunblock altogether simply because we had stocked up on aloe the day before. Aloe may be great for soothing the pain of sunburn, but not getting sunburned in the first place should always be the preferred course of action.

The same principle of prevention applies to when we teach a child how to ride a bike. Do we make sure our children always wear helmets? Yes, of course. Why? Because there is a very high likelihood in those very early days of learning how to ride that they are going to crash, tumble, and fall. But the helmets are on their heads to help mitigate the impact of them hitting the ground. It does nothing to prevent them from toppling over. What helps to prevent them from falling is making sure the bike is in good working condition and that the children understand the mechanics of how a bike works. We ensure they understand the concepts of inertia and momentum. We make sure they understand the rules of the road. We help them to anticipate the actions of others. There are hundreds of things that go into the action of riding a bike in a safe and successful manner. None of them have anything to do with wearing a helmet. The helmet is for when those preventative safeguards fail. The helmet is for what comes after.

The Broken Record of Protective Strategy

Stop me if this sounds familiar: something bad happens that ignites the public fear; there is an outcry to "do something"; a show of force is unleashed. Within hours, we see heavily armed cops on street corners. The National Guard is called in while stadiums ramp up their security screenings. Movie theaters and shopping malls hire extra security guards to help their customers feel securer. Everything is ramped up to instill confidence and regain the public trust. But then, a week or so later, everything returns to normal. Now if there was any protective validity to having the National Guard, the police, and extra security on hand, wouldn't they be there all the time? Of course they would. But they aren't, are they? So why, then, in those very moments when we need our protectors to be out there doing what they do best, do we want them to be pulled away from those core functions to do something that actually makes us less safe?

The truth is, after a threat has been realized is statistically the least likely time for another threat to occur. Why? Because there is an immediate psychological shift to hypervigilance instead of pushing efforts to prevent these kinds of threats from ever happening again. Case in point: the most dangerous time to fly was September 11, 2001, but the safest time to fly was the very next day. While there were almost no protective safeguards on the day of the attack, the very next day, it was all hands on deck. We over-deployed our protective assets to "protect" us when *there was no threat*. Whoever wanted to cause harm had already gotten away with it.

The most disturbing revelation of this scenario is that the false sense of security isn't being assumed by our own decision-making processes at all. What is actually happening here is the false sense of security is being prescribed to us by those in public office who clearly know better. They have simply chosen to placate the emotional fears of their constituents so they don't get voted out of office. It is almost as if our elected officials care more about securing their reelection than they do about protecting their constituents. The Safety Trap here is that when we continually allow this cycle to repeat, we as a people are not left any better off than we were before. In fact, we are even less secure than we were before, because our silence is our acquiescence. By allowing ourselves to be placated by this common push toward *security theater*, we are all but allowing ourselves to be pacified by the over-publicized posturing of our protectors.

Think about this for a moment: After a school shooting occurs, townships will have police cars positioned in the school parking lot. If a middle-class home is burglarized, city council officers will want to appease their constituents. So what do they do? They make a show of concern by having police cars make more obvious patrols down the neighborhood streets. Of course, they don't have these patrols happen at night or during the workday when home invasions are most likely to take place because the homeowners are away at work. What good would that do? Instead, they make sure those patrols are circling through the neighborhoods at the hours those homeowners are leaving for and then returning from work. They have them patrol past those houses during the times when the homeowners are sitting down to dinner and then again around 9:00 p.m. before they close their blinds for the night. They don't really want to prevent crime; they want to promote the public posture that they are preventing crime.

This is what we in threat management refer to as *security theater*—it is a practice meant to make people feel safe but in doing so distracts from the core capability of what actually keeps them protected. It is window dressing. It is smoke and mirrors. It is nothing more than an attempt to reconstitute the public confidence by resurrecting the same redundant deployment of assets and the same rehearsed sound bites of "We're doing everything we can to ensure a safe return to normal." The reality is, had New York City had a heavy presence of cops on the city streets on 9/11,

THE SAFETY TRAP   159

they would have done nothing to keep those planes from flying into the towers. Same for the police car in the school parking lot. Had it been there on the day of the shooting, it would have done nothing to have kept the troubled teen from acting out in a violent manner. Same still for the middle-class home. It would still have been robbed if the police car had been circling the neighborhood. The robbers would have just waited for it to pass by and then went on about their business just the same. The patrolling car would not have been a deterrent. It would have just been one more fact for the bad guys to consider in their attack plan.

This kind of response is *not* intended to promote a protective posture. This is not intended to supplement any kind of effective policing. This is just what has always been done. Which means, this is what community leaders are expected to do. It is nothing more than *check-the-box security* in an attempt to quickly return to normalcy after a breach of safety.

The Dignitary Protection Model

So much of safety is about mindset. Back when I was a young agent providing close personal protection to my celebrity clients around the world, one of the very first things I learned was to always assume the absolute worst would happen. I could never, even for a moment, allow myself to become complacent. Ninety-nine percent of the time, things went without incident. Thousands of book signings, speeches, movie premieres, sporting events, too many shopping trips, vacations, and nightclubs to count, and I can count on a few fingers where anything really ever got too close for comfort.

What helped to set me apart from my peers was that I learned very early in my career that I was a million times more valuable to my clients when I could *prevent* rather than effectively *react* to a concern. Being a protector isn't about being a bouncer in a bar. A protector doesn't stand around and wait for a fight to start before running into the crowd to break it up. A true protector looks for the warning signs. We look for the behaviors that indicate an individual intends to do harm.

To help me achieve this goal, I learned the importance of a good plan. So what would I do? I would think like a bad guy would think. Plan like a bad guy would plan. I would show up as early as I could. Sometimes I would have days. Sometimes I would only have hours. But I would walk the routes, get a feel for the stage, map the room. I would plan the attack, and then I would reverse engineer the attack plan to make sure I had the necessary safeguards in place. I learned to achieve this by implementing as many concentric rings of security as possible.

The goal was to cocoon ourselves in safety everywhere we went. For instance, when I was with a celebrity giving a speech onstage, the first ring would be me by their side. The next ring would be the ropes and stanchions around the stage or some other buffer between the stage and the audience. Then it was how the audience was seated in the room—those we knew up front, those we didn't toward the back. After this was access control—how we monitored who got into the room. Farther out: the security teams around the perimeter of the event, the parking lot attendants, even the way the tickets were designed helped us to differentiate friend from foe. We would even cross-reference ticket sales against the names on our watch list. (No sense in selling a ticket to the guy who's been emailing us death threats.)

The point is, each one of these circles of security helped me succeed in keeping my client safe. Each additional ring meant I had a higher likelihood of identifying a threat far enough away from my client that we could prevent whatever the bad guy was trying to achieve.

TV and movie dramatics aside, most people weren't trying to kill my clients. In this age of instant information, protective strategies are implemented with equal attention paid to protecting the brand as to protecting the client, which, in today's evolving threat matrix, is not always easy to do. The always-watching eye of social media presents its own set of challenges. On the more favorable side, it meant fans were often trying to get my clients to pose for selfies, kiss them, hug them, or give them some kind of a gift. But on the unfavorable side, it meant pursuers were equally likely to attempt an attack with a shoe, smash their face with a pie, or "bomb" them with blood, glitter, or some other type of vile smear. But yes—like the movies—certain others did have more violent motives in mind.

But what I was not willing to do was strictly rely on my ability to shoot straight and punch hard. As one of my mentors once taught me, "When it comes to protecting your principal, getting them out of harm's way is always preferable to holding your ground. If you have time to draw your weapon and fire, then you have time to cover and evacuate." I never wanted my confidence in being able to react to ever get in the way of my ability to prevent. After all, for a protector, prevention was my bread and butter. If I had been a baseball player who hit five out of every ten pitches that came within the strike zone, I would have been inducted into the Hall of Fame. But as a protector, I didn't have the luxury of having those same odds. If I introduced myself to a client saying, "Don't worry, you're safe with me. I've protected five of my last ten clients from harm," I would have found myself choosing another career path rather quickly. I never wanted to be just another protector. I wanted to be one of the best. So I worked every day to learn everything I could about what security and safety really meant and how those two competing philosophies could be dually achieved.

What helped me to be successful? I learned to remove denial from my decision process. If anything ever triggered my internal "Spence Defense," whatever it was . . . it was investigated. I *never* assumed things would go as planned. I expected things to go wrong. And when they did, I was prepared to handle them: I had a plan, I knew where to go, I knew what to do. I always hoped for the best, but I always expected the worst. I wasn't being paranoid. I was being practical. I was taking control. I was actively participating in the protection of my clients—and my own as well.

An Ounce of Prevention, a Pound of Crime

In the wake of violent threats, there is often a costly, ill-advised, and *reactionary* approach to breaches of security, rather than a well-thought, proactive, and *preventative* approach to safety. While this pattern in practice remains a cross-spectrum concern impacting soft targets like shopping malls and movie theaters, businesses like retail stores and office parks, and organizational infrastructures like military installations and government buildings, the perpetuation of this practice is most readily visible in schools, where a tremendous amount of money is dedicated to promoting the fatal flaw of preparing to respond rather than preparing to prevent.

If the definition of insanity is to continue doing the same thing over and over while expecting to find different results, the decision-makers in charge of school safety may be due for a psychological evaluation. It has been more than twenty years since the tragic school shooting at Columbine High School took the lives of twelve students and one teacher. Yet the current solutions have not had any impact on resolving their current concern. In fact, their ill-fated solutions may be contributing to the cause. Why? Because whenever we become overly reliant on our ability to react to a problem—and in doing so reject any preventative measures—we condemn ourselves to reinventing the same concern back into our lives again and again.

Even When Confronted with the Reality of Reactive Failures, Schools Double Down on Reactionary Measures

On October 25, 2016, a fourteen-year-old boy shot an older teen twice in the head during an after-school confrontation. The following responses to a *Washington Post* survey were provided by Canyons School District spokesman Jeffrey P. Haney.* I have made bold the key comments that underscore the heavy reliance on a reactive approach versus preventative measure.

What type of drills, if any, had the school done before the shooting (classic lockdown, active-shooter, ALICE, or something else), and how often had they been practiced?

"Union Middle, an 830-student school of sixth, seventh and eighth graders, has completed at least four emergency-preparedness drills a year since 2009. . . . The school conducted a drill for a 'lockdown,' which is called when there is a direct threat to campus, roughly one month before the traumatic incident on campus."

As it turns out, these "preparedness drills" are not preparedness drills

---

* John Woodrow Cox and Steven Rich, "Armored School Doors, Bulletproof Whiteboards and Secret Snipers: Billions Are Being Spent to Protect Children from School Shootings. Does Any of It Work?," *Washington Post*, November 13, 2018.

at all. They were in fact reactionary drills—they did nothing to prepare the school administrators for how to identify the warning signs of harm and then keep them from escalating into violence; they simply prepared the students and teachers for what to do *after* something had already been revealed as violently real.

What other types of safety measures, if any, did the school have in place before the shooting (metal detectors, SROs, special door locks, pepper spray, armed teachers, etc.)?

"Union Middle, built in 1968, has been retrofitted with security measures such as a surveillance system, ID-access-only external doors, and the presence of a certified and armed School Resource Officer whose salary is co-funded by Canyons School District."

The problem here is that systems of protective intelligence like surveillance cameras and access-controlled doors are very effective at providing key warning signs of harm, but only if the actionable intelligence gleaned from those protocols is being properly audited. Otherwise, these systems are only beneficial in helping investigators to understand what happened after the fact. When your bank calls you after they notice a suspicious transaction on your credit card, they are acting in a preventative manner to make sure your card has not been stolen or your card number has not been compromised. This is how a proactive safeguard is supposed to work. If the credit card company had the ability to monitor your transactions but didn't bother to do their due diligence until *after* you disputed a charge, they would be seriously underutilizing the preventative safeguards they had in place to protect your financial certainty.

Did students and staff follow the drilling procedures they'd practiced?

"Yes. The students followed the directions of the administrators, counselors and teachers who responded to the incident. The students were immediately shepherded into classrooms and warned to take cover away from windows and doors until told otherwise. After students were safely inside the building, the doors were locked to safeguard those inside the school from external threats."

Again, "doors were locked to safeguard those inside the school from external threats," but the threat was already *inside* the school! Locking the doors would only mean they would thwart the quick response of the first responders. Bullets travel through doors and windows very easily. It's great to see they have a shelter-in-place plan, but having a cookie-cutter plan for all crises is not the correct response. The correct response would have been to evacuate like they would for a fire drill.

What ultimately ended the shooting?

"A teacher who had been assigned to after-school duty was the first on the scene after she started walking toward a group of students who were gathering as if they were going to watch a fight. She heard a sound, and then began running toward the group of students. As she ran, she saw a student with a weapon. Some students yelled, 'This is a prank,' but as she approached, she realized that one student was severely injured. At that point, the boy with the handgun slumped to the ground."

The preceding comment in particular proves the Safety Trap of Effective Response when it abates the fear of not having a proactive plan in place, even though the school had what they believed to be proactive safeguards in place: surveillance cameras; access-controlled doors; a well-rehearsed lockdown plan; an armed resource officer on staff. These were all in fact reactive measures that did nothing to help prevent their realistic risk from rising to reality.

In retrospect, what—if anything—do you believe could have been done to stop the shooting from happening at all?

"At this point, *we're focusing on preparation. Students and teachers must know how to respond* to all kinds of emergency situations. Yes, it's unfortunate, but that's where we are. We operate under the assumption that tragedy can strike anywhere, if someone is determined to cause damage."

Once more, an overreliance on being prepared to respond instead of being prepared to prevent. Awareness + Preparation = Safety is about being aware of the realistic risks you are most likely to face so that you can prepare by putting *preventative* safeguards in place. A sole reliance on preparing to respond to these risks will only allow for those same risks to continually reescalate into reality.

There Are No Standardized Tests for Security

In the wake of a school shooting like the massacre in Parkland, Florida, which left seventeen people dead, it is perfectly understandable that parents and students alike demand action. School safety requirements are mandated at the state level, but local school boards still have a lot of discretion in how those directives get implemented. Virginia, for example, requires schools to have a security audit conducted every year, but not all states adhere to these same standards. Furthermore, not all states place the same emphasis on the safety of their students. Some schools choose to have their audits focus on property-related concerns like computer theft and vandalism rather than student safety.

But school shootings, while tragic, are exceedingly rare. As Harvard University instructor David Ropeik wrote for the *Washington Post*: "The chance of a child being shot and killed in a public school is extraordinarily low. Not zero—no risk is. But it's far lower than many people assume, especially in the glare of heart-wrenching news coverage after an event like Parkland. And it's far lower than almost any other mortality risk a kid faces, including traveling to and from school, catching a potentially deadly disease while in school or suffering a life-threatening injury playing interscholastic sports."[*]

But those facts do very little to help reduce the fears most parents feel every time another school shooting news banner streams across their TV screen. To make matters worse, many schools are wasting good money on ineffective and unproven solutions. Public school spending on security features is estimated to be upward of $2.7 billion. While these expenditures include everything from access-controlled and self-locking doors to video surveillance capability, this amount does not include the billions of additional dollars spent on armed guards and other hefty price tag à la carte options like bulletproof blackboards and active-shooter rehearsal programs. Federal spending on school security is also rising. Homeland

---

[*] David Ropeik, "School Shootings Are Extraordinarily Rare. Why Is Fear of Them Driving Policy?," *Washington Post*, March 8, 2018.

Security has even gone so far as to award a $2.3 million grant to train high school students how to act like first responders in the event of a mass casualty event like a school shooting.

The problem with these security options is that they do nothing to prevent a student's harmful ideation from escalating to a violent action. What may be making these decisions even worse is that the decision-makers facilitating these decisions are mostly not well educated on the best practices of threat management solutions and also heavily influenced by political and emotional considerations. As a 2016 Johns Hopkins report on school safety concluded, "Decisions about whether to invest in school security technology for a school or school district are complex. Many choices about the technology selected, however, may be made with incomplete information or with information that is influenced more by political or reactionary consideration than by local conditions."*

What Does "Preparing to Prevent" Look Like?

After every school tragedy, I am always asked the same question: What can we do to stop this from happening? The answer is simple: help those who are hurting.

Most children don't have the emotional maturity to ask for help. So they act out, begging for you to notice them, but society loves to shirk responsibility. It's easier to scold than to care, so the response to their behavior is often punitive, and the student is ignored even more. Instead of a one-on-one conversation, they are given detention—put in a room after school where they are forced to endure even more isolation: "Sit here. Stay quiet. You're not worth any more of my time."

Schools can implement all the reactive protocols they want, but school shootings will continue so long as we do nothing to address the emotional turmoil some students endure and the harmful ideation they fantasize as a remedy to their grievances. My hope is that someday soon,

---

* Johns Hopkins University Applied Physics Laboratory, "A Comprehensive Report on School Safety Technology," National Institute of Justice, October 2016.

schools with a systemized clearinghouse for observable concerns and a dedicated team of threat management professionals to help reduce risk and prevent violence will be as common as cars having seat belts. But, until this becomes the norm, we need to help those who are hurting. This isn't about the stigma of reporting. This is about our willingness to help those children in need. No student is ever harmed by someone providing them with the resources they need to communicate their concerns so they can begin to overcome whatever issue they are struggling to endure.

PROTECTIVE PREPAREDNESS

The following are some best practices to keep you from falling into the Safety Trap of Effective Response:

1. **The cardinal rule of crisis management: don't get into a crisis.** Throughout my professional career, I have had the good fortune of working with some of the best crisis management and public relations gurus advising today's tier-one clientele. They always say the same thing: they can't make a crisis go away. They can only help their client to manage the crisis at hand. While there are some exceptions, the number-one reason a crisis is allowed to arise is because somewhere along the line someone made a series of bad decisions. Sometimes it's ignorance; sometimes it's idiocy; often it's both. Bottom line: if you're not making the problem better, you're probably making the problem worse. When in doubt, heed the doctors' oath to first do no harm.

2. **Sunblock is better than aloe.** Beware the pitfalls of remedy. Do not allow for yourself to become so comfortable with the cure for a concern that you willingly forgo the practical prevention that will negate that cure from ever being necessary.

3. **Avoid a death from a thousand cuts.** Get sunburned once and it hurts. Get sunburned a few more times and you've increased your risk of skin cancer. Same goes for stubbing your toes. The first time, you might hurt yourself. The tenth time, you might break it. Truth is, if you've stubbed your toe ten times or gotten sunburn more than once, whatever you're doing to protect

yourself isn't working. Audit your solution and find out where the flaws are. Make the necessary corrections and try again. If it happens again, you haven't fixed the problem. At this point, you may want to seriously consider asking for help. You don't have to fix what isn't broken, but you should definitely try to prevent what is clearly hurting you.

4. **Don't get complacent with tech.** Every time I give a talk to homeowners, I ask how many of them have security cameras installed at their homes. Almost everyone's hand will go up in the air. Then when I ask how many of them routinely monitor the security feeds, most of their hands go back down. When I follow up with a question about how many use their camera feeds as an investigative tool *after* something happens, all the hands go right back up again. Great as it is to have security cameras, if you are not employing their scope of service as they were intended, you cannot expect them to serve you as you would prefer. Do not allow yourself to fall into a false sense of security just because you have some cool tech employed at your home. Remember, a home security system does not prevent your home from being robbed. It is simply there to alert you to the fact that you *are* being robbed. The responsibility to notify is on the system. The responsibility to prevent is on *you.*

5. **Don't allow yourself to be placated by security theater.** Whenever you ask the right questions, you and your loved ones get safer. Don't be satisfied with being told that "everything is being done" to keep your children safe at school or your neighborhood safe from crime. Ask the tough questions. Get specifics about what is being done. Who made those decisions? What were their qualifications? What other options are available? Why were other options not considered? What were the failings of the safeguards that were already in place? Why are we doing more of the same? What are we doing to make a change? **Remember,** the responsibility to participate in your own protection is always on *you.*

[11]

FALSE EQUIVALENCE

What Happened

A few years ago, I conducted some threat assessment audits for a collective of credit union owners. They had some concerns about the way access control into their vaults was being regulated. They also expressed some concerns regarding the residential security of their key leadership. A recent story in the news had given them good reason to be more cautious. A bank manager and his family had been recently held hostage after a pair of bank robbers broke into their home. The two robbers held the family at gunpoint overnight. The next morning, under threat of violence to his wife and children, they forced the bank manager to return to the bank, empty the contents of the vault, and then return home to them. When the bank manager returned with the money, a brief scuffle took place, but the bank robbers were able to get away with the money. Once they were captured, one of the robbers was revealed to be a customer of the bank. That was how he had been able to gain the insight needed to hatch his plan. The suspect's girlfriend worked at the courthouse, and he had convinced her to use her access to law enforcement records to obtain the bank manager's home address.

It was a simple plan. The robbers knew the layout of the bank. They knew the bank manager had access to the vault. They knew he could get into the bank by himself and that he could access the vault without raising any alarms. All they really needed to know was where he lived and the best place to stage a confrontation. That part of the equation wound up being surprisingly easy. With a few clicks of the girlfriend's keyboard, they were able to find out everything they needed to know. After that, it was just a matter of researching the bank manager's home, monitoring his daily routine, and then making sure there were no insurmountable obstacles to overcome. Once they realized there were none, within a few days' time, they were ready to execute their plan.

As is the case with most safe neighborhood homes, the bank manager had zero protective safeguards in place. None whatsoever. They didn't even lock the back door. While the robbers, in legal terms, broke in, they really just walked in through the back door. With no need to break a window or trip an alarm, they were able to enter the home without anyone being any wiser. After that, it was a waiting game. When the wife came home with their two kids, they simply held them hostage until the bank manager came home. After that, they just had to wait for morning. Their likelihood of success was high, because the bank manager had never once thought he could ever be considered a target.

Regrettably, this trend is likely to continue over the coming years. From the wealthy to the rest of us, everyone has an assumed level of risk. The Safety Trap of False Equivalence lies in believing that simply because we are not as wealthy as others in our social circle, we are thereby not at risk. "Well, that may happen to other people, but it could never happen to me." This false equivalence does more harm than good. The simple fact is that if you are the holder of value and someone else believes that value can be taken from you or traded for you, you are at risk. Regardless of circumstance or scenario, your risk will always be lower than for some but higher than for others.

PROTECTIVE TAKEAWAY
Your risk rating may be lower than for some, but it will always be higher than for others.

PROTECTIVE AWARENESS

Optimism Bias

If you were asked to estimate how likely you are to experience divorce, losing a job, being the victim of a crime, or even getting into a car accident, you would likely underestimate the likelihood of such a concern impacting your life. This is not uncommon. Everyone likes to believe they are the exception to the rule. We all like to believe we are above average—maybe not better than everyone, but certainly better than most. Problem is, everyone else feels the exact same way. We can't all be right.

In nearly all aspects of life, there is no shortage of things in which we believe we are above average. We all like to believe we are above-average drivers. We like to believe we perform our job at an above-average level. And while we may not believe we are worthy of being on the cover of a fitness or a beauty magazine, almost all of us believe we are above average in terms of our physical appearance. The same holds true for popularity, health, likability . . . the list goes on. In fact, there are so many things we believe we do better than average, there is even a term for it: *optimism bias.*

Optimism bias is the belief that each of us is much more likely to experience good outcomes than we are to experience bad outcomes. The key to optimism bias is that we disregard the reality of an overall situation because we think we are excluded from the potential negative effects. This very reason is why the sale of lottery ticket continually goes up, and the effectiveness of warning labels continually goes down. The optimism bias is why we are more prone to saying, "I feel lucky," when we are projecting the likelihood of something good but are more likely to say, "That can't happen to me," when we are projecting the likelihood of something bad. In fact, the optimism bias may even be part of the reason why we are predisposed to finding some amount of entertainment in negative news. While we may feel a slight increase in our anxiety each time we are made aware of something bad happening to someone else, the fallacy of "It can't happen to me" is equally reinforced.

When We Feel Overly Optimistic, We Make More Poor Decisions

Whenever a negative event is perceived as unlikely—even if the risk *is* *likely* (like a smoker getting lung cancer)—we still tend to be unrealistically optimistic about the risks. Why? Because we believe that much of what we experience is under our direct control. It's not that we believe things will magically work themselves out; it's that the optimism bias allows us to fool ourselves into believing we have the capability and the skill sets to make it so. This is why we don't immediately panic when the warning lights in our vehicles tell us that we are running low on gas or that we are due for an oil change. We know that we have time and that we still have the opportunity to make things better. The problem is that we know better. We know we should never have let our car get below half a tank. We know when our car is due for an oil change.

Perception Is Reality

One of the more common responses I hear when I make security enhancement recommendations to clients—especially to public figure and public-facing clients—is their tendency to benchmark their risk as compared to the risks of others on a higher rung of the hierarchy. Stars of television and movies will admit they are famous but will counter that they aren't a worldwide phenomenon. Business magnates may mention their mansions on both coasts but will downplay their wealth by bemoaning their absence from the *Forbes* wealth list. But my famous and well-off clients are not the only ones who cling to the Safety Trap of False Equivalence.

When we are evaluating our risks, we tend to compare our own situation to that of other people in our social orbit. If we have a nice house but not the nicest house on the street, we may incorrectly predict our risk to be lower than that of our neighbor. If we have a nice car but our neighbor has a nicer car, we may falsely believe that their car is much more likely to be targeted for theft than our own. But in almost every circumstance, we would be wrong. When it comes to being targeted for a crime, what we think has nothing to do with it. What matters most is the perception of what other people believe to be true. It doesn't matter how wealthy you are, what matters is how wealthy others believe you to be.

Even if you are of modest means like the bank manager, if you have access to or if it is believed that you can be easily ransomed for a large sum of cash, you are very likely on someone's radar as a target of opportunity. And it's not just cash. Any level of access to anything of value makes you a target of opportunity. Veterinarians who have access to medicine at private hospitals and pharmacists who have access to the drugs behind the counter are equally at risk for being targeted by those looking to make a quick score. While these cases are rare, the fact remains that they do happen.

Tech Exec Tragedy

In October 2019, the body of a fifty-year-old tech executive was found a day after he had been abducted from his Northern California home. The executive was forced from his home at gunpoint, put into his girl-friend's SUV, and later found shot in the same SUV a few miles away at another property he owned. The motive for the crime was believed to have been robbery. The abduction sent a shock wave of fear through the hearts and minds of the tech world's wealthy but otherwise anonymous engineers and entrepreneurs. How could this have happened? Did this mean they were all at risk?

A month later, no suspects had been identified, though police were able to calm some of the neighbors' nerves by communicating their belief that this abduction was an isolated incident. Their investigation thus far had revealed the executive may have been targeted because of a new business venture in an entrepreneurial cannabis enterprise. It was speculated that his business interests had unfavorably let it be known they kept large reserves of cash on hand to help contend with "the illegal black market elements in the cannabis industry," where "if you don't pay them, bad stuff happens."*

---

* Josh Copitch and Phil Gomez, "Body in Pleasure Point Kidnapping Identified as Missing Man, Motive Released," KSBW8, October 3, 2019.

Tragic as this incident may be, it serves as a clear example of how many people have a false sense of security because they believe—regardless of their own particular set of circumstances—that they are not as at risk as others in their own social circles.

Promoting Your Own Protective Posture

I was recently contacted by a global business venture. They were curious about learning more about my approach to vulnerability reduction. They were very clear to articulate that they were still very early in the exploratory phase but were interested in hearing my thoughts on "a hypothetical" they were prepared to pose. This made my ears perk up. At their level of global enterprise, the time afforded for the "framing of a hypothetical" was not often granted. C-suite decision-makers don't waste time on developing a strategy to manage something that is not on their radar. And if this were a contingency concern, the executive on this call would not be the point person. That tasking would have been delegated to an organizational risk manager a rung or two on the ladder below. Added to this was the fact this call been scheduled via referral from a public relations firm that specialized in strategic communication. Put it all together and my immediate read on their need leaned one of two ways: a chink in their armor had already been exposed, or they had found one themselves and needed it to be closed. Fortunately for them, it was the latter, rather than the former.

Identifying an inherent vulnerability and then taking the necessary steps to making that bad thing better is infinitely more preferred to the realization that this vulnerability existed only after it had been exploited. Just as the best time to buy insurance is before the crash and the best time to put on the seat belt is before the accident, the best time to take an honest look at where you are vulnerable is before your vulnerability finds you.

One of the best ways to identify inherent risk is through a vulnerability assessment, which will provide an in-depth overview of personal and/or professional practices. The takeaway of these assessments is to provide a snapshot of the overall security framework that exists at that time, to identify those areas most likely to be exploited by those with nefarious intent.

Conducting Your Own Vulnerability Assessment:
The FOIL Method

But not everyone needs or could even afford a professional vulnerability assessment. What everyone does need is to take a realistic look at their own security situation, identify their own chinks in their armor, and then do their best to make a bad situation better. One of the most efficient ways to go about this is to use what I call the FOIL method.

While we may not remember everything we learned in our basic algebra class, most of us *do* remember being taught how to solve for x—some of the more mathematically gifted among us may remember FOIL as the mnemonic for the standard method of multiplying two binomials. I was horrible at math. Just wasn't my thing. But what I was really good at was taking something learned in one discipline and then leveraging those principles to solve something else. While this process is not a replacement for the more comprehensive and full-spectrum security audits you may need for ensuring the security of your organization and the safety of your employees, it is an excellent framework for you, your family, your team, and your colleagues to use as a tool for increasing their awareness and mindfulness while in an otherwise familiar environment. It may also serve as a new-hire team-building tool to see what takeaways a new point of view may provide beyond what decision-makers may be preconditioned to see.

Firsts: Take a look at what it is you are trying to secure. It doesn't matter if it is your home, your office, a school, or an office park. All that matters is that you position yourself at a vantage point that gives you the best field of view. What are your first impressions? What are the first things you noticed as you arrived? How many takeaways could someone discern from a simple drive-by? Is this place wealthy, poor, or middle class? What kind of cars are in the driveway? Do they look like they are run-down or well maintained? What about the venue itself? Is it well maintained? Does it look inviting, or does it look standoffish? What do the traffic patterns look like? Are they busy or sparse? Are people out walking their dogs? Are kids out riding their bikes? How much pedestrian traffic is there? Take some notes. Imagine that you were planning to attack this location. What obstacles would you need to overcome? Does this location take their security seriously? Do you see guards? Do you see cameras? Do you see motion lights? Do you see any dogs? Do you see any barriers to entry? Is there a gate? Does that gate require a key card to access? How visible is everything from the street? Is there a lot of traffic? Are there neighbors? What about security features in the surrounding area? Do the neighbors have security cameras or motion lights? Is this location easily accessible by foot? Is there any public transportation nearby? Is the location within a quick response time of police or would it take them a while to get here? What about the windows? Can you easily see inside? Does anyone notice you out here doing research? Or are you able to hide in plain sight?

All of these are questions a bad guy would be asking if he were casing your location to determine his likelihood of success. What would you want his takeaway to be? What were your first impressions? Are you an easy mark, or are you a mark that isn't worth his effort because you have too many safeguards in place? Are you an inviting target of opportunity, or does another location offer a higher location of success?

Outers: For this stage of the assessment, you will want to move closer. Walk the grounds. Circle the property a few times. Really give yourself a good feel for the area of operation. In the military, we would call this SLLS: stop, look, listen, smell. Bringing your senses to the forefront of your consciousness will help to make them more in tune with your assessment. What do you hear? Do you hear your footsteps making noise as you step down? Are you walking on gravel or grass? Paved concrete or rough rocks? Would a bad guy walking around make the same amount of noise, or would there be a way for him to quiet his footsteps? What do you smell? Is there something in the air that may mean someone is nearby? Do you smell food being cooked? What time of day is it? Food being cooked nearby may mean nosy neighbors. It may also mean people around here don't keep to normal working hours. Or maybe it's a nearby food truck or a restaurant, which would mean a higher degree of traffic in the area. These are all things to consider. Write these notes down too. What else do you hear? Is it quiet or noisy? Take a few minutes to really observe all the key features of the outside. Pay particular attention to the structures and the layouts. How many doors do you see? How many of them are being used primarily for arrival and departure? Which ones are the most popular? What other ways are there to get in and out? Is there a service door? Is there a loading dock? Is there a door that leads to the kitchen? What about emergency doors? What about windows? How are they secured? Are any of them propped open? Can you see from the outside how the windows are locked? Do they have that tab at the top of the window that indicates if they are locked or not? Can the windows be used as a means of entry? Look inside the windows too. What do you see? Do you see anything of value? Do you see anything that would be worth your time to steal? What does the backyard look like? What could you not see from your vantage point before? What tools or toys are lying around? Can you tell what these people do here? Can you predict how many people are engaged in activities here? Can you predict their age range? Is there a shed? A garden? A playground? How many different clues can you put together to paint a picture of everything that goes on here?

But don't just limit yourself to thinking about how a bad guy would break in. Also think about how someone could escape out. How many different ways are there for someone to exit? What about from the upper floors? Is there a stairwell? A fire escape? Is there a tree they could climb down? Once people are out, how easy is it for them to get as far away as possible? Is there another area of containment? Will they run into a fence? A wall? Train tracks? How easy is it for anyone inside to escape?

What about first responders? How easy would it be for them to get to you? How many different ways are there for them to arrive? What if one of those avenues of approach was intentionally obstructed? What could you do to help improve the timeliness for first responders to arrive?

Inners: Now it's time to move inside. What do the insides look like? Is the floor plan open, or is it closed? Do you have free rein throughout the entirety of the property once you are inside, or are there different levels of access? Are there any areas of critical infrastructure like a server room? A pump room? What kind of Wi-Fi signal are they using? Is it secured? Has the router name been changed, or is it one you can look up online and maybe find a way to gain a back door into the system? Do you see any safes? How big are they? Are there any signs of weapons in the house? Any military artifacts or memorabilia? What about books? What kind of books are they reading? Are there any rooms inside where someone may believe to be large sums of cash or valuables? How are these rooms secured? Did you notice any cameras inside or outside the building? Where do the cameras feed to? Is there a command or security room? Is there a public address system? Is the PA system a phone or a dedicated telecom? Who has the authority to make an announcement?

Lasts: What are your lasting impressions? All things being equal, could you get in and get out with relative ease? How difficult would it be? What kind of odds would you give yourself for being successful? What questions do you still have? What do you want to go back and double-check? Then later, after you put all of this down on paper, what are those concerns that still keep creeping back into your mind? What can you do to address them?

Whenever I present this FOIL method to an audience, one of the first questions asked will almost always be about how long this entire process should take. The answer is: as long as you can afford to give it. If you can dedicate an hour, dedicate an hour. If you can dedicate an entire afternoon, dedicate an entire afternoon. The honest answer is that the more time you can dedicate to conducting this assessment, the more comprehensive your takeaways will be. Conducting a vulnerability assessment is a lot like putting together a jigsaw puzzle. When you first sit down, all the pieces look the same. After a few minutes, you can start to see how the pieces go together. Assessments operate much the same way. The more time you can dedicate to looking at everything, the more you will notice how all the pieces fit together.

Something is better than nothing. Don't ever feel like you have to get everything done in one sitting. If you can dedicate an hour this week, and an hour the next week, and an hour the week after that, you will be surprised how much you begin to notice how many things stand out to you that you didn't even notice on your first or second pass. The most important takeaway is to audit yourself with honesty. The more realistic you can be about your own real-world risk, the better your decision-making will become about the most effective safeguards to put in place, and the better you will become at identifying the warning signs of future harm.

Reducing Likelihood of Success

The other benefit of conducting your own assessment is that it promotes to others just how seriously you take the security of your home and the safety of your loved ones. The more you are able to promote to a bad guy that they will have a better chance of being successful if they target someone else, the better off you will be. A lion stalking a gazelle in the wild doesn't attack the strongest of the herd. They prefer to attack the gazelle who has gotten lost and looks weak. Bad guys are no different. If one bank or one house looks easier than another—and the loot reward is believed to be the same—the target that is easier to hit will get chosen. The fact that the other one may be a closer drive to their home will rarely if ever factor into the equation.

Kidnap Concerns

Today's kidnappers are professionals who are dedicated to their craft and willing to invest the necessary time, effort, and resources into identifying, observing, and attacking their target. There is a common misconception that only the wealthy are targeted. In reality, the most frequent targets for kidnapping are middle-class executives.

Kidnap for ransom is the number-one source of financing for terrorist organizations. In developing, impoverished, or war-torn countries, where government and law enforcement authorities are weak and corruption is rampant, kidnapping is an easy way for criminal and terrorist organizations to make a lot of money.

Since 2008, more than $125 million in ransom has been paid to Al-Queda and its affiliates for kidnapping, making it the most lucrative component of their fundraising mission.

"Kidnapping for ransom has become today's most significant source of terrorist financing," said David S. Cohen, the Treasury Department's under secretary for terrorism and financial intelligence, in a 2012 speech. "Each transaction encourages another transaction."*

---

* "Remarks of Under Secretary David Cohen at Chatham House on 'Kidnapping for Ransom: The Growing Terrorist Financing Challenge,'" U.S. Department of the Treasury, October 5, 2012.

Globalization and instantaneous wire transfers enable kidnappers to transfer funds anywhere in the world. Technology has also emboldened their resolve. A leader in Morocco can now manage a kidnapping band in Syria; a kidnapping may be committed in Nigeria but the ransom paid in London. Today's kidnappers often take full advantage of social media, burner phones, online proxy servers, countersurveillance monitoring equipment, and numerous other marketplace advantages.

Reducing Your Vulnerability

In most cases, the intended victim is a variable the kidnapper is willing to interchange if their likelihood of success improves. An individual taking even the most basic safety and personal security precautions can significantly reduce their vulnerability. Something as simple as modifying your daily movements, taking alternate routes to and from work, school, or the gym or even every so often driving around your block before pulling into your driveway sends a clear message to anyone taking notice that your actions are not overly predictable. Prior to any overseas travel, it is advised that all business travelers review a country assessment report that provides the most up-to-date information related to their area of travel and to not publicize their travel plans on social media. Paying attention to your surroundings and identifying safe havens—those places you know you can go to be safe and find help—should be common practice. Sometimes even the smallest of changes to your routine becomes the biggest reasons a would-be kidnapper decides easier targets are available.

If You Are Abducted

During an actual attack, focus on those actions and attitudes necessary to maximize the chance of survival. Everything else is unimportant. Money, jewelry, and other possessions can be replaced—your life cannot. Your survival is the only acceptable outcome. The first tactic to employ in any criminal situation is calm cooperation. If the attacker feels that you are not resisting, chances are greatly improved that the potential for violence will be reduced. The best opportunity for escape may occur in the first moments of a kidnapping. Kidnappers will sometimes let down their guard momentarily or do something that can afford the victim the opportunity to escape. The kidnappers may not have considered that a victim may react by fleeing or taking a chance. If circumstances permit, try to get away.

Additional Concepts to Consider

Employ any action or mindset that will maximize your chance for survival.

Understand that every attempt is being made to rescue you.

Tell yourself as often as possible that you will survive.

Any chance to escape or seek help should be taken.

Maintain as high a level of fitness as possible, and exercise your mind by making mental notes of every possible detail and then practice committing those details to memory.

Cooperate as much as possible with demands. Understand that compliant behavior may lead to increased trust or privileges, which may aid in your escape.

Assume whatever is offered is not tainted. Eat and drink as much as you can to stay healthy.

Corporate Response

The first hours following a kidnapping are of critical importance to the successful negotiation of hostage release. Every company should have a crisis management team (CMT) in place with a clearly outlined to-do list should one of their employees be kidnapped.

These early decisions should be made by decision-makers at the corporate level in consultation with expert security advisers, not by the local representatives or field office managers where the kidnapping took place.

In the United States, it is important to involve the authorities at the earliest possible opportunity. In the United States, kidnap for ransom is very rare, police corruption is very low, and there is a comprehensive law enforcement network that can support a timely resolution.

If overseas, it is important to immediately contact the United States embassy, not the local authorities. Many international kidnapping cases revealed that local authorities were in league with the kidnappers. Any assistance from local authorities should be politely declined.

If your company has kidnap insurance, immediate notification should be made so that your professional kidnap-and-ransom (K&R) specialist can begin negotiating the release of the hostage. If a professional security company has not been retained, one should be hired immediately.

PROTECTIVE PREPAREDNESS

The following are some best practices to keep you from falling into the Safety Trap of False Equivalence:

1. **Set realistic safety standards.** We tend to set unachievable standards for ourselves. When we fall short of these standards and there are no consequences to face, we become more comfortable with falling short in other areas of expectation as well. When it comes to the safeguards intended to keep us safe, this can be a fatal pattern in practice. To help minimize these risks, try making the standards you set more achievable. Instead of saying that you will always keep your gas tank as full as possible, make it a standard that you will never let your car go below a quarter tank. Instead of waiting for the batteries in your smoke detectors to chirp that they need changing, set a calendar alert to have them changed every ninety days—same for your emergency flashlights and any other battery-powered safety tool. In all things, try to shy away from major overhauls and time-draining necessities and instead replace these strategies with short, easy, and more manageable support, which will in turn help you and your family to make more informed safety-centric decisions moving forward.

2. **Take an honest look at your current protective measures**. Most families are aware of the risk inherent to their current geographic environment or socioeconomic status, but very few families take the necessary steps to mitigate these risks. However unlikely it may be for you and your family to be directly

targeted, the reality is that too few families have taken any pro-active measures to effectively reduce their vulnerability. Today's heads of households have a responsibility to understand the limitations of antiquated and reactive security measures and learn as much as they can about more proactive practices that today's family safety requires. The modern marketplace offers a host of consultative and technological advantages to help ensure the safety of all involved.

3. **Trade out your keys for electronic locks.** Keeping people out is easier than getting them out. Effectively controlling who's allowed through your front door is especially important if once someone is allowed inside there is nothing preventing them from having free rein throughout the rest of your residence. The problem with keys is that they work all the time. Keys are cheap, frequently lost, and easy to copy. Keys don't validate their user the way card readers and key codes do. If possible, install motion-activated scene and keyhole cameras to add an additional layer of security. This way you will not only be able to notice who is coming and going but be better able to verify who has tried and failed.

4. **Remember that predictable routines are risky.** Whenever possible, try not to make yourself so predictable. Any opportunity to introduce a new variable into your life is a positive protective practice. Change up your gym times. Change up your workouts. Try to not have that one "signature" thing that makes it easy for someone to pick you out of a crowd. Even the seemingly benign things like always carrying the same purse, or wearing the same hat at the gym, or parking in the same spot at the mall, may make you more identifiable to someone. The more you are able to change up your daily routines may not only help to keep you safer, it may help make you smarter too. By keeping your brain actively engaged and off the default setting of autopilot, you force your neurotransmitters to find new pathways, which will help make your problem solving in a high-stress scenario that much more efficient.

5. **A sentry-trained dog is the best protection money can buy.** When it comes to home security, tech tools are great, but a well-trained dog will prove to be worth their weight in gold. In addition to being an unconditionally loving component of any family dynamic, a well-trained, naturally territorial, and sentry-trained dog like a German shepherd, Belgian Malinois, Doberman, or rottweiler will be able to provide a full-spectrum security service. Through their highly developed senses of smell, they are able to detect something or someone out of place far before they will be seen or heard, their physical presence can serve as a visual deterrence, their barking may serve as an early warning of harm, and, if necessary, they will be able to physically confront an intruder. When it comes to staying safe, a dog will never negotiate against their instincts. They will protect you and your family at all costs.

12

COMPLACENCY

What Happened

In 2002, I spent some time operating out of Forward Operating Base (FOB) Chapman, which is located in the Khost province of Afghanistan. During my time there, I became intimately familiar with the layout of the base. I knew how the access points were controlled out of both sides of the base. The main village road was a few hundred meters out from "the wire"—the barbed-wire fence that served as the final demarcation line between what was "ours" and what was "theirs."

To slow the flow of any traffic leading from the road to the base, military-grade HESCO baskets were emplaced in Lombard Street and chicane turns to prevent a vehicle from being able to speed up and slam through any of the perimeter gates. There were multiple checkpoints along the route where U.S. soldiers stood sentry from elevated watchtowers while local recruits from the Afghan Armed Forces positioned themselves behind ground-level barricades.

Military convoys heading out and returning from combat missions were waved through the checkpoint. For U.S. assets, speed was a vital component of security. Everyone else was stopped and thoroughly checked. Regardless of who anyone claimed to be, no matter how sensitive the information a local villager or agency asset claimed they had to share, no matter how legitimate a reason for desiring access onto the FOB they claimed to have, *everyone* was checked, doubled-checked, and then checked once more. The procedure was as strict as it was secure. Drivers of vehicles and any passengers were required to exit the vehicle and were subjected to a very thorough physical search of their person. Their vehicles were subject to an even more thorough level of screening. K-9s smelled for explosives. Soldiers searched for weapons and contraband. Anything that could have possibly been inspected, searched, or rummaged through was fair game for inspection. If there was a backup of vehicles waiting to enter, so be it. Our lives were on the line, and no one was taking any chances. This was, after all, a war zone, and a stark reminder of this fact was that the very name of the FOB Chapman was named for Sergeant First Class Nathan Chapman, who was the first American soldier to be killed in combat in the war in Afghanistan.

I don't have a lot of photos from my time on that base, but I do have two that have stood the test of time. The first is of a map post with arrows pointing to the different cities of significance with the distance in miles labeled underneath. The arrow for Kabul, Afghanistan, pointed to the east: 92 miles. The arrow for Fort Bragg, North Carolina, pointed to the west: 7,309 miles. The arrow for hell pointed straight down: "Closer than you think." The second is of a sign that was placed just before our combat convoy of Tacoma pickup trucks would pass through the wire leading us out into the great unknown. It was a makeshift wooden sign, painted red with black letters that read COMPLACENCY KILLS. That sign was a sobering reminder that we were in a war. That the risk of harm was real. And that this wasn't a video game we were about to go out and play. There would be no do-overs, no resets, no "Let me try that one again." In this game, the stakes were very real, and getting killed meant you were dead forever.

In 2011, nine years after my time at FOB Chapman, it was a surreal feeling to find myself on a movie set outside of Amman, Jordan, which had re-created—in very intricate detail—that very same location. I was working as a security adviser for the movie *Zero Dark Thirty*, which was filming a scene that reenacted the suicide bombing that had targeted CIA officials two years earlier.

The event that had transpired was as tragic as it was preventable. On December 30, 2009, a Jordanian doctor named Humam Khalil Abu-Mulal al-Balawi was scheduled to meet with U.S. intelligence officers of the CIA to discuss sensitive information relating to U.S. interests in the war on terror. Al-Balawi had been able to establish trust with his Jordanian and American handlers because of actionable information he had been able to provide as a result of his "infiltration" of Al-Queda cells in Pakistan. Having proven his value as an asset and with claims of having information more valuable than he had been previously able to share, the CIA agents who had invited him to meet at the FOB Chapman airfield wanted to show him a sign of respect by allowing him to bypass the security checkpoints that were in place at the entrance to the airfield. Unbeknownst to the CIA or Jordanian intelligence officials, al-Balawi was actually a triple agent with loyalty to Al-Queda and strong sympathies toward Islamic-extremist ideals.

The security teams tasked with ensuring the safety of the base fought back against the decision to allow al-Balawi to be waved through. They wanted to search him and his vehicle as he arrived at the first checkpoint and then allow him to pass through the remaining checkpoints once they were certain he posed no risk to the camp. Their argument was sound: their security procedures only worked if they were followed every time. In the end, they were overruled. Upon arrival, al-Balawi's car was waved through all three security checkpoints. When his car finally came to a stop deep inside the center of the airfield in front of many high-ranking intelligence officers, al-Balawi got out of the vehicle, took three steps toward those who had come to greet him, and then detonated the suicide vest he had hidden beneath his clothes. According to official reports, al-Balawi and nine other people were killed by the blast. Seven were CIA personnel: five officers, including the chief of the base, and two contractors. One was a Jordanian intelligence officer, and another was the Afghan driver. Six other CIA personnel were seriously wounded in the attack, including the deputy chief of the Kabul station.

PROTECTIVE TAKEAWAY
We are most at risk when we feel most safe.

PROTECTIVE AWARENESS

Hiding in the Wide Divide Between Policy and Practice Lies the Risk of Harmful Consequence

Whenever I conduct security audits, one of the most consistently realized concerns always relates back to complacency. I see it all the time. Complacency is most commonly found in the wide divide between policy and practice—between what an organization says it will do versus what it actually does.

Let's take access control into a school as an example. When I look at the policy and procedure for how someone is to be granted access onto school grounds after classes have begun, there is very often a very detailed, step-by-step process that is mandated to be followed. Let's say little Sally forgot her lunch and her mom wants to drop it off. Sally's mom will call the school and say that Sally forgot her lunch and that she will be dropping it off around 10:00 a.m. At 10:00 a.m., Sally's mom will drive to the school and will request access onto the school grounds. Then she will walk up to the door and press the buzzer to announce who she is and what she is doing there. From there, her identity will be confirmed, prior to her being granted access. Then Sally's mom will go to the office, get checked in, be issued a visitor's badge, and then be escorted to Sally's classroom. You get the point. There is a very specific plan in place that is intended to ensure the certainty of safety for everyone involved.

This is all fine and dandy, except that this is rarely—if ever—what happens. In reality, Sally forgetting her lunch was likely the fiftieth time a student forgot their lunch that week. Odds are the parent doesn't even call the school, because let's be honest, parents are too busy to make a phone call they aren't mandated to make. So the parent just shows up at the school. Most of the time, they won't even bother to park in the parking lot. They are in such a rush, they leave their car running outside the school while they just dash inside. Of course, the administrator responsible for granting access inside the school is just as busy. They too are inundated with a plethora of priority tasking. So what happens? The very sophisticated policy and procedure for controlling access into the school gets reduced to a Pavlovian response of buzzer pressed and access granted.

The parent is then free to bypass the front office, dash to their child's classroom, drop off the lunch, and then back out to their running car they go. No harm, no foul, right? Wrong! This very same complacent approach to access control is the very same dereliction of duty that allows for those with nefarious intent to exploit inherent vulnerabilities—sometimes with unimaginable consequences.

Man Vanishes with Sixteen-Year-Old Girl He Signed Out of School Ten Different Times

On March 5, 2018, a forty-five-year-old married man with two children who was engaged in an illicit and inappropriate affair with a sixteen-year-old child in Pennsylvania signed her out of school, and the two of them soon went missing. On March 7, the following request for assistance was posted on the Facebook page of the Allentown Police Department:

WE NEED YOUR HELP! PLEASE SHARE!

Amy Yu age 16 and Kevin Esterly age 45, have been reported missing and could possibly be traveling together in a 1999 Red Honda Accord, 2 door bearing PA vehicle registration of KLT 0529. Amy Yu is described as being an Asian Female, 4-11 in height and weighing approximately 90 lbs. Kevin Esterly is described as being a White Male, 5-09 in height and weighing 185 lbs. Both persons were last seen on or about Monday, 05 March 2018 and could possibly be endangered. If seen or located you are strongly urged to call 911, your local police department, or the Allentown Police Communications Center at 610-437-7751 and report their location to the Allentown Police Department. #AllentownPolice

A school may have a ten-step process for signing out students, but if no one enforces it, this can easily happen. A teen who wants to slip out of school only has to outsmart a paper trail. Another problem is that many schools are still doing things in a way that is riddled with vulnerabilities. Parents sign out their children on a piece of paper, and many teachers still take attendance by hand instead of electronically. In either case, how often are the records audited and updated? Who is following up on protocol? The real problem is that many school policies are stricter on paper than they are in practice.

Thankfully, U.S. federal agents and Mexican authorities caught up with the missing child and Esterly in Playa del Carmen, a Mexican coastal resort town, after a passenger noticed an inappropriate amount of contact between the older man and the young child.

After being extradited back to the United States, Esterly struck a deal in which felony charges against him were dropped. In exchange, he pled guilty to corruption of a minor, a first-degree misdemeanor, and was sentenced to two and a half years in jail. His plea bargain also prevented him from having to register as a sex offender.

What was most disturbing about this case was that Esterly was already known to the school. He had last been seen on school property a month prior, when school records showed he had signed out the child for a ninth time. When her mother found out what had happened, the police were notified, and Esterly was ordered to stay away from the child. If he was seen on school grounds again, the police were to be immediately notified. So how had this been allowed to happen a tenth time? In a word: *complacency*. After every instance of harm, one of the most eye-opening lessons for an organization to learn is that security standards do not rise to exceed the expectation of your policy. Instead, they falter to the lowest level of acceptable practice.

Complacency Versus Hypervigilance

Of course, what happened next was a complete overhaul of how the school enforced its access control policy. This is something else I see all the time too. After complacency is realized, there is a rush to overcorrect. This is an observable response to almost every concern that arises from complacency. It doesn't matter if the issue has to deal with guns, immigration, alcohol, prescription medication, or the simple act of brushing your teeth. More often than not, the standards and practices that were already in place would have been more than enough to prevent whatever concern had been realized. But somewhere along the line, the rigid adherence and commitment to following those prescribed practices was deemed unnecessary or, at best, discretionary. Like the sign in my dentist's office says, you don't have to floss all your teeth, just the ones you want to keep.

But instead of brushing our teeth for the recommended two minutes, we brush for thirty seconds. Instead of flossing every day, we floss when we feel like it. Instead of swishing with mouthwash for the full minute, we slosh it around until the bad taste becomes too much to handle. Then we get a cavity. And then it's off to the races. We go out and get a new $200 dentist-recommended toothbrush when the $2 one from CVS would have worked just fine. We get a power flosser, a tongue scraper and dental pick, and whatever else we can afford to overcompensate for our own unforced errors. But then, after a while, we'll slide right back to where we were. Thirty seconds of brushing here, a swish of mouthwash there, a floss when we feel like doing so.

Staying safe is no different. In almost every aspect of our lives, we can find instances of allowing ourselves to live on the fringe of a pendulum swinging between complacency and hypervigilance. We are either saying, "Nothing is going to happen," or we're patting down Grandma as she enters the ballpark. We need a move to the middle. A healthy sense of skepticism and vigilance that keeps us both comfortable yet cautious. We must unburden the weight of our anxiety and replace it with the empowerment that grows from being aware, capable, and prepared to participate in our own protective strategy.

Never Turn Your Back on Burning Fire

A few years ago, a group of us rented a cabin up in the mountains for Thanksgiving weekend. The house was part of a private development on a large parcel of land near a river known for fishing. A few hours after our arrival, while we were all gathered on the back deck enjoying the view of the open sky, we heard screams for help from a nearby neighbor. As I looked up, dark smoke began to rise from the nearby tree line.

As we went through the house and exited the front door, it was clear what had happened. The steel drum the neighbor had been using to burn the leaves and branches he had raked up from around his property had turned over, and the fiery contents had found renewable fuel on the forest floor. To make matters worse, strong winds were not only pushing the fire up the mountain, but the fire was spreading wider and creeping ever closer toward our rented cabin.

As I ran to grab the fire extinguisher from my truck, I yelled for one of my friends to call 911. I heard the neighbor yell that his wife had already called and confirmed that the fire department was on their way. As I opened the door to my truck, I could hear the sirens of the fire trucks in the valley down below, but they were still at least a few minutes away.

There was nothing we could do to stop the fire from blowing up the mountain, but for the next ten minutes, we all worked tirelessly to keep the fire from burning closer to our respective homes. The wind was working against us. Every time we raked, shoveled, stomped, and sprayed the fire extinguisher along the newly created firebreak, a gust of wind would seem to circle back around us and breathe new life into the fire, allowing the flames to "jump" over our man-made blockade.

It was a terrifying effort in futility.

The fire department arrived on scene with a full squad of firefighters armed with backpacks and power hoses, surrounding the fire in a containment pattern while another crew ran their large hoses up the mountain alongside the fire. I followed the fire hose up to where I had tossed my empty fire extinguisher along the fire line. When I bent down to pick it up, I noticed the still-flaccid fire hose behind me had gotten caught up on a stump. The firefighter at the top of the hill was trying to flail the hose free, so I turned around and knelt to help unhitch the hose from the stump.

As I was kneeling, another firefighter came up beside and pulled me from under my shoulder, directing me to kneel on the other side of the hose. "Never turn your back to the fire," she directed. "Fine to fix the hose, but always face the fire." And with that, she slapped me on the shoulder and continued up toward her team on the upper ridge of the mountain.

She was right. As I was kneeling to unhitch the hose, the fire had been creeping up behind me. It had only taken a few moments for me to help pull the hose free, but if it had taken a few minutes, the fire would have caught me by surprise, and I would have been in a world of hurt.

The fire department made quick work of the fire. They had it contained and cleaned up in under an hour. Other than the runway of blackened forest and the lingering smell of burned ash that still lingered in the air, the event was all but over.

I have found myself in quite a few harrowing scenarios in my life, but that was the first time I had ever had to fight a fire. The words of the firefighter who had turned me around stuck in my mind. Later that night, I ran through the event in my head.

The neighbor had confided in us after it was all over that he had gone inside to use the bathroom and had left the burn barrel unattended. He didn't know how the barrel had gotten knocked over, but as soon as he came back outside, he knew he was in trouble. He hadn't even bothered to get the hose out. He had run through this routine so many times before, he didn't think this time would be any different.

But this is what happens when we get so used to doing things without consequence. I'm betting the next time he uses that burn barrel, he'll weigh it down with rocks before he puts anything into it. I'll bet he'll have a fire extinguisher or two on hand and a new hose with a high-powered nozzle at the ready. His mindset will swing way back across that wide divide separating his former stance of complacency back over to his newly claimed perch of fire-marshal vigilance.

But how long will that last? How many more iterations of burning leaves, trash, and whatever else was in those barrels will he cycle through before his mindset slowly creeps back toward complacency? How long before he'll justify in his mind that he can get away with "I'll just run inside real quick" to use the bathroom again? After all, how bad had things really been? He had neglected his responsibilities to prevent the problem in the first place, but that's what the fire department was there for, right?

Complacency Creep

Complacency, of course, is much more easily identifiable in hindsight. One of the ways complacency is allowed to creep in is because it almost always results from a habitual routine that is able to be performed without consequence. Nothing demonstrates the pitfalls of complacency like car crash statistics. There is a reason most car accidents happen within a five-minute drive of home. There is a reason that most of those collisions involve the driver hitting a parked car. It isn't because these drivers were intentionally reckless or careless; it's because they felt too safe—they allowed themselves to become too complacent.

It's easy to understand how complacency can build up over time. Our first time driving, many of us gripped the wheel with white-knuckled enthusiasm. We made extra sure our hands were held at the prescribed ten-and-two positioning. Our side-view and rearview mirrors were checked and double-checked for blind-spot avoidance. We kept our heads on a swivel as we proceeded to turn over the ignition. Then, with overt caution and defensiveness in mind to the myriad of variables around us, we slowly put the car into gear and began to pull onto the road. But then, with ten thousand hours of driving under our belts, our heart rates barely elevate. We drive with two fingers, and sometimes a knee, while we check our email and respond to text messages while traveling sixty miles an hour down a freeway. More often than not, we find ourselves on autopilot, and our ability to notice changes, recognize pre-incident indicators, or even the caution signs of hazards begins to drift and fade away. Next thing we know, we're hitting a car, and not even one that's moving.

It's Not Over Until It's Over

One of the worst things a protector can do is get complacent as an event draws to a close. Why? As an event gets closer to being over, the risk of something happening doesn't get lower; it gets higher. While a bad guy who enters an event with the intention of doing something may have all the courage in the world at the onset of the event, the fact is, they are still looking for their perfect window of opportunity to strike. As the event draws closer to the end, their window of opportunity also begins to close. This makes the end of an event the most critical time to combat complacency. The end of an event is when a protector needs to be most vigilant, most on guard, most on point and ready to respond.

Even in today's twenty-four-hour entertainment news cycle, most public figures are able to go about their daily lives without a protective detail following their every move. Unfortunately, their lives do become inherently more complicated whenever they agree to a planned public appearance. Whenever the general public has a reasonable expectation of a precise time and place a public figure can be found, effective personal protection should always be employed as a preventative measure.

These are events like book signings, charity events, fundraisers, movie premieres, speeches, or any other event that has been made public in advance. It is important for both the protector and the public figure to understand why these events have an increased level of risk. Unlike an off-the-record or impromptu appearance (think President Obama making a pit stop at Shake Shack) where the likelihood of an attack would be considered low, events that are publicized in advance give a would-be attacker critical information like dates, locations, and, perhaps most concerning, time to plan.

As any protector worth their body armor will tell you, it's easy to walk behind someone and look confident. It's something else entirely to plan a protective mission from conception to completion, all while reducing non-required exposure, risk, and vulnerability for every conceivable scenario. Every possible contingency must be conceived, planned for, and prepared for, and one thing must always be understood: the game clock starts the moment the public figure departs for the event and does not stop until they are secured back at home. Each passing second is another moment for the would-be attacker to gain confidence. The stakes only get higher as the event winds down and their window of opportunity grows smaller. The mindset of the protector must not end with the "good night" applause.

Too many times in history has the end of an event been met with violent consequence. Prime Minister Yitzhak Rabin, Benazir Bhutto, and President Ronald Reagan were all attacked after their "official program" had ended but before they had successfully departed. In Boston, the marathon bombs exploded hours after the race had been won and the day seemed all but over. Complacency kills and has no business entering into the mindset of those entrusted to be vigilant.

I remember driving a client home one evening after a long day with a complicated itinerary. From the back seat and still forty minutes from having him home, I heard him say to me, "It was a good day today. Good job!"

"It'll be a good day for me once you're home safe, sir," I responded politely.

In the rearview mirror, I saw him nod in agreement. "You're right," he said. "Thank you!"

Anything worth doing is worth doing right, and doing it right means seeing it through all the way to the end.

PROTECTIVE STRATEGIES

The following are some best practices to keep you from falling into the Safety Trap of Complacency:

1. **Never let your guard down.** It is perfectly fine to hope for the best, but it's equally necessary to recognize risk. Are you going to get into a car accident driving home today? It's not very likely. But you're still going to put on your seat belt, use your turn signal when changing lanes, and come to a complete stop at each red light and stop sign. Every other aspect of your life requires the same level of awareness and participation. The more complacent we become in our everyday lives, the more risks we invite in. A healthy sense of skepticism, a moderate dose of vigilance, and a pinch of participation will go a long way to helping you ensure your safety today, tomorrow, and every day moving forward.

2. **Don't be a zombie.** Know this: you matter, your contributions matter, your life has meaning, you are stronger than you think, you are smarter than you know. Not trying, giving up before you begin, and negative self-talk are all ingredients in the cake called *complacency*. All these self-sabotaging strategies are grounded in a shitty sense of self-worth. The more you commit yourself to growing and nurturing your own emotional well-being, the more you will avoid the downhill coasting into complacency that has only contributed to your emotional turmoil of ill will. Get off the bench, and get back in the game. You need you.

Your family needs you. Your tribe needs you. Dig deep, step up to the plate, and start swinging for the fences. The world needs more winners.

3. **Never stop improving.** Always strive to be learning something new. Start by setting ambitious yet realistic goals. It doesn't matter if those goals are to learn a new language, teach yourself a new instrument, or pursue a new hobby, you should always have a goal you are striving to achieve. Never stop pursuing a new passion. As soon as one goal is reached, you should have another one at the ready, waiting for you to dive right in. Always be moving in an onward-and-upward direction. Slow and up is always better than fast and down. The more you focus on improving one area of your life, the more likely you are to improve in other areas of your life as well. The more dedicated you become to bettering yourself, the less complacent you are likely to become.

4. **Break the cycle of complacent routine.** There is a difference between being dedicated to discipline and regimented in routine. Being dedicated to discipline is about constantly looking for ways to improve yourself. The foundation of discipline is grounded in the rooting out of complacency. Becoming regimented in a routine is about dumbing yourself down to doing that which you already know you do well. You didn't get smarter by reading the same book over and over again. You became smarter by starting with a nursery rhyme and then eventually getting to the point where you could read a novel. Never conflate your discipline in learning how to read for the comfort of routine in always reading the same book.

5. **Never underestimate the opposition.** The successful mindset of business can also be applied to a successful mindset for staying safe. Always assume someone is out there working even harder to take away what is yours. Practice becoming your own protector by asking what-if questions. Look for the dark corners of danger to uncover blind spots. However unlikely an encounter or crisis, have a plan, know what to do, know where to go, know how to get there. To underestimate the enemy is to court disaster.

13

OVERCONFIDENCE

What Happened

Back when I was in Ranger School, I had an instructor who was giving my class a block of instruction on room clearing. *Room clearing* is the way by which a squad of soldiers will go through a building with multiple floors, rooms, and hallways to make sure it has been cleared of any threats. We had just run through a scenario where we were clearing rooms that extended down either side of a narrow hallway. I had just gotten "killed" on a run-through, and this was my after-action review. What had happened was one of those things you're happy to have happen in training, because if it had happened in the real world . . . let's just say I wouldn't be here to tell you about it today.

What had happened was this: I came in through a door and saw the muzzle of a rifle held by a bad guy who had been crouched in a corner. I fired three rounds into the cardboard cutout and then announced the room as cleared. I turned around to come back out of the room and announced, "Coming out," to the rest of the squad. As I entered the hallway, one of the other instructors who had been watching from the rafters above shouted down to me, "You're dead, Coursen!"

What had happened? Hadn't I just won? Hadn't I just expertly performed the very thing we were in here training to do? I looked up at the rafters with confusion.

The instructor must have been able to read my mind. "You never finished clearing the room."

He was right. I was wrong. I had been so relieved by "surviving" the threat and become so immediately overconfident on my own capability that it never occurred to me there was another threat lurking behind the door in the room. But there was. And I missed it. Lesson learned.

What had happened to me was no different from what we have all witnessed a hundred times over in sporting events. How many times have we watched a race where the runner in the lead gets overconfident and begins to celebrate too early, only to watch in horror as they are surpassed at the last moment just before crossing the finish line? How many times have we watched a football game where the ball carrier is nearly to the end zone and performs a celebratory high-step trot, only to be tackled before getting the touchdown?

Overconfidence is a real problem that we all have to contend with, and when we don't account for it in our decision-making process, the likelihood of us failing in that very venture we were so certain we would succeed becomes a near certainty. Overconfidence can have a negative impact on our health, our wealth, and even our own success. And if we do not learn how to keep our confidence in check, we may very well sabotage our own safety as well.

PROTECTIVE TAKEAWAY
As the saying goes, "It ain't what you don't know that gets you into trouble. It's what you know for sure that just ain't so."

PROTECTIVE AWARENESS

What Is Overconfidence Bias?

A significant part of overconfidence is grounded in our illusion of control—where we believe we have control over things, but in reality we have no power to control. When we are overconfident, we tend to misjudge our own values, opinions, beliefs, or abilities, and we have more confidence than we should considering the objective parameters of the situation. For example, it may be appropriate to have confidence in one's control over things that involve skill, like taking the game-winning shot with only a second left on the clock, but to then also believe you have control over luck or fate where skill has no influence—like a roll of the dice—simply because you made the game-winning shot, would be an over-confidence bias.

When it comes to our decision-making, this overconfidence can cause problems, because this false expectation may lead a person into a danger-ous situation they are not equipped to handle.

Some Examples

A person who is naturally athletic but who has never swum before is out on a boat with some friends, then jumps in the water without a life jacket because he is overconfident in his athletic ability. Once in the water, he sinks like a rock and nearly drowns before his friends are able to save him.

A presidential candidate begins to believe they are going to win in a landslide victory, so they don't bother to aggressively campaign in key areas of the country. They become so overconfident they will carry these votes without any extra effort that they begin to divest efforts into the next phase, rather than dedicate resources to ensuring a strong victory in this phase. Meanwhile, their opponent doubles down in those very same swing states, and the overconfident candidate winds up losing the election.

A mom pulls her car into the driveway and is so distracted with her hands full of kids and groceries that she accidentally leaves her keys in the car. Later that night, she realizes she left the car's key fob in the cup holder but is overconfident that nothing will happen because they live in such a safe area. The next morning, she awakens to realize her car has been stolen.

On a snowy day, a food delivery driver parks his vehicle on the main road and attempts to make a delivery on foot to a home set back from the road. He becomes lost along a dirt trail but is so overconfident in his own sense of direction that he winds up wandering off five miles in the wrong direction. He is lucky to be found by search and rescue hours later but requires medical treatment after being exposed to the cold and wet weather.

An over-the-hill military veteran who was once very capable of being able to handle himself in a physical confrontation is overconfident he hasn't lost a step. Looking to teach a younger "tough guy" a lesson, he is badly beaten after stepping into the sparring ring at his local gym.

In fact, some may argue that what initially made *American Idol* such an immediate success was due in part that they not only allowed those who were supremely talented to audition but that the showrunners also chose to showcase those who were so tragically overconfident in their own singing skills. So many of the clips that went viral on social media from the early years of that show were the result of someone who had no talent at all but who believed they had a great voice. They were so overconfident, they wound up becoming nothing more than a punch line on national TV.

Overconfidence Is a Multipronged Problem

The problem with overconfidence is the less you know about something, the more likely you are to overvalue your skill level. An example of this would be when we set out to complete a "simple task" we expect to have completed in no time at all—like putting together a piece of furniture or doing final edits on a report—but then soon realize the task is much more involved and will realistically require ten times the investment of time we had previously predicted.

The second problem with overconfidence is that it is the disease of expertise. If incompetence is certainty in the absence of expertise, then overconfidence is certainty in the presence of expertise. Overconfidence stems from people doing something with such repeated success that they believe there is no way for them to lose by simply repeating the same thing that has bestowed them a successful outcome time and time again. In fact, the more successful someone becomes at a particular task, or analysis, or performance, the more likely they are to be overconfident in just how successful they will be.

In fact, the more experienced someone is, the more confident they are in their skill sets, the higher the stakes, or the more additional stressors are placed upon them in a critical moment, the more likely an individual is to be overconfident in everything working out as it should.

This is one of the reasons why eyewitness testimony is so unreliable for investigators. The everyday person on the street believes themselves to be smarter than the average citizen, be more aware of their surroundings, be better at problem solving, calmer under pressure, and have a better memory than their peers. This is why they are so overconfident when giving eyewitness testimony to an investigator after a crime where they are 100 percent certain that the getaway car parked outside the bank was black (when it was really blue), the bad guy was "super tall" (when in reality he was under six feet in height), and they heard at least ten gunshots (when only two spent casings were found).

Science has proven time and time again just how awful our memory really is, but because we are so used to being able to remember the movie poster we saw in the grocery store with clarity under perfect conditions, we naturally become overconfident when the stakes are even higher.

The Police Hit Rate

I sometimes have to warn my clients about the hazards for having a handgun in the home for self-defense. Statistics prove that in most cases, a weapon in the home only increases the odds of that same weapon being used to harm or even intimidate the homeowner. Why is this the case? Because the homeowner is overconfident in their skill set. Having a few reasonably successful rounds at the firing range after the initial purchase of the firearm may constitute a training block of familiarization, but it by no means makes you a trained shooter. But it will make you feel overconfident that you can handle yourself should the need arise during a home invasion. The problem is that course of fire you conducted at the range, when it was the middle of the day, in a well-lit room, when you were wide awake, poised, calm, and had all the time in the world to mentally prepare yourself for the task at hand, is not at all what the conditions will be like when you are startled awake in the middle of the night and then have to reenact those same shooting performance protocols in poor lighting, while scared, panicked, and shaking.

Even outside of the homeowner concern, a perfect example of this overconfidence in a real-world, high-risk, and high-stakes environment may account for the very low hit rate of police when they are involved in shootings. The most recent FBI study on police-involved shootings has identified the police hit rate at less than 20 percent.* Think about that. For every hundred shots fired at a suspect in the real world, only twenty hit their intended point of aim. Why? For the very same reason. Most police departments conduct shooting drills on a range. Their officers shoot the same course of fire over and over and over again. The officers get good at hitting the target because it's the same target, at the same distance, in the same conditions they have been aiming at their entire careers. So naturally, it's easy for the officers to become overconfident that if they were ever in a real-world shooting, they would perform better than expected. In reality, they perform much, much worse. There are literally hundreds of case studies to choose from as documented in the FBI's report, but a very clear example is the shooting that took place when the police had the Tsarnaev brothers cornered on a side street in Watertown, Massachusetts:

> Police training dictates that officers consider several key factors when making the decision to fire their weapons. They must assess the danger posed to bystanders, residents, and fellow officers; they should know the position of fellow officers; and they should stop to reassess the situation if they can, rather than simply continuing to pull the trigger. But on Laurel Street, rounds flew into parked cars and police vehicles and chewed up fences and trees. A round entered the home of Andrew Kitzenberg on the north side of the street and lodged in a chair. Another ripped through the exterior wall of Adam Andrew and Megan Marrer's house and landed on their living room floor.

---

* "National Use-of-Force Data Collection," FBI, www.fbi.gov/services/cjis/ucr/use-of-force.

The exact number has never been released, but according to Watertown Police chief Ed Deveau, "Between 200 and 300 shots were fired."*

Calibration

Overconfidence ultimately manifests itself in the wide divide between how accurate you believe your ability to be versus how accurate your ability really is. An example of someone who is well calibrated would be if we took two people out to the batting cages and asked them to predict how many of the ten balls they would hit as they came out of the machine. If the first person predicts they would hit "about half" and then they hit five of the ten balls, we could say that person was well calibrated. Conversely, if someone else at the batting cage predicted they would hit "most of them" but then wound up hitting only one out of ten, we would argue that person was miscalibrated.

Again, relating this to the police hit-rate problem, most officers would be miscalibrated in their overconfidence of how many times they would actually hit their target versus the actual number of hits.

Illusions of Control

An illusion of control stems from believing that in addition to having control over your own ability, you also have some control over things that you can't influence—like fate and luck. This illusion of control is grounded deep in our human DNA. While we know that we can never fully control what happens to us, we simply feel safer when we believe we can.

As early humans, we sought shelter in caves to protect us from the elements, we wore clothes to protect our skin and shoes to protect our feet, and we learned to grow crops and build tools to hunt game. We had control over a great many facets of our society, but we were never able to

---

* Alexander Abad-Santos, "New Secrets of the Forgotten Watertown Shootout, Revealed," *Atlantic*, April 23, 2013.

control the weather. In Latin, there is a phrase *post hoc ergo propter hoc*, which is translated to "after this, therefore because of this," and it is this informal fallacy that first impacted early man and took hold of our future selves.

At some point in our history, our ancestors began to believe they could have some control over the weather by performing some kind of ritual. In some cultures this was a sacrifice, in some it was a prayer, while in others it was some sort of performance. If the ritual were performed well, the rain would come, the sun would shine, or whatever our ancestors would want to happen would happen. Or so they believed. But this is the very definition of the illusion of control.

Today, similar rituals are considered superstition, but they nonetheless play a very important factor in promoting overconfidence in performance. A gambler may believe their lucky hat will help them to win a poker tournament, and a baseball player may believe his lucky bat will help them to win the World Series, but this overconfidence is grounded not solely in their skill but in their ability to control factors we all know are outside our human sphere of influence.

Victory Disease

But there is still yet another factor of overconfidence that must be explored, and that is the symptom of *victory disease*,* which has been historically studied as it relates to military decision-making by commanders, but has more recently—especially since the 2008 financial crash—also been detailed in large organizational structures like those found on Wall Street, and even into the realm of big business and the interworking of mergers and acquisitions. But for today's purposes, the military example shall suffice.

Victory disease occurs when military commanders believe that tactics that proved successful on a former enemy will work just as well on a new

---

* Timothy Karcher, "Understanding the 'Victory Disease,' from the Little Bighorn to Mogadishu and Beyond," U.S. Army, Global War on Terrorism Occasional Paper 3, Combat Studies Institute.

foe—resulting in disastrous result (e.g., one-hundred-plus hours in the Gulf War versus ten-plus years in Iraq). As Machiavelli famously said, "Wars may begin where you will, but they rarely end where you please."

When I joined the army in 1999, there was an overconfidence throughout the U.S. military that any future campaigns that may take place in a desert landscape would be easily won by artillery and air campaigns. This overconfidence would arguably set the effectiveness of U.S. fighting forces back by a full decade—a mistake that many servicepersons would pay for with their lives.

For several years prior to the infamous fiasco of 1993, on which the book and movie *Black Hawk Down* were based, military intelligence had been forecasting to the powers that be that the high likelihood of future battles taking place in Middle Eastern environments would be similar to what was experienced in Mogadishu. Despite these warnings, and quite possibly because the careers of many commanders had resulted from riding the coattails of previous victories involving more conventional military applications, the decision was made to remove the desert phase from Ranger School. The faulty framework of military decision-making did not refocus the collaborative efforts required to meet and beat the modern enemy until many of us were already on the ground in Afghanistan wearing desert-patterned uniforms with jungle-patterned body armor.

Why was this the case? Because up until that fateful day in September, the vast majority of infantry troops were still heavily invested in perfecting the practices that had helped us win the previous wars. We weren't learning how to identify roadside IEDs or learning how to effectively maneuver a squad through a trench-warfare mock-up. We weren't learning how to use a flash-bang to stun an enemy on the other side of a thin and projectile-penetrating baked-mud wall; we were learning how to toss and roll a hand grenade into a WWII-style bunker. We weren't running shooting simulations aimed at teaching us how to differentiate a hostile threat from hostile intent in an urban setting; we were on a three-hundred-yard marksman lane shooting at little green pop-ups that had no way of indoctrinating us into the world of confusion and chaos where we would soon find ourselves just a few short months later.

PROTECTIVE PREPAREDNESS

The following are considered best practices for avoiding the Safety Trap of Overconfidence:

1. **Audit yourself with honesty.** Know your limitations. Carefully consider your capabilities. Calculate reasonable risks.

2. **Listen to "think twice" advice from smart people who disagree with you.** It can sometimes be difficult to see the forest when all you can see is the trees. If those who would generally support your decision-making ask you more than once if you think what you are about to do is a good idea, odds are it is not.

3. **Brainstorm what you don't know.** Accepting we don't know everything and questioning what we think we know can help us to get a better perspective on our situations. The clearer our perspectives, the more effective our decision-making steps for how to best move forward.

4. **Check yourself before you wreck yourself.** Don't just look before you leap; test yourself on less risky levels first. If you want to jump off the high dive, first make sure you can swim. Crawl. Walk. Run.

5. **Accept the reality that what worked once may never work again.** Just because you won the lottery once by playing numbers drawn from your birthday and zip code does not mean you figured out a way to game the system. Be especially mindful that the decision-making process you are employing to reach your conclusion does not overvalue your influence over uncontrollable factors like fate and luck.

14

BEING TOO POLITE

What Happened

I had a young female client text me from the back seat of the ride-share town car she was in because she was getting a weird feeling about her driver. We had just spoken on the phone not thirty minutes prior, because she had just wrapped up a corporate speaking gig in Orange County, California, and was heading to LAX for her flight back to New York.

As she would relay to me through our text convo, her driver was talking in graphic detail about a woman he had driven earlier in the day who said she was an actress but whom he was convinced was a porn star. He then kept telling her about a true-crime podcast he had been listening to about how many sex workers went missing in California. He told her it was almost like a how-to guide for disposing of a body.

I immediately had her share her trip details with me and then had her ping me her location. I had her send both so if the driver canceled the trip, I would still have her location available. I pulled up Google Maps on my iPad and texted her back saying there was a was a hotel nearby. I instructed her to edit her trip destination and get dropped off at the nearby hotel. From there, I would arrange to have another car take her the rest of the way to the airport.

She texted me back saying she felt uncomfortable doing that because she was afraid it would "hurt his feelings." So I told her I would call her phone and to put me on speaker so that I could pretend to be a friend of hers who was also in town and invite her over to the hotel to meet me for a drink. Thankfully, she agreed. Using the phone call as cover, she felt more comfortable playing along with our ruse and then made the change to her trip. I stayed on the phone with her until she got dropped off outside the front door of the hotel and made her way into the lobby. Then I had her go into the hotel bar to calm her nerves with a drink. In the meantime, I called the concierge at the hotel to have one of their designated hotel cars take her the rest of the way to the airport.

She texted me once she was in the hotel car and back on her way to the airport.

"I hope I didn't overreact," she wrote.

Was the guy a threat? Maybe he was, maybe he wasn't, but there was no need for her to stay in the back seat of a car with a strange man who had already given her enough warning signs that something wasn't right. She definitely wasn't overreacting; she was simply caught up in the Safety Trap of Political Correctness.

PROTECTIVE TAKEAWAY

Your willingness to defend yourself should always be stronger than your unwillingness to offend another.

PROTECTIVE AWARENESS

My client in the back of the town car already knew what she wanted to do: she just wanted permission to protect herself the only way she knew how and, if possible, not come across as looking like a bitch as she did so.

A few months later, we ran into each other at a fundraiser in New York, and she joked with her date about the driver.

"Do you think he knew?" she asked.

"So what if he did?" I told her. "His feelings weren't my concern. Your safety was."

"I admire your emotional strength," she told me. "Maybe it's just because I'm female, but I look up to someone who is able to separate emotions from reality!" Then she chuckled to herself. "Not sure if I said that right, but you know what I mean."

Indeed I did. The thing is, we all have the same capability. It's simply how we choose to employ our abilities that differs from person to person. Our internal sense of defense is so finely tuned for ensuring our personal safety that it automatically acts as a safety net for what is good and what is bad. But we as a people have socialized ourselves to rationalize our intrinsic survival instincts away from our better judgment. We negotiate against our natural ability to protect ourselves for fear of offending the feelings of another.

Yes, Being Too Polite Can Be Dangerous

Bad guys prey on vulnerabilities. What are they looking for? Bad guys are looking for someone they can take advantage of, so it is important to know if you are the type of person who tends to be too nice for their own good. This niceness can make you an easier target. If your default setting is to be overly empathetic or if you have a hard time saying no, you are statistically more at risk than someone is more comfortable being "disagreeable."

This does not mean you have to stop being nice and start being mean, but it does mean that you should act with more realistic expectation that while *being polite is a courtesy, protecting yourself is a priority.*

One golden rule to remember is: trust your gut. If the situation feels wrong, it probably is. Gut instinct can improve safety if we learn how to channel it. *Situational awareness* is really just another term for *mindfulness.* It's about living in the here and now and paying attention to the world around us. When we pay attention to our surroundings and we afford ourselves the opportunity to be more in tune with what's going on around us, we immediately become much less vulnerable and much safer. More often than not, a healthy sense of skepticism and a moderate dose of vigilance are all most people need to stay safe.

Each and every one of us has our own very well-calibrated and highly in-tune self-defense mechanism that is both purposeful and accurate in most situations. But when we ignore these warning signs and override this Gift of Fear* with the assumption that everything will be okay and work itself out or, worse, we negotiate against our own feelings because we don't want to be assessed by others as being impolite, we all but allow ourselves to be a willing participant in violence against us.

The Fear Factor

Fear often informs our decision to be "too polite," because it is often our most practiced skill set. We all have a desire to be agreeable and to not upset the social fabric in whatever circumstances we find ourselves. This desire holds especially true once we have regrettably realized we have already gotten ourselves into trouble.

When we get into an argument with a family member, a significant other, or a trusted friend and we are all but certain there is no risk of harm, we are much more willing to risk escalation in hope of achieving the higher ground. But this is almost never our preferred strategy when there is a risk of harm. In a social engagement with a lot of unknown variables—say, with a stranger—most of us will choose to de-escalate the situation and try as best we can to placate our way out of our current concern.

But how did we get here in the first place? Part of the problem is how we are informed about threats. TV and movies often represent those who wish to do us harm as being overtly mean, controlling, and violent. The bad guy always looks menacing. His face is contorted into a sneer, his face is unshaven, he looks intimidating, and his actions are often controlling and overpowering in nature. The monikers of these characters conjure an immediate image in the mind's eye: the mugger, the burglar, the robber, the bully.

But in real life, those who wish us harm are much more often hiding in plain sight. They don't look like the types of people who would want to do us harm. They come to us as wolves in sheep's clothing. They hide their true intentions in plain sight. They are the delivery guy, the limo

---

* Gavin de Becker, *The Gift of Fear* (Boston: Little, Brown, 1997).

driver, the coworker, the gym guy, the bartender, the Tinder date. It's not until we look back that we realize they had laid out a trap for us, had we only thought to notice. But now we feel stuck, as if one of our feet is suddenly trapped in a snare.

But this isn't the time to be polite. This is not the time for you to apologize to them. This is the time for you to stand your ground and make them realize that *they* made the mistake. Never allow for your previous politeness to be mistaken for weakness. Now is the time to stand your ground and muster the courage to defend yourself more than you ever have before.

The Underpinnings of Our "Too Polite" Personality

Our personality is formed by a lifetime of emotions and experiences that ultimately project their own influential ingredient into how each of our own unique personalities are formed. The three predominant influencers are biological, cultural, and experiential.

Biological

Much of the current understanding of personality from a neurobiological perspective places an emphasis on the biochemistry of the behavioral systems of reward, motivation, and punishment. Human neurobiology, especially as it relates to complex traits and behaviors, is not well understood, but research into the neuroanatomical and functional underpinnings of personality are an active field of research. Some recent behavioral psychological studies argue that some of us may be genetically predisposed to be more open and accepting, while others of us are more predisposed to be more closed and rigid. Why the duality? Simply stated, survival of the species requires both. If everyone were open and accepting, the society would be less likely to survive, as they would be more likely to be conquered and overrun by outsiders. On the flip side, if the society were completely rigid and closed off, they would be more likely to never evolve because they would fight off and kill any outsiders who tried to engage in the exchange of goods and services, which are required for a society to learn and grow. This research has also argued this same biological rationale may be the reason why some of us are more inclined toward a conservative outlook versus a more liberal leaning. Dozens of behavioral studies have found "conservatives consistently test high on psychological measures of personal need for order, structure, and closure while also showing greater sensitivity to fear and disgust. In contrast, liberals test high on psychological measures for tolerance of ambiguity and complexity, and for openness to new experiences."* So yes, on a very biological level, some of us may be more genetically inclined to be nicer than others.

Cultural

While there is no question that some people—especially women—are socialized to prioritize the needs of others (men) before their own because of a particular religious influence or cultural norm, the influence of political correctness on society can also not be understated. Make no mistake: political correctness is most certainly part of the problem. As it was intended, political correctness involved a sensitivity to the suffering of minority groups who were historically overlooked by the dominant forces of society. Its purpose was to help spread awareness and empathy to the systemic disadvantages these minority groups must contend with on a daily basis so that everyone could work together to help promote a fair, just, and equal playing field for all. We can all agree this was a noble and valiant effort. Of course, as with many social endeavors, the intent of this initiative was not well supported by its ineffective implementation. While political correctness intended to bring empowerment and justice to those who were historically marginalized, the true impact it had was to overpromote politeness so as to avoid causing any emotional suffering to anyone. College campuses—which were once the battleground for intellectual debate—are now the "safe space" and "trigger warning"–free safe havens for the emotionally frail and intellectually paralyzed participants who want nothing more than to live in an echo chamber of their own design. Today's "cancel culture," which seeks to silence not just anyone who

---

* D. M. Amodio, J. T. Jost, S. L. Master, and C. M. Yee, "Neurocognitive Correlates of Liberalism and Conservatism," *Nature Neuroscience* 10, no. 10 (2007): 1246-1247.

says anything insensitive but anyone with an insight or takeaway that differs from their own, does not help to promote a society forward. Our cultural acceptance of this behavior only serves to enhance the deafening silence of acquiescence to those voices who would otherwise feel empowered to rise up and speak their mind in disagreement. Instead, they are socialized into learning that speaking up will only serve to do more harm than good. And while these patterns in practice may be perfectly fine to allow free rein while confined to the safe and secure campuses on which these persons roam, once they enter the real world of consequence, they are much more likely to come face-to-face with an offender who doesn't care at all about how willing their victim is to speak up on social media when they demonstrate zero willingness to speak up in person at all.

Experiential

The beliefs we form in our childhoods form our core beliefs later in life. They are the strongest factors that influence our personalities. One study in child development found that "the type of emotional support a child receives during the first three and a half years has an effect on education, social life and romantic relationships even 20 or 30 years later."[*] Of course we all know that our early experiences affect us, and we know some people are more sensitive to certain interpersonal dynamics than others, but what we may not know is that the once-rigid belief that your personality can't be changed appears to have been disproven. Of course, the degree of change is specific to each person. The more we are exposed to different experiences, the more likely we are to change our belief structures and the more likely we are to change our personalities. Just because our experiences as children led us to believe that being overly polite and courteous to everyone we meet, regardless of circumstance, would serve us well does not mean that we will hold that same belief system should we experience something that disproves this rule. Our personalities,

---

[*] K. L. Raby, G. I. Roisman, R. C. Fraley, and J. A. Simpson, "The Enduring Predictive Significance of Early Maternal Sensitivity: Social and Academic Competence Through Age 32 Years," *Child Development* 86, no. 3 (2015): 695–708.

ultimately, are as malleable as we would like them to be. We just need to decide for ourselves how much of a change we want to make.

How Do I Know If My Default Setting Is "Too Nice"?

Let's say you've just left the grocery store and you're walking to your car when someone asks you for the time or directions. Are you more likely to stop and answer them or to keep moving while you give them an answer? Is your default setting to say, "I'm sorry, no, I don't," while never slowing your stride, or is your default setting to stop and help this supposed stranger in distress? Let's be honest, most people today have a mobile phone that will very likely have a map application and will most certainly have a clock. Which means if someone is asking you these questions, it is highly likely they have an ulterior motive in mind.

Bad guys on the street, domestic abusers at home, bullies at school, and sociopaths at work are all very skilled at assessing those who prioritize being polite over those who prioritize their own empowerment. How do you know if your personality is "too nice"? Three ways: if you are the kind of person who is more concerned about what others think of you than what you think of yourself; if you are more concerned about other people's feelings than you are about our own; and if you are more concerned about giving people the benefit of the doubt than you are about trusting your own gut instincts, then you are very likely being too nice too often.

People who are polite are often overly compliant. Have you ever been in a crowded room where someone without first identifying themselves walks in and asks for a show of hands for some randomly benign question like, "Please raise your hand if you drove here today." People who are too compliant are the ones who will immediately partake in this sort of assumed power dynamic. They don't bother with asking themselves who this person is or why they are asking the question. They simply assume it's perfectly fine for them to play along. They do what they are told. They've learned that it is easier to do what someone asks than to question what's going on. They don't want to risk an argument.

People who are too polite also tend to be too passive. They are often afraid to stand up for themselves, causing them to be easily manipulated and controlled. They are afraid to speak their minds either out of the fear of hurting someone else's feelings or out of fear of being rejected or hurt themselves.

People who are too polite are also less likely to voice a strong opinion or position on a particular issue because they are afraid of confrontation. People who are too polite would rather be people pleasers. But in doing so, they will often agree with one person but then turn around and agree with someone else who has the exact opposite belief. This isn't about them playing some kind of Machiavellian power play of manipulating both sides against the middle. It is merely their own inability to be disagreeable, so they hide behind their politeness instead of allowing their preference for politeness to stand behind their own true preference or belief.

PROTECTIVE PREPAREDNESS

The following are considered best practices to help you avoid the Safety Trap of Being Too Polite:

1. **You are the agent in charge of your own protection team**. You are the captain of the team called Me, Myself & I. If someone is trying to run a sneak play, a fake-out, or some other game of getting one over on you, it is first and foremost *your* job to call for the foul-call demand that the game be over.

2. **Own your agency.** Set better boundaries. Never allow others to perceive your kindness as weakness. You are an intelligent and empowered individual with the capacity and responsibility to act independently and to make your own free choices.

3. **Stop feeling guilty for taking control**. When it comes to staying safe, your needs take priority over someone else's desires.

4. **Anticipate the problem so you can prepare your solution**. A key tenet of leadership is to anticipate the needs of others. When it comes to staying safe, always remember that Awareness + Preparation = Safety. Think about those times in the past where you were "too polite" or "too nice" in a situation where

you would have preferred to have acted more in your own best interest. If that same situation were to come up again, what could you do differently? What could you say? How would you make your needs known? The more we prepare today, the safer tomorrow will be.

5. **Be more disagreeable.** Being disagreeable isn't a bad thing. In fact, the more disagreeable you are, the more successful you are likely to be. To be clear, being disagreeable does *not* mean being unpleasant. What I do mean by being disagreeable is not needing the approval of others for your decision. If you're a woman in a bar and a guy you're not interested in begins to flirt with you and asks you for your number, you are not being mean when you say no. Even after his friend tells you what a great guy he is, it is perfectly acceptable for you to stand your ground and be disagreeable. Better their pride be wounded than your desires be coerced. There is nothing wrong with being disagreeable. In fact, it's really quite good.

15

RELIGION

What Happened

I remember being a child in church and hearing a sermon from our priest about a man who had been caught in a flood calling on God to save him from atop his roof. The sermon was presented as a teachable moment about how to understand the difference between what to expect when calling on God to save you and the reality of knowing how God could save you. As the priest explained to our congregation, "A faith in God may save your soul, but saving yourself is up to you."

I'm quite certain this story has many different versions, but this is how I remember hearing it: A man was stuck on his rooftop in a flood. The waters were rising, and the man was praying to God for help. A few moments later, a neighbor in a rowboat came by and shouted to the man on the roof to jump down to the boat so they could both row to safety. But the man on the roof shouted back, "No, it's okay. I'm praying to God, and he is going to save me." The neighbor shrugged, then rowed on. A little while later, another neighbor with a motorboat sped up to the house. Again, the man on the roof was offered a ride to safety, but same as before, the man on the roof shouted down that he had faith that God would save him. And so the motorboat man sped off. As the floodwaters were almost to the top of the man's roof, a helicopter flew overhead. The pilot dropped a rope and yelled down for the man to grab hold so he could be hoisted up to safety. But the man again replied that he was praying to God and that he had faith he would be saved. The pilot sighed and then reluctantly flew the helicopter away. Not long after, the floodwaters rose higher than the man's home. The man was washed away and drowned. Upon his arrival in heaven, the man was angry he was dead and confronted God for betraying him. The man demanded to know why God had failed him. But the man's questions were only met with a disappointed expression. God sighed, then replied, "On three separate occasions, I tried to save you. I sent you a rowboat, a motorboat, and a helicopter. What exactly was it you were waiting for?"

PROTECTIVE TAKEAWAY

Houses of worship were once a safe haven in which to pray, but without modern-day sheepdogs to keep the wolves at bay, the flock inside will remain targeted as easy prey.

PROTECTIVE AWARENESS

One of the biggest risks to houses of worship is the belief by the congregation that while inside their divine sanctuary, their God will watch over them with a ready sword and smite anyone who may try to harm them. Much as we would all love for this wish to come true, the reality remains that despite the best efforts of even the most devoutly faithful among us, the intervention of an almighty is never as direct an action as our time of need would require. As the Broadway tune "Now You Know" would sing to us, "It's called thieves get rich / And saints get shot / It's called God don't answer prayers a lot."

What faith does provide, however, is an elevated level of courage to confront the evils of the world and to help us play our parts to make the world a safer place. There are a lot of benefits to having faith, and while a belief in a God is a gift I have never been blessed to receive, I still find value in the role religion plays in helping all of us to live better lives.

Are We Safe When We Attend Services in a House of Worship?

Shootings in houses of worship are part of an overall—and alarming—increase in mass shootings within the United States. In many respects, houses of worship are simply a convenient target of opportunity for attackers who have a grievance against former lovers, spouses, or friends. Many sanctuaries have regular schedules, lack robust security, and proudly promote open-door policies. In fact, a core mandate for many houses of worship is to offer open arms to those who are "lost"—even if that sometimes comes with terrible consequences. Those who are driven by hate prey upon gatherings of people with the intent to do harm when they are least expecting and most ill prepared to respond.

Like school shootings, attacks at houses of worship are rare. They are horrific because of who and what they target. Also similar to school shootings, victims of church shootings are likely to know their attackers. In the most recent cases, nearly half of the offenders were affiliated with the church, and nearly a quarter involved an escalation of a church attendee being involved in ongoing violence with an intimate partner.

There is most certainly a need for heightened awareness in regard to security in houses of worship so that all can feel assured that they can worship in peace. Churches have long been a place of refuge where, historically, doors were never closed. Things are different today. Churches lock their doors when not in session to guard against vandals, theft, or harm to others.

It seems particularly repugnant for someone to murder others in a place where they come to seek peace and a connection to love and justice. Yet churches seem no more protected from violence than any other location.

Who Is It That Is Attacking Our Houses of Worship?

Predators who attack places of worship are (statistically) not looking for fame. They rarely leave behind manifestos. Those who target houses of worship with violence are almost always angry men in crisis. Their attacks tend to be poorly planned and often end in their own deaths or suicides.

Those who choose to attack places of worship seem to fall into two separate groups: those who are motivated to intimidate, and those who are motivated to retaliate. The intimidators seek to strike fear into a specific subgroup. They are motivated by hate, which often includes anti-Semitic, anti-Islamic, or anti-Christian sentiments. The perpetrators of these kinds of killings are not typically known to members of the congregation. They generally have grievances with the world and target a specific group of people to blame for their disappointments.

An example of this would be the mass shooting in Charleston, South Carolina, where on June 17, 2015, a white supremacist murdered nine African Americans and injured three more during a Bible study at the Emanuel African Methodist Episcopal Church.

Another example would be the mass shooting that took place at the gurdwara (Sikh temple) in Oak Creek, Wisconsin, where, on August 5, 2012, a white supremacist fatally shot six people and wounded four others before committing suicide by shooting himself in the head. All the dead were members of the Sikh faith.

The second group of perpetrator is motivated to retaliate by an overwhelming need to resolve a personal grievance. For these retaliators, the church is selected for the initiation of their violence simply because a girlfriend, spouse, or some other target of their grievance happens to be worshipping there. In fact, most house-of-worship shootings stem from a continuation of intimate partner violence. For example, an abusive partner who has been looking to strike back against the victim who is trying to leave him may know his target will be at church on Sunday morning, stalk her there, and then use the house of worship and the location to stage their confrontation.

An example of this would be on November 5, 2017, when an armed assailant entered the First Baptist Church in Sutherland Springs, Texas, and murdered twenty-six people and wounded twenty more. Investigators said the shooting was not motivated by racism or any proclaimed prejudice against religion but rather a predetermined continuance of domestic violence. According to police reports, the shooter's estranged second wife sometimes attended the First Baptist Church with her family. Prior to the shooting, the shooter had sent threatening text messages to her mother. His wife and her mother were not at the church when the attack occurred, but he did kill his wife's grandmother at the church.

Another example of a retaliation-motivated attack that did not have a domestic violence component would be the shooting at the West Freeway Church of Christ in White Settlement, Texas. The man who attacked the church was known to the parishioners and was repeatedly given food by the congregation. But the man grew angry when church officials refused to give in to his demand for money. The man's anger grew into a grievance, and then, as we have discussed before on the pathway toward violence, escalated into a harmful ideation and then ultimately into a violent act.

Modern-Day Sheepdogs

While the presence of an armed security team inside a house of worship has been proven to reduce the number of casualties to the congregation once violence by an armed offender has been initiated, there is little evidence to support that the presence of an armed security team inside the house of worship has any impact on preventing violence from initiating in the first place. As previously stated, those who attack houses of worship plan poorly and are often so hell-bent on displacing their own anger onto the target of their violence, they consider little else beyond the likelihood of success in their attack plan.

Another consideration that cannot be overlooked is that in almost all cases where a church security team did intervene in thwarting a violent offender, these "protectors" were present in an ad hoc capacity. In most cases, the sheepdogs—those responsible for protecting the congregation—were themselves participating in the worship service. The protective practice of "participate in prayer until you are called on to protect" is a methodology most houses of worship choose to adopt for the simple fact that the likelihood of violence erupting during a service is so low. For most budget-conscious houses of worship, the cost of a professional and designated protection team is not within the realistic constraints of their operating costs. So it comes as no surprise that most houses of worship choose to adopt this sheepdog approach to safety. Regrettably, the impact of this mixed model is akin to adding water to wine. It reduces their effectiveness from proactive prevention to an overdependence on effective response. Which, as discussed before, is another safety trap in and of itself.

Still, there is no arguing that the presence of an armed response does save lives. The West Freeway Church of Christ shooting in Texas had a security team in place for nearly ten years and, according to investigative notes, was made up entirely of members of the church's congregation who were not only licensed to carry firearms but practiced shooting regularly. Eyewitness accounts testified that during the service, the gunman was "acting suspiciously" and drew the attention of the church's security team. The shooting—which was captured on video because the church regularly posts its services online—supports their testimony. The video—which is now posted online as a teaching tool for church safety staffers to demonstrate just how quickly a service can go from calm to chaotic—shows the gunman stand up during a quiet moment and briefly speak with someone standing against a wall. The shooter is then seen to brandish his shotgun and immediately begins to fire into the pews of the parish. Frightened and panicked congregants can be seen crouching down in their pews. A member of the church security team is shot and killed, but a second security member of the congregation manages to kill the shooter. From the initiation of violence, until its conclusion, the entire incident lasts just six seconds.

This ability for the West Freeway Church to effectively respond stands in stark contrast to the First Baptist Church shooting, also in Texas, where the shooter fired seven hundred rounds in an attack that lasted almost eleven minutes. Instead of the shooter being challenged by a security team immediately following his initiation of violence, the church video cameras show him being slowed down only by the time it took to reload his rifle.

PROTECTIVE PREPAREDNESS

The following are considered best practices for avoiding the Safety Trap of Religion:

1. **Know where all the exits are.** There is more than one way to skin a cat, and there is more than one way to exit a building. Educate yourself as to where all the exits are, and whenever possible, always keep at least two of them at the forefront of your mind. Remember: windows are always an option.

2. **Assign clear roles and responsibility.** Have a team of trained volunteers identified to watch for unusual behavior and people who don't belong. House-of-worship shootings are often the continuation of domestic disputes that may have never been brought to the attention of the congregation. This is sensitive because the church is where we want the hurting to come—so it can be difficult to decipher the two.

    Train these eyes and ears to notify the appropriate person(s) if they see any questionable behavior. Predetermine in an emergency who will call 911, who will talk to authorities, and who will talk to the media. Assign backups and redundancies for each role.

3. **Conduct tabletop drills.** Hard questions like "What if it happened here?" is a great place to start. Be honest with your answers. Do not be overconfident in your ability to respond. Be realistic. Know your limitations. Put a practical plan in place. As was demonstrated in Texas: Awareness + Preparation = Safety.

4. **Recruit local assistance.** Invite local law enforcement to help identify inherent vulnerabilities. Do your best to better understand potential risks and work toward solutions that will help you create a secure environment for all to feel safe and welcome.

5. **Do not allow protectors of the service to participate in prayer.** Dedicate a team of protectors during worship services to greet the congregation, monitor unlocked doors, keep an eye on the parking lot, and monitor security feeds. These protectors may be members of the congregation, but they should not be

participating in the prayers or the service. If you are a protector, do not expect during service to be able to both pray and protect. Pick a lane and stay in it. If you are there to protect the flock, protect the flock. If your job is to watch over the congregation with a ready sword, your task is simple: protect now, pray later.

Part III

Putting Threat Management into Practice

16

THE ESSENTIALS OF THREAT MANAGEMENT

What Happened:
It All Began with Celebrity Escapism

Soon after broadcast television became the preferred promotional tool for celebrity culture, the American desire to know everything about the lifestyles of actors, athletes, and musicians became insatiable. As a result, production companies and talent agencies did everything they could to feed this frenzy. Actors would show off their homes. Actresses would showcase their wardrobes. Musicians would share what inspired the lyrics for a popular song. Within a very short amount of time, the number-one form of American escapism was to experience all the fame, glitz, and glamour that Hollywood had to offer. For the very first time, Americans were able to live vicariously through the eyes of their favorite celebrities from the comforts of their own homes. Since that day, the demand for celebrity content has only intensified.

Once having a television set in the home became the norm across America and the influences of celebrity culture became more identifiable throughout the American landscape, the emotional desire for the masses to have an even greater personal connection with their favorite stars began to grow. Fan clubs began fan mail campaigns, where letters would be written in praise and support of their favorite actor's most recent project. Fans shared stories from their own lives that were similar to the stories the celebrities had shared in the interview. For the fans, an interpersonal connection began to develop. This emotional connection was only intensified when sometimes their favorite stars would write back. Every now and again, the celebrity would respond with a thank-you letter and maybe even include a headshot. On a rarer occasion, the most prized possession would be included: their autograph. It didn't take long for this two-way engagement to completely reframe the experience. Once fans realized they might be rewarded for their efforts, their investment of time, effort, and energy intensified. But as more and more fan mail began to arrive at the celebrities' homes, their publicly listed addresses were changed to reflect the addresses of the studios. Which meant that the return on investment for the public had again been reframed. The responses they now received were not from the celebrities themselves but from the studios, who had received their letter on the actors' behalf. For some fans, this was perfectly acceptable. They never expected to hear anything back from their favorite celebrities. For many fans, the simple act of reaching out held the same thrill as buying a lottery ticket. They didn't expect to win anything, but it would certainly be a treat if they did. And after all, you couldn't win if you didn't play.

Even as recently as when my career in protection first began, the most common way the general public communicated, or at least attempted to communicate, with a celebrity, a politician, an athlete, or some other popular public figure was to write them a letter. More often than not, they were addressed to the studio that produced their movies, the stations that broadcast their shows, the stadiums that hosted their sports, or the offices they held as part of their public office. Very rarely were these letters ever sent to their homes.

Many of those who wrote letters were fans who simply wanted to express their support. Others cared to share their appreciation. Some wanted to offer a sincere thank-you for the joy brought into their lives watching them in a particular role, playing their sports, or for being true to their word on particular political issues.

Even today, with as much as we know about the evils of how entertainment is contrived, there is still something undeniably enjoyable
about the charisma of a celebrity. All the best movie stars, politicians, and
entertainers have the innate ability to capture the attention of adoring
fans. Even through the screen, they can make you feel like you are the
only one in the room. The downside to this personality trait is that some
people mistake this carefully crafted ability to communicate through
the screen as a legitimate connection.

Regrettably, some people became infatuated with a celebrity. They
became obsessed with learning as much as they could about them. Some
would even allow themselves to go so far down the rabbit hole that they
were able to convince themselves that they and the celebrity are destined
to be together. Then they would write to the celebrity to tell them this.
They would say things like, "If you would only just meet me, I promise
you would see." Some would provide receipts of the new suit they had
bought so they could "look good for their girl." And then, when they
did not receive a response, they would increase their efforts. They would
book a flight. They would send copies of their travel itinerary. They
would let the celebrity know where and when they planned to meet them
at the studio. The would write things like, "Don't worry about sending
me the address, I already know where it is."

Concerning as these communications were, not everyone was a love-
sick fan. Others who wrote letters had a darker agenda. They didn't love
the celebrity. They hated them. They hated the reminder of "how good"
the celebrity's life was and "how bad" they believed their own lives to be.
Since the authors of these communications believed the celebrity had
so much money, maybe they could "do the right thing and send some of
that green my way." Then when they didn't hear back, they would write
them again, "Or maybe I'll just come out there and take it."

I truly believe that most people have good in their hearts. I sincerely
accept that most people who want to contact a public figure—whatever
their reason may be—are doing so out of a legitimate gesture of good
faith. I understand that most people have no expectation of ever hearing back from the public figure they attempted to contact. They simply
wanted to say what they wanted to say and send it. That was all it was

ever meant to be. Most people who do good are happy enough with the emotional reward that comes from sharing positivity. Unfortunately, this is not the default setting for everyone. Regrettably, not everyone lives with love in their hearts.

Today, the communication game has completely changed. People still write letters (I still review quite a few of them), but the simple act of writing letters is for the most part an antiquated practice. Digital communication has elevated the sheer volume of communications to an entirely new and previously unfathomable level of discourse. When I first began my career, it was unprecedented for a public figure to have received upward of ten thousand communications from fans over the course of their entire career. Today, a public figure may receive that many communications in a single day. Which is not to say that all these communications are threatening in nature. In fact, most of these communications are somewhere on the spectrum of ultra-positive to otherwise benign, but even one threat in a batch of ten thousand is a concern to be taken seriously.

It was not so long ago that threat assessments were reserved for the well-known politicians, the celebrities, and the public figures who were prominently featured in TV shows, the evening news, and the Saturday matinée. Not anymore. Social media and digital communications have changed the threat management landscape forever. As a result, any business or person perceived as being aligned with a dissenting opinion is at risk of becoming a target for unsolicited viciousness and vitriol—and in some cases violence. It is easier today than ever to communicate a grievance. It is easier than ever to bully, harass, torment, and threaten a target online than it would ever be to do in person. The other unfavorable reality is that this form of harmful ideation is impacting the lives of everyone. From the classmate, to the coworker, to the ex-lover, to our families and friends, every single interpersonal relationship in our lives is connected online in one way or another. And if any of us find ourselves on the receiving end of these disruptions, it can be devastating to our ways of life. When we don't know how to deal with something, we will sometimes choose to simply avoid having to deal with it and then hope the situation will somehow make itself better.

So what is someone to do? How should these communications be handled? How is the everyday person on the receiving end of these disruptions supposed to know who is just joking, who is being an asshole, and who is a serious threat? Well, that is exactly what we are going to discuss right now. Threats are my business, and over the course of this chapter, I am going to provide you with the basic framework for understanding the essentials of threat management so that you can begin to understand the building blocks and take a lead role in securing your own safety.

PROTECTIVE TAKEAWAY

Threat management is about reducing risk and preventing violence. Above all else, the role of threat management is to identify the hazards on the horizon *before* any ideations of harm are allowed to evolve into an aggressive act.

PROTECTIVE AWARENESS

What Is an Inappropriate Communication?

An *inappropriate communication* is any form of communication that could be considered outside the bounds of what a rational person would expect to be normal.

Let's say a woman was just dropped off from a first date by a man she had met on a dating app. The date went well, but there was no intimate interaction beyond the hand-holding on the walk home followed by a warm hug and a soft kiss on the cheek good night. She was not sure if she would see this person again, but she was open to the idea if he asked her out again. Soon after getting home, she hears her phone chirp with a text message. The display on her screen says that it's from the guy she was just with. She's happy to see this, as she is expecting him to say that he had a nice time, and would like to see her again, but instead she finds a text message which reads:

No sex? WTF!!! Next time you better be naked.

Not really what she was expecting to read, was it? Welcome to the world of inappropriate communications. This communication is a concern for three reasons:

The first concern is that his drafting and sending this message is a key indicator of emotional instability. The second concern is his word choice: *No sex?* followed by *WTF!!!* is a clear indicator of a grievance, and as we discussed earlier, the identification of a grievance is the first step on the pathway to violence. Finally, the message contains a conditional threat: *Next time you better be naked* communicates a willingness to apply consequence for her not having fulfilled his sexual desire.

At this point in time, the best approach would be to do nothing. The man who sent this message is annoyed and frustrated and is clearly acting in such a way to displace his own frustration onto another—in this case, his date. Any response from her will only serve to instigate him. When in doubt, no response is almost always the best response. In fact, no response is its own response. Always better to put a period at the end of a conversation rather than an ellipsis. Despite our best intentions, engaging an irrational actor with what we believe to be a rational response works as well as telling someone who is angrily agitated that they "just need to calm down." If someone is insistent upon overcommunicating to you their emotional turmoil, document and record their behavior, but do not respond. Do not reward their bad behavior with a response. Very little will come from engaging in a back-and-forth banter of escalation.

It is important to understand that an inappropriate communication is the very first indication that something is wrong. In some cases— especially when there is a clear communication of a grievance—they serve as the first ping on our radar of risk. Do *not* allow yourself to fall into the Safety Trap by believing that this kind of a thing will "work itself out" all by itself. Sometimes it may, but more often, it will not.

Will every inappropriate communication require vast sums of time, effort, and energy? No. It will not. That said, each and every inappropriate communication does require some level of effort. Even if the only effort required is your willingness to acknowledge the communication was inappropriate and your promise to save it in case it becomes more relevant later is a significant first step to ensuring your safety.

Pro Tip: Always keep anything that may appear to be an inappropriate communication. Those communications you receive through personal accounts like texts, emails, call logs, social media comments, and direct messages are all important things to document for future reference. Preserving the original communication is always preferred as best practice, because they offer an extra level of metadata that can sometimes be useful in an investigation. Screenshots are also useful. Anything that can be used to document a pattern in practice of harassment or the escalation of an emerging concern is always helpful when framing the narrative should the time to involve law enforcement or legal advocacy become necessary.

As with most things in life, *you* will always be your own best arbiter for what constitutes a concern. Any communication you believe to be an inappropriate communication *is* an inappropriate communication. No one understands the totality of circumstances encompassing all the variables in your life better than you. Should you ever find yourself on the fence about deciding if a communication is inappropriate or not, there are a few takeaways that will surely fit the bill. Such communications may contain or convey a direct, indirect, conditional, or veiled threat; a desire to do harm; an expression of an extreme emotion like love or hate; a reference to a debt that is owed; a reference to information that is not in the public domain; a reference to historical acts of violence; a reference to historically violent people; a reference to any religious themes; any reference to mental illness; any reference to death or suicide; an expression of an obsessive desire to meet; any reference to another public figure who has been attacked, harmed, or killed; any reference to the author of the communication being someone greater than or other than who people believe them to be; or any reference to bodyguards, security, or protective safeguards.

If at any point in time, you find yourself on the receiving end of an inappropriate communication, *do not ignore it*. Do not allow yourself to fall into the Safety Trap of Avoidance by allowing for your concern to dispute but then allowing for the risk to remain. You are very likely prioritizing a million other tasks. Ask for help. Tell a friend. These are not the concerns you want to fall between the cracks. Protect yourself. Safety first.

What Is a Threat Assessment?

A *threat assessment* is the process for determining the likelihood of an expressed threat to escalate into a harmful or otherwise violent act (the assessment phase) and then to help manage that concern toward peaceful resolution (the management phase).

Pro Tip: Waiting around for the direct threat of "I'm going to kill you" to be communicated is like standing around and watching as someone who's clearly pissed off at you goes to the store to buy a gas can and a lighter, fills the can with gas, breaks into your home, and then pours the gasoline all over your bedroom—but then never taking them seriously until they pull out the lighter and say, "Dare me to do it?" Don't wait until it is too late to take the threat to your safety seriously.

One of the biggest misconceptions about threat assessment is that it is all about one creepy communication. It is not. Threat assessment is about the totality of circumstance much more than it is about evaluating a singular communication within the framework of an isolated incident.

Personal Versus Impersonal

Another critical consideration when making your determination is to understand the nature of the relationship between the author of the threat and the target of their communications. There is a significant difference between knowing someone and knowing *about* someone. Not only is it important to understand the dynamic of the relationship between the author and the target, it is of equal importance to understand the relationship of the target to the author.

Personal
Author <————————> Target
Impersonal
Author————————> Target

A significant impact that social media has had on threat management is the increase in emotional investment some people have instilled in those public figures, public office holders, and public-facing businesses. While the recipients of this attention may be grateful for the support and fandom they receive, their managers are more likely to view the engagement as a collective (which can be monetized) rather than as individuals—each with their own unique relationship to the public figure. After all, while their fan base may be counted in the millions, the public figure is just one person. And while it would be impossible for the public figure to know as much about their individual followers, the high degree of emotional investment and the belief by their fans that the connection is strong and their relationship is real only serves to intensify the feelings of betrayal when they do something in such a way that runs counter to how an individual fan may prefer they would.

Intent and Motivation

Another important step is to understand the motivation behind the communication and to identify the author's intent. While motivation is the emotional driver behind their action, the intent of their communication is what really helps to frame the takeaway of what the author was trying to achieve. Does the author of this communication want to physically harm the target of their communication, or are they more than happy to simply try to disrupt the target's efforts by throwing a wrench into their scheduled activity? There are two overarching concerns in this world: disruptive efforts (those who express a threat) and predatory practices (those who pose a threat).

Expressing a Threat

The simplest way to understand the difference between the two is to imagine you are driving home from work. Now no matter how safe a driver you are, at some point in time, another driver is going to curse, scream, flip you the bird, and damn your soul to hell. They'll honk and holler and then speed off. You'll never see them again. These people are disruptors. They have, in that moment of anger and despair, chosen to express a threat for the sole purpose of displacing their own emotional angst onto you, but they have zero intention of escalating that hostility beyond their emotionally charged display of disapproval.

Posing a Threat

On the other side of that coin is the driver who feels like you cut them off in traffic but says nothing. Instead, they go white-knuckled and stare. They slow down behind you and start following you home, but then they speed off as you pull into your driveway. Later, you notice them checking your LinkedIn page, which means now they know where you work. Now they know more about you than they reasonably should. This driver poses a threat. Their behavior is deliberate and methodical. Their actions are not emotional; they are predatory.

Of these two categories of concern, those who pose a threat are much more dangerous. For the most part, those who orally express threats have made a conscious decision to employ fear and intimidation rather than violence. They chose words that alarm over actions that harm.

Pro Tip: In an organizational setting, the difference between expressed threats and a posed threat is especially common in scenarios involving bomb threats. The purpose of a bomb threat is to instill fear, panic, and disruption—not to do harm. If their intent were the physical destruction of their target, then why would they call in the threat? Simply stated, they wouldn't. A would-be offender who is able to acquire the materials, build the bomb, circumvent security to get inside, place the device, and then successfully escape undetected would not go through all that hard work only to sabotage their success with a phone call.

Disruptive Endeavor Versus Predatory Planning

There are those who express a threat (the disruptors) and there are those who pose a threat (the predators). The best way to frame this picture in your mind and distinguish the difference between the two is to think of the behavioral motivations between when a dog has decided to bark and when a dog decides to bite.

If your dog is in the living room and the mailman comes to the door, your dog will very likely run to the door and establish his dominance as the protector of your property by barking its bloody head off. In this scenario, the dog is expressing a threat of violence but has made the conscious choice to not attack.

The K-9 attack dogs of the military and the police are trained and deployed in a very similar fashion. While the K-9 is on the handler's leash, they express their innate desire to take you down. They lurch forward, they bark, they bare their fangs. This is a tactic a K-9 handler may employ to convince an otherwise noncompliant suspect to obey the officer's commands. However, should the suspect not comply, as soon as the handler frees the K-9 from the tethers of the leash, well, that K-9 is done barking for the day. They are now in full-tilt attack mode. Fast, aggressive, deadly.

Just like dogs will often bark before they bite, dogs do not bark while they are biting—they growl. Human disruptors on the path of becoming a predator will often employ very similar tactics.

The Disruptors

More often than not, those who direct their individual angst, disgust, and emotional turmoil have no intent of doing you harm. This class of disruptor finds empowerment in their belief that their actions will cause chaos in the target's world. And since it is unlikely they will ever really know how much of an impact they have had, they will imagine that their success was extraordinary.

An excellent example of this was during the ramp-up to the 2016 election, where anyone found in even the remotest corner of the political ecosystem soon discovered that their social media and email accounts had become a push-notified minefield of inappropriate communication. Anyone who was even peripherally perceived to be an advocate for or against any of the candidates for office was immediately targeted by opposition groups as being either "Fake News," part of the "Deep State," or any of the other incentivized hashtags-of-hate monikers assigned to news organizations or political party platforms. Even those whose roles had historically been to report on the election cycle—the journalists—had not been spared from these attacks.

An overwhelming number of these communications were what we referred to as the *Crusaders.*

By and large, these Crusaders did not know the targets of their communications. They lived in a fantasy world of their own creation and found personal validation in their efforts because their imaginations allowed for them to have a far greater impact on the world than their reality could ever offer. They communicated as a way of advancing some cause they perceived to be larger than themselves. They threatened political and social opponents in the hope of disrupting their target's operations, business, or social activities. These Crusaders were also very specific in their choice of target. They targeted individuals who represented a political or social stance they opposed. Crusaders were often motivated by religious, moral, or political beliefs, which their communications would often misconstrue as justification for their threats, as in some warped worldview of an "ends justifying the means" argument or as being "a necessary evil in a larger war." In the minds of these Crusaders, the "purity" of their motives—especially when believed to be directed or instructed by "God"—somehow served as justification for the extremity of their harassment.

Here's a recent example of a voice mail that came across my desk:

—Begin Call—
Yooo . . . Takin' a class-action loss out . . . lawsuit out on you bastards.
Yup! Lyin' on the United States of America and the president.
Callin' him a racist.
Class-action lawsuit for every citizen of the United States.

Disparaging. Our. President.

Who the fuck are you freeloaders?

What the fuck!?

Oh, the president's a racist . . .

You wore it out.

Nobody believes it no more.

Just like the Mueller shit . . .

You're just a bunch of weirdos.

A bunch of weirdos who don't work for a living.

Never had a real job.

You bags of fuckin' dooty-poop.

<laughing>

I crack up every time I see a bunch of you losers.

Why don't you go there with ANTIFA?

Oh, that's right, you probably are ANTIFA.

. . . ya fuckin' shitbags.

Have a wonderful day.

See ya in federal court, fuck-face.

—End Call—

The Predators

Predatory communications are those communications that reveal insights or secrets about a target's private life that the general public should not know. These insights are particularly worrisome because they reveal that the author of the communication may have been engaged—or hired others to engage—in an unlawful activity like stalking or surveillance.

Social engineering is the psychological manipulation of people into performing actions or divulging confidential information. This is a very common tactic and is used to either obtain information about a target that may not be publicly available or, worse, to manipulate a gatekeeper of their target's time to grant the predator access.

Haven't you ever wondered how Sacha Baron Cohen of *Who Is America?*, *Borat*, and *Da Ali G Show* is able to keep getting famous guests for his show?

Simple. He does the exact same thing a bad guy who would want to do them harm would do. He just chooses to make them look like fools instead.

> **Pro Tip:** Successful stunts are teaching tools of terror. Always keep in mind that if someone is able to find a way to breach security to conduct a stunt—a gag interview, sneak into a Super Bowl game, jump onstage at a concert, streak across the field, and high-five a player—it might be funny in the moment, but bad guys aren't laughing; they are incorporating what you just taught them into their attack plan.

The process is fairly simple. He identifies famous guests who have weak gatekeepers and a low barrier to entry. Then he finds something they would already want to talk on camera to a televised audience about, and then he offers them the invitation to do just that. Only thing is, he creates a false persona, fake media credentials, and a fake website to make it all appear like he's the real deal and that this is a legitimate offer for engagement.

Producers of Cohen's show send their target a letter "which explains that an entity named Somerford Brooke Productions is creating a six-part series called 'The Making of Modern America (working title).' Lauding the recipient's 'unbridled reputation,' the letter invites him to appear on a show that will 'present issues in a fresh and innovative way that will engage young viewers.' It says that the producers hope the show, ahem, 'won't just be seen in the UK but world-wide.'"*

Not too difficult to see where whoever gave this invitation the green light fell face-first into the Safety Trap. Now I can't say for certain, and it's very possible that I am wrong, but I'm pretty damn sure that an elected official has a pretty rigorous process in place for vetting the names and

---

* Sam Schechner, "Respek! How Does Ali G Keep Conning Famous Guests?," *Slate*, September 20, 2004.

organizations for any media requests. Maybe the ones who have a bill-board in Times Square get a pass, but everyone else—especially foreign press—is most certainly expecting to get vetted.

Can you fake a website? Of course. But what is much more difficult to fake is everything else, which would have been rather obvious to no-tice had anyone bothered to look. Since they granted the interview re-quest, I'm comfortable speculating they did not bother to do so. Again, maybe I'm wrong. What do you think? Which is more likely: they did their due diligence and were so satisfied by the very little available to be found that they felt certain enough in their safety to move forward, or they heard the buzzwords of *TV, worldwide,* and *engage young viewers* and decided their fears were abated enough that they need not worry about whatever risk remained? I don't know about you, but I'm betting heavily on door number two.

Pop quiz!

Okay, now that you know what we are looking for, imagine someone you don't know sends you a direct message. Which of these communica-tions do you believe to be more concerning?

#1—"Y'all just a bunch of bastards, and I'm gonna luv watchin' y'all burn."
#2—"You're not gonna be bikini ready for Mexico eating all that late-night ice cream."

Did you guess number two? Why? If your answer has anything to do with having insight into information that isn't publicly available, you're on the right track. All things being equal, the first communication is clearly intended to be disruptive and instill fear. They are expressing a threat. The second communication doesn't say anything outright harm-ful, but the author of this communication poses more of a threat be-cause they reveal insights about your life that are not publicly known. How did they know you were planning a trip to Mexico? How did they know you prefer a bikini to a one-piece? How did they know you were bingeing on ice cream last night? While both communications should certainly be flagged for follow-up, insider information—which may indicate that someone has been stalking you—is the far greater concern between the two.

Social Media Is a New Threat Medium

Social media provides an accepting, sympathetic, and sometimes supportive forum for the expression of real, perceived, and imagined grievances. While most violent offenders will not directly communicate threats to their intended target, many will make ominous posts about their attack ideation.

Recent news reports of social media threats escalating into real-world hazards only makes the fear more real. Even the Supreme Court is involved in determining where free speech ends on social media and where prosecutable threats begin.

Perhaps the most challenging aspect of online threats and harassment is that the different social media services are only aware of the concerns reported on their own sites. They have no way to monitor the behavior of predators who jump between communication platforms. At present, Twitter, Facebook, Tinder, Instagram, and personal communications like email and text messages have no way to share the reported concerns of their users. This void allows for those intending to harass, stalk, or threaten their targets to jump between platforms with the near certainty of anonymity.

PROTECTIVE PREPAREDNESS
The following are the top five things you need to know about real-world threat management:

1. **Those who wish to do harm do not just snap**. Targeted violence is the result of an identifiable and observable process of thinking and behavior that when identified, assessed, and managed has been proven to prevent violent outcome.
2. **Violent offenders will not only make direct threats toward their intended target, they will also express their intent to others they believe will be agreeable, supportive, or even sympathetic to their**

belief that they can do something to resolve their grievances. While the expressions of these grievances may take place in an interpersonal context, they are increasingly taking place on internet forums and via social media platforms.

3. **On the pathway to violence, those who wish to do harm must first engage in some form of research and planning to determine the likelihood of success for their intended action.** A key component to bringing a threat assessment case toward peaceful resolve is identifying the subject's attack-related behavior. These are the self-identifying patterns on the pathway to violence that include research, planning, weapon acquisition, training, and logistical considerations. The research-and-planning phase provides the best protective intelligence to determine if the subject poses a realistic threat that is likely to escalate into violence. This phase also offers the most observable monitoring of the time, money, and effort being invested in the subject's willingness to do harm. This phase is crucial in determining if the offender will continue on the path toward violence or if they will transfer their ideation toward a more easily accessible target.

   It is important to keep in mind that to the violent offender, likelihood of success is the most significant factor in the decision to move forward with their intended action.

   This is one of the predominant factors as to why schools are so frequently targeted by their own students and why workplace violence offenders attack their own offices. The offenders know these locations well. They know the terrain. They know the active-shooter response plan. They know the layout of the structures. They know what the security response is likely to involve. They know how effectively access control is regulated, and they are able to carry out a dry run without raising much suspicion.

4. **Understand the difference between a threat that has been expressed and those who pose a threat.** While those who make threats have made a conscious decision to choose alarming words over harmful actions, those who pose a threat are of a

much greater concern, as their self-identifying behavior is consistent with predatory actions that are commonly associated with hazardous outcomes. A dog who barks is expressing a threat. A lion laying low in a pounce position poses a threat.

5. **Effective threat assessment is about a totality of circumstance.** This is more about the pattern of behaviors over space and time than it is about the assessment of a specific incident in the context of a singular occurrence. These practices of identifying, monitoring, and assessing patterns of behavior are not new methodologies. They have been utilized by financial institutions to track market trends for central banks and private investors for years. Similar methodologies are used by governments to identify destabilizing geopolitical realities that often precede terror concerns.

Until now, these methodologies have not been readily employed to reduce risk and prevent violence in our homes, schools, and places of work. Today is different. We are smarter today than we were yesterday.

17

CASE STUDY:
THE BAD BREAKUP

Model Mayhem

When people I don't know ask me what I do for a living, I typically tell them I have my own consulting firm and that I specialize in threat management. If they ask what that means, I will tell them one of two things: "I help good people make bad things better," or "I help my clients to return to normalcy after a breach of safety." Every once in a while, I'll say both. It depends on my audience.

Truth is, for all the red carpets and runways of my younger days in protection, today, the bulk of my business is spent reading illicit emails, listening to vulgar voice mails, contributing to news stories, giving speeches, conducting audits, writing assessments, or I'm engaged in some similar effort in support of helping my clients to ensure the certainty of safety for everyone involved.

What I love most about my chosen profession is that it is a guaranteed escape from the typical nine-to-five career I spent my entire professional life trying to avoid. I have been lucky enough to make my passion my profession, and to be perfectly honest, even though I am often working eighteen-plus hours a day and haven't had a true weekend off since I don't know when, it still never feels like "work."

Maybe that's because I'm still learning, still growing in my field of profession, and still receiving the positive feedback that comes from a job well done. Another part of the satisfaction is that when I spend my days dealing with the more inappropriate side of what humanity has to offer, my days may be long, but they are rarely, if ever, boring.

The bulk of my business is threat management, and like I said before, when you boil it down, it's about helping good people make bad things better. For the most part, good people don't go out looking for trouble, but if you are a public-facing organization, if you are a public figure, or even if you are an anonymous but otherwise high-net-worth individual, trouble always seems to somehow find you.

We've already discussed emerging trends in threats relating to social media and the inability for a certain cross section of our society to accept that the societal norms of the digital realm do not cross over to the real world.

The other concern I would like to take some time to address may have been with us for a much longer time, but it is still grounded in the unwillingness—mostly by men—to accept the fact that a relationship is over and that it is time for you to move on.

Across the board, bad breakups—especially those breakups that had a history of intimate partner violence—have consistently resurfaced as one of the most challenging concerns to manage.

Don't Speak

The people who know us best—especially those recently relinquished intimate lovers—know all too well the emotional triggers they can manipulate to their advantage. Lustful memories. Embarrassing moments. Friends. Family. Coworkers. If it has even the remotest chance of eliciting a response, it's fair game. Nothing is sacred. They will tear at each and every tie that binds in a desperate ploy to retain their own sense of control. These are people who seek to maintain what they had, and they will obsessively pursue whatever small fragment of what once was because they are wildly unwilling to move on. These are people who express a fanatical inability to accept their target's decision to move away from their previous relationship. They use intimate knowledge of their former partner in their efforts to win back the relationship. Nothing is off limits. Since they have personal insight about the private life of their target, they will exploit that personal knowledge in an attempt to instigate a response. They will do anything and everything to maintain some level of communication with their target because they believe that any hold they may have leads to the possibility of their perceived return to normalcy.

If you have walked past the magazine rack at a bookstore or glanced through the window of the airport grab-and-go, you have most certainly seen her. Dark hair. Light eyes. High cheekbones. Yoga-toned arms. Beauty personified. Beautiful as she was, she was also lonely. Her level of celebrity and notoriety did not make dating easy. And she traveled a lot—not as much as some but definitely more than others. Her social media commentary was full of half-serious gestures of romance, but she couldn't remember the last time someone actually asked her out on a proper date. So it came as no surprise that her new relationship began as most relationships do—a just good-enough combination of mutual attraction and convenience. The initial introduction began innocently enough. They both lived in the same building, but on different floors. Her apartment was higher, but they both had the park-side view. He was successful. Did well for himself. Something to do with investment banking. They met in the elevator. They were both dog lovers. They would often see each other during morning walks. They soon started taking those walks together. She was interested, but she was taking things slowly. She was being hesitant. Cautious.

A week or so later, her dog sitter fell ill before a trip. They were out on one of their morning walks with the dogs when she got the call. She confided her dilemma to him. He offered to help. They exchanged numbers. This was typically reserved for her as a true sign of trust. She chose mostly to communicate with newly associated acquaintances through social media. She had found people—especially men—easier to delete that way. But this one she felt she could trust. She found herself liking him.

He lived in her building. He was offering to help. So she let down her guard and decided to give him a try.

Soon, he became her go-to friend. He would watch after her German shepherd when she was traveling. They exchanged access codes to each other's homes under the guise of "doggy emergencies"—but they both felt there was something more. When she returned home from a trip maybe a month or so later, she invited him over for dinner as a thank-you for being such a good guy.

One thing led to another. A glass of wine, then two, then the bottle. Soon, their self-prescribed vows of not ruining a friendship gave way to the promise of going back to being friends once the sun came up. It was an easy lie to agree upon to help them get through the night, then the next night, and the night after that. They enjoyed the casual comfort of closeness. A late-night text. A soft knock on the door. Before they knew it, their onetime random night of passion had turned into a regular routine.

But nothing lasts forever. Reality sets in. The chance encounters in elevators that used to spark joy on their random occasion now seemed to become more frequent and planned. Somewhere between comfort and claustrophobia, the relationship broke bad. It just wasn't as fun as it used to be. He wanted more. She wanted less. He was drinking more. He was becoming more demanding of her time, wanting to know where she was. What was she doing? Who was she with? It always made her wonder why he was never out. She didn't understand why he didn't have friends. Why was a good-looking, wealthy guy in a city full of beautiful women never unavailable for her? She didn't want what was easy.

He was simply always here. Waiting for her to want him. And that was not what she was looking for in a man. Then one night, he got too drunk. He started crying. He felt like he was losing her. He did not understand why she did not want to be seen with him. Never let him take her out. Never out for a date. Was he not enough for her? Was she ashamed of him? Afraid to let the world see how much he loved her?

She wanted to laugh. It was all she could do not to. So she chose instead to roll her eyes and turn away. She threw her hands up. This was just too much. She'd had enough. She walked into the bedroom. He followed her inside. *Okay,* she thought. *This is over.*

She broke up with him right there. He wouldn't take no for an answer. And instead of choosing what was right, he became wrathful and chose what was wrong. He made a move toward her in aggression. She had never encountered this before. As his right hand raised up and was fisted, her German shepherd burst in through the door. And before his threat to her life could be realized, her German shepherd had him down on the floor.

In the half second between the realization of her fear and her complete unpreparedness to protect herself, her German shepherd bought her the two precious seconds she needed.

She escaped into the bathroom and locked the door. She heard his scream of shock. His moan in pain. Heard the low growl of her German shepherd as he guarded her bathroom door. She balled up on the floor and was crying. She only came out once she knew it was safe, when her four-pawed protector was scratching on the door. She opened the bathroom door and let him inside. They spent the better part of the night on a robe-lined floor.

The next morning, he called. She sent him to voice mail. He called again soon after. She did the same thing. Then a text saying how sorry he was. He was drunk. He apologized. He'd quit drinking. Please don't leave him.

She ignored those too.

Then her dog barked at the door before she even heard the knock. He was at the door. He was trying her code, but she sighed as she remembered activating the no-entry option so he couldn't get in. But he was pleading with her to let him in. He kept trying the door. Did he know she was in here?

He was calling her phone again. Texting her. Begging her to "just talk."

So she decided to talk. She walked over to the door and told him that if he didn't go away, she would call the police. He begged her to open the door. Pleaded with her to say it wasn't over.

Her final response left no room for interpretation: "Fuck straight off and leave me alone."

He left. But the text messages continued. *I will never leave you. I will fight for you until the day I die. I beg you. Please talk. Just talk.*

She didn't want to stay there. She didn't feel safe. She logged in to her building's resident portal. Yes, her building had security, but she wanted more. This wasn't her first time dealing with a creep. She and every other model she had ever worked with before had been forced to deal with some brand of stalker. Most were just obsessed fans. A few were bad breakups. But this one was different. This former friend turned lover wasn't just another run-of-the-mill stalker in the making. This one was too familiar and literally too close to home. If he was threatening to never leave her alone, she wanted to have a camera that could see what was going on outside her door.

Fuck. Now he was calling her again. *Well, that's enough of this shit,* she thought. She blocked his number. She blocked his social media—everything.

She decided she was going to leave. Just get out of there for a few days. Check into a hotel. She had a trip coming up end of the week anyway, which she felt would be good. Give him some time to simmer down. Get the fuck over it. Move on. Leave her alone.

She just wanted to run away. She felt as if she were in prison. Trapped. Too terrified to leave. Too afraid to come home. She was certain he was around every corner, hiding in every shadow, behind every door.

She spent the next few nights at a hotel. She had her dog with her whenever possible. Her life may have become an agonizing hell, but her dog was living his best life—enjoying all the newly committed pampering and attention. She loved him. She needed him too. The only male in her life who had never let her down. She even had her agent update her travel rider so that her dog was part of her package.

"And what if they balk?" her agent asked.

"You can tell them whatever you want," she replied, "but no dog, no me."

She spent the next few nights at a downtown hotel. She checked the Ring security camera that night and saw that he had passed by her apartment door. He was trying to act like he was just walking down the hallway, but he looked freaked when he saw the camera on her door, and he quickly tried to cover his face with his hand. But that was it. He didn't try to knock on the door. He didn't try to enter.

A week later, she was in Los Angeles with work. She wound up staying for a few extra weeks on her own dime. It was a perfect time of year for her to enjoy the beach. And her dog loved the sand, loved jumping into the waves, playing in the surf. But every time her phone rang, every time an email alert chimed, every time another social media mention pinged its notifying alert, her fear renewed. Her anxiety rose. And her psychological rationale for not going home was recommitted.

Fortunately, work was keeping her busy: Miami, then Chicago, and then back once more to LA.

Six weeks had gone by. Nothing out of the ordinary to report. A few random phone numbers had tried to ring through, but they had all been ignored. No one she wasn't personally connected to could reply to her stories. And even if he had created an account to follow her or comment on her photos, she wouldn't have even known. They were too numerous to mention and not worth the effort to explore.

She was checking the Ring camera footage every night. She saw nothing. She needed to decide.

On August 3, she bought a plane ticket.

On August 4, she moved back into her apartment.

And for the next two weeks, everything went fine. She didn't see him at all. Maybe he moved. Maybe he moved on. Maybe he was just finally ready to leave her alone. Her life, she felt, was finally getting ready to return to normal.

On the morning of August 17, she was meeting up with a friend for a workout at the Equinox on Prince Street, followed by lunch at Mercer Kitchen. She was sipping a green-tea protein smoothie when her Ring doorbell notified her that someone was at her door. She thought nothing of it as she clicked it on.

She regretted it as soon as she did.

There he was. Standing in front of her door with an obnoxiously oversize bouquet of flowers in one hand and an equally inappropriate-size teddy bear in the other.

"Oh hell, fuck no!" she blurted out loud to her friend while sharing the screen view of her phone.

And as small worlds would have it, her friend sitting with her was the TV star from earlier who had been forced to contend with her own stalker.

A Friendly Referral

To be honest, I almost didn't take the call. I didn't have whatever number the TV star was calling me from programmed into my phone. But she came up with a Santa Monica area code, and I had been hopping back and forth on calls to LA in support of another matter. I assumed one of them was calling me from an office line instead of the mobile phone.

It took me a second to recognize her voice. It had been a while since we had last spoken, and even when we were in the middle of all of that, I had mostly been working on behalf of her agent. Which is not to say the TV star and I did not have the chance to talk or establish a good rapport—we most certainly did. It's just rare for a talent in need to reach out to me at the onset of a concern so directly. More often than not, the initial contact is made by a handler, an agent, a lawyer, or a studio rep. That said, referrals are the driving force behind any successful business model, and I was more than happy to know that I was who she first thought of and was first to call.

The two of them were still sitting at lunch. The TV star handed her phone to the model, and after a quick few minutes of general overview, she asked if I might be able to help.

I told her I could. I told her I would forward my contact card to the TV star. She could then get it from her. That way, if she would like to talk more, she would have the best number to reach me. At the onset of a concern like this, I never know how it will play out. Regardless, there was no need for me to have her information. And it would have been not only unprofessional but inappropriate for me to even ask.

For all the obvious reasons, public figures are very particular about who is able to have what level of access to their personal devices. In their world more than many others', circles of trust change often. Contact cards change more than fashion trends. Friends change more than seasons. And power partnerships, like the two of them there at lunch, are often intended to promote the public's perception in support of an upcoming project more than a long-standing history grounded in friendship and trust.

Another reason for putting the onus on the model to call me is that over the years, I have learned how important it is to have those asking for help to initiate the first call. Time is an excellent measure for how serious they believe something to be. In my profession, the timeliness by which someone calls you after having extended the invitation to do so tells you everything you need to know about the perceived severity of their concern. If they call you immediately, it's a priority problem. If they say, "Okay, thanks, I'll call you back later today," it's not.

Her concern was more serious than most.

The model texted within the hour, asking if I would be free for a call in fifteen minutes. She beat the text from the TV star saying they had talked about this some more and that she would be reaching out soon by a full ten minutes.

What Does Winning Look Like?

The first call was short, just enough to get a more complete understanding of the overarching concern followed by a framing of her expectation for "What does winning look like?"

Short term: Was she in any real physical danger? And if so, what were her options?

Long term: The permanent removal of this guy from her life so she would never have to see, hear, or deal with him again.

Both expectations were reasonable. Making a bad thing better can often have a vast scope of interpretation. For some people like the model, it's enough to just have the concern be permanently put in the rearview mirror. They just want it over so they can move on. Others may want more. Some people will say they want an apology. Other people will say they want to sue. A few people will want to have the hounds of hell unleashed on them, their families, their second-grade teacher, and anyone else who may have had some semblance of value in their life. They all but ask for the scorched-earth option.

But most of these requests are driven by emotion. They are motivated by fear. They are manifested by the fantasy of retaliation. So the best way to manage these expectations is to frame the process as a multitiered strategy.

The Solution Phase

First, let's make sure you are safe.

Second, let's bring this concern to a close.

After that, we have a suite of options that may be both legally and morally available to you based on the findings of our investigation, the assessments those findings reveal, and the likelihood of this concern being reignited somewhere down the line. But more often than not, if you really want for this to be over, then you really have to decide if you want to put a period at the end of this sentence or if you want to continue the conversation. My advice is almost always the former. The latter is rarely worth the effort. Trust me, the cost of vengeance is always expensive, never fulfilling, and always leaves you wanting more. Revenge is a devastating descent into suffering.

Best advice: those with lives worth living will always be best served by living those lives.

The Game Plan

It was important for the two of us to be on the same page with regard to the playbook and the overarching strategy we would be employing to win.

As we discussed before, we are not dealing with a rational actor. These personality types have tied their own sense of self-worth to you and your relationship, and they will stop at nothing to get you back. They will try anything even if they think it has only the slightest chance of success in initiating a response. Anything they believe they can use as leverage to get you to respond can and will be used. But remember, as soon as you concede and respond, it's right back to square one all over again. Stay strong. Breathe deeply. Stay the course. The more time and distance you can put between you and them, the better.

Difficult as it may be to accept, it is considered a best practice to *not* block their email, phone number, or social media accounts. Here's why: we do not want this to escalate into a game of cat and mouse. As we move forward in this process, we want to be able to build as strong a case file as possible. The more information we have to support your claim of harassment and emotional abuse, the better. This means we need to have the capability to assess, document, and manage all their efforts to contact you. We need to know what they do, how they choose to do it, and, perhaps more importantly, how often. If we block their ability to contact you, they will simply attempt to contact you through other means of communication. While this may also happen, our ability to add that factor to our case file will only serve to support the pattern in practice of their inability to leave you alone. As likely as they are to continue their efforts, we want to be even surer that we are being as effective as possible in ensuring your safety and bringing this unfavorable circumstance to its most favorable resolution as soon as humanly possible. Rest assured, all of this is being done to maintain and promote a strong, positive, and protective posture that simply communicates one thing: your life only moves in one direction—forward.

The Pursuer Mindset

Up until this point, the model had him all but blocked from being able to communicate with her. As the floodgates of his emotional engagement were now free to rush through an open door, I wanted to frame her expectation for what she was more than likely to find.

Communications from those who were once intimate partners but are now unrequited lovers engage their target for the sole purpose of instigating a response. When these communications are written, they will very often be able to be classified into one of these following categories.

BAITING: They will often try to chum the waters in an attempt to get you to respond. Nothing is off limits. They will try anything to get you to respond. Leverage is everything. But remember: as soon as you concede and respond, it's right back to square one all over again. Stay strong. Breathe deeply. Stay the course. Sometimes this approach will be coy: "Can I just ask you one last question?" They may be more sinister: "Your mom still has the 8349 number, right?" Other times, they may be just downright indefensible: "TMZ will pay a pretty penny for these" attached as a caption to an intimate photo taken during a more trusting time.

BARGAINING: These are communications that will be used to make the pursuer appear more reasonable than their earlier demands may have framed. They know that you are unwilling to give them what they want but will try to negotiate their desires down to the point that you may be willing to engage with them in a back-and-forth of terms and conditions.

BINDING: These are communications that refer to the more positive touchstones of your relationship. They will sometimes be about a shared experience of fun, but more often than not, they will infer the more intimate moments of sexual gratification and physical pleasure that were shared between the two of you alone.

MAINTAINING: These are the communications that almost seem as though nothing is wrong at all. They are simply reaching out about things they saw and wanted to share or details about how their day went, but mostly make no reference to there being any kind of elephant in the room with regard to the current status of your relationship.

The Data Dump

It was important that we had everything documented as part of a historic record.

We began this process by having the model write out her narrative with as much attention to detail as possible. I did my best to reemphasize this point as much as I could. Every. Detail. Matters. While she began to author her narrative, I began to create the profile template I would be putting together on her ex-boyfriend.

The profile template I prefer to use is basically a spreadsheet of my own design that allows for me to include photos of the individual in question, details about their background, pedigree information, criminal records, DMV records, court reports, and any other information the private investigators are able to glean from all available records. This template also affords me the ability to document the key details about the relationship that I would pull from the narrative the model was writing. But perhaps most important, now that the model had unblocked our subject from all her access points, this template would also serve as the clearinghouse for those activities, actions, and communications, which were most certainly going to take place moving forward.

So now that we had everything set up and ready to go, we were able to begin.

Unfortunately, the amount of information we had in this file at the end of that day was very minimal.

There had been no reporting to the police about the attempted assault. There had also been no report made to her building about either the attempted assault or the following day's attempt to enter her apartment. Don't get me wrong, I 100 percent understand why she didn't report the attempted assault to the police. While he may have been the aggressor, he was also the only one with the bruises. She was trying to protect her dog. This was the same reason she didn't report him to the building. She was terrified of the thought of them taking her dog away from her. Her dog was her only real sense of security. He had protected her when she needed saving the most. She loved him. She needed him. He had proven his loyalty to her, and she was certainly not going to betray her love and trust in him.

We did have the Ring camera capture of him walking past her door for no apparent reason, but there was no report made to the building about that incident, and there had been no notification made regarding the flower delivery from the day before either.

Unfortunately, the flowers were something else we didn't have in our possession. We had him captured on the Ring camera in front of the door, and we had him leaving the flowers and the bear in front of her door. But it wasn't until I asked to see what he had written in the card that she informed me that he had come back to her door about thirty minutes later and taken them back. We had the video, but nothing extra to go on. Still, something was better than nothing.

So we had what we had. And we were both willing to work forward from there.

The next day went much better. During our research, we found an old entertainment news article in which she had given an interview about a movie she was in. That article linked to the IMDb movie page, and on that movie page there had been a few back-and-forth comments from those who were part of the crew for that movie and who had also seen the entertainment news story that linked to this page. The comments section had become something of an ad hoc crew reunion, as different members began to tag other crew members from that production across a few other social media platforms.

What made this discovery relevant was that one of the crew members had found an old call sheet that had the names and contact information of all the cast and crew. When we cross-referenced the cast and crew sheet with the model's name, she was right there in the middle of the page. The thing was, the email address listed on that contact sheet was not one of the email addresses we were monitoring for activity.

So we asked her about it. Sure enough, it was an old email address that she had created for the purposes of that production, but she couldn't even remember the last time she had checked it. Lucky for us, it didn't take long for her to remember the password. Even better, we found the pattern in practice we needed to make our protective strategy that much more effective.

A Pattern In Practice

15 June 2018 22:15 Breakup / Attempted Assault

16 June 2018 09:35 Uninvited Appearance / Attempted Entry

18 June 2018 11:35 Attempt to Approach
Ring Capture

19 June 2018 02:10 Maintaining Email
"I've been calling and calling . . . Just talk."

19 June 2018 08:32 Bargaining Email
"Okay. I get it. But . . . something inside me tells me it's true. I love you . . . Just talk."

20 June 2018 08:32 Baiting Email
"Hope you have a great weekend."

09 July 2018 13:04 Baiting Email
"I still don't understand why you blocked me."

10 July 2018 08:59 Bargaining Email
"Get me a therapist and I will go. I'll do anything you want me to do."

10 July 2018 12:54 Baiting Email
<Link> "These 10 Ways In Your Relationship . . . Not Real"

11 July 2018 12:25 Maintaining Email
"I'm sorry . . . selfish person . . . I'm sorry I hurt you . . . alcohol. You're right, I do change when I drink."

12 July 2018 10:17 Binding Email
"I'm cleaning out pics in my phone." <attachment>

13 July 2018 17:33 Maintaining Email
"I realize you are mad at me . . . could really use your help."

13 July 2018 19:11 Maintaining Email
"I will call you tomorrow."

15 July 2018 15:48 Binding Email
"God, this is us! Come on!" <attachment> "A Real Relationship . . . Some Good Ass Sex."

17 July 2018 21:14 Bargaining Email
"Do you really hate me that much? Am I really that terrible of a person?"

18 July 2018 13:46 Baiting Email
"I'd rather bad times with you than good times with someone else."

18 July 2018 15:40 Baiting Email
<Meme/Attachment> "We're All Just Looking for Someone as F*cked Up as We Are"

17 August 2018 12:10 Flower Delivery (In Person)
Ring Camera Capture

17 August 2018 12:50 Flower Delivery Retrieval (In Person)
Ring Camera Capture

I sent the model my overview of initial findings. With the emails she was able to find on her old email account, we had a solid foundation from which to build our case file. His behavior had provided enough of a pattern in practice to work on. He was clearly on the *social loner* side of the house—those who have the capacity for social normalcy but who prefer to exist in an isolated social setting, unable to immediately fill the void with outside social support. This meant he was still trying to fill the vacuum of loss with whatever remnants he could salvage from their previous relationship.

Bottom line: it was favorable that the indicators showed he was not getting worse, but they were unfavorable in that he was likely to continue.

The model was taking this all in stride, handling this all much better than I honestly would have expected, especially since she was the one who was having to field all these communications and then send them over to me for review. That was why I really wanted to drive home that point— again and again—for how critical it was she never engage. I was trying to frame and manage her expectations as best as I could. But she needed to know and understand that this was going to continue, not forever, but at least for the next few weeks. The thing with stalkers like this . . . these personality types are traditionally of low emotional intelligence, which is only made more complicated by any false hope given to their methodology. Which is to say that if they leave nineteen voice mails, but they are then able to get through to their target to answer on call number twenty, they will recalibrate their baseline effort to a twenty-call foundation. This is why it is so important to disengage entirely from any response. You do not want this to evolve into a game of cat and mouse.

She said she understood. I was certain she did. It didn't take long for him to continue.

20 August 2018 06:55 Maintaining Voice Mail
"Good morning—um—to the most beautiful . . . not sure if you even get this."

2 September 2018 N/A Bargaining Letter / US Mail
Handwritten Letter
"The couples . . . meant to be . . . go through everything . . . tear apart, and come out strong."

8 September 2018 21:35 Baiting / Missed Phone Call
No message

9 September 2018 18:09 Bargaining Email
"I never loved someone like you. . . . I know I sound like a broken record."

The voice mail and the letters were something new. This very likely meant he knew she was back at home. I let the model know that as we had previously discussed, it was still unfavorable that he had not yet moved on—but it was favorable that he was at least acknowledging that he was not expecting a response but that he was also expressing an appropriate measure of realization that his time and energy would be better spent elsewhere. The language he was choosing was also consistent with evolving transference as indicated by his choice to verbalize *missing you* more than he was ahead of *loving you*. It was also favorable to see that he was not ending the communications with more "the end" type sign-offs like "Bye"—which is consistent with closure—instead of a future planned encounter such as "Talk to you soon," "See you around," or "Until next time."

Still, the end wasn't near. At least not yet. He was still circling back. The voice mail bothered me. The handwritten letter did too. Hard to tell. And with no overt act of aggression and no clearly communicated threat, we still had to just watch and wait and see what happened.

These things don't always move as quickly as we would like, but hardwood takes time to grow, and we both felt confident that so long as we stayed the course, we would eventually have all the evidence we needed to make our case as strong as possible.

Ten days later, we got what we wanted.

While the model was out of town, he came to her door.

19 September 2018 20:10 Uninvited Appearance at Residence
Ring Camera Capture
Building Security Notified / Protective Advisory Documented

He was warned by building management to stay away from her at all costs, because the next time, the police would be notified. Two days later, he did the same thing again. Only this time, he tried the old code that used to work to get inside. He was drunk. He was desperate.

21 September 2018 16:55 Uninvited Appearance at Residence
Ring Camera Capture
Building Security Notified / Protective Advisory Documented
Police Notified
Arrested—Criminal Trespass / Attempted Breaking, Entering

21 September 2018 23:59 Acceptance Email
"I'll never bother you again after today. But after you read this, maybe you'll see why I've had a difficult time letting go. I'm sorry for everything. Best wishes. Goodbye."

<Link to Article>"I Don't Want to Get Over You and That's My Problem"

Sweeping up the Pieces

After the arrest, things moved fast. He was a man of means, and his lawyers were effective at making the prosecutor think twice about pressing charges against "a man of his standing in the community" for doing nothing more than knocking on his ex-girlfriend's door.

The model was still out of town on an assignment when the victim advocate called her from the prosecutor's office to see what she wanted to do. When the model explained that this was just one incident in an escalating pattern of harassment that had been going on for three months, the advocate's tone changed. When I got an email from the model asking me to please forward the prosecutor our assessment report, I was only too happy to help.

And when those findings were also provided to the ex-boyfriend's high-priced-retainer defense attorneys, they took one look at what their client had to say for his actions versus what the prosecution was more than ready to prove and worked very hard to have their client understand just how deep a hole he had dug. As any good defense attorney will tell you, there is a big difference between someone who is telling a story versus someone who is trying to sell you a story. And one of the biggest tells between the two lies is the intent and motivation that underscore what brought you into your story much more than what your story is trying to say.

Onward and Upward

For all the obvious reasons, the specific details of this case are better left to the agreements and settlements that took place within the confines and the confidentiality of a judge's chambers. But what I can share is that when the model returned home to her apartment one week later, her ex had already been completely moved out for a full three days. And on that very same day, the model's life returned to normal, while the ex's new normal was just becoming realized. Needless to say, she got what winning looked like, and she never heard from him again.

Part IV

Personal Threat Assessment
Checklists

18

HOME

What Happened

When my parents retired to a beautiful mountain home in Pennsylvania overlooking the Delaware River, home security was the last thing on their minds. Their property sits on fifteen acres of God's country that is only accessible via a quarter-mile-long driveway that winds up the side of a mountain.

In the early-morning hours, a family of deer comes down from the crest of the mountain to drink from the valley stream, and they will often stop to graze their morning breakfast from the low-hanging leaves and bud-sprouting branches. Hummingbirds swarm the feeder that swings from an overhang on the front deck.

It is a beautiful, safe, and tranquil environment, and it is all but untouched by man. Other than family, a near-daily Amazon package delivery, and the occasional washing-machine repairman, no one comes here. Few could ever find the place even if they wanted to.

This part of rural Pennsylvania is a throwback to a time of days gone by. Most townspeople still park their cars and leave the keys sitting in the ignition. Windows are always open, and doors to neighborhood homes stay mostly unlocked. Maybe it's because the area is so remote. Maybe it's because everyone in town knows everyone by their first name. They wave to each other as they drive down the street. Being there is like stepping into another world.

As I began writing this chapter, I was reminded of an incident from many years ago when I was home on a visit, on leave from the army. My parents were out of town. I was at the house all alone one night when I heard the front stairs begin to creak. As I said before, the home is in a secluded area. Had someone driven up the driveway, I would have heard them. At the very least, I would have seen the headlights dance on the trees out the living room window as a vehicle approached.

I muted the TV and listened again. Someone was definitely coming up the stairs. The distinctive creak of the steps leading to the front deck was unmistakable.

Well, I thought, *if you want to try to sneak up on me, I guess I'm going to try to sneak up on you.*

In those days, I was almost never more than an arm's reach away from a weapon. So I retrieved the Sig Sauer .40 pistol from the small of my back and made my way to the side of the house where exiting out the sliding door would place me in a flanking position to ambush the soon-to-be-sorry somebody who was trying to sneak up to the front of the house.

So there I was. Barefoot, on the hardwood deck so as to not make a sound, creeping ever forward in a low-profile tactical advance with my pistol at the ready. As I began to "pie" the corner—a tactical maneuver for coming around the corner in an armed engagement—I had every confidence that I was going to get the drop on this "bad guy" and surprise the living daylights out of them.

I was wrong.

The surprise was all mine.

As I slowly began to turn the corner, I realized just how ironically dead-on-the-nose my predator assessment had been. The dark brown coat of a brown bear glistened in the moonlight as it batted at the bird feeder that was swinging from the overhang.

I viewed the bear through the now seemingly puny sights of my pistol and slowly backed away in a tactical retreat. If I was going to initiate this fight, I was going to need a bigger gun. Shooting him with what I had on hand would only serve to make matters worse.

I backtracked my steps and slid back inside, then watched from the second-floor window as the bear grew tired of the bird feeder and lumbered back up the side of the mountain and then disappeared into the woods.

When I told my parents, they responded like it happened all the time. "Oh yeah," my dad said. "We sometimes see two or three of them coming down. Not sure what they are finding to eat out there, but they sure are big!"

And that was that. None of us thought anything more about it—that is, until a few years later—when my mom left a Crock-Pot of beef stew on in the kitchen and came home to find a bear licking the knocked-over contents from the kitchen floor.

That was a wake-up call.

You see, up until that time, the front door had handles that served as a lever, which was great for when you were trying to come in through the front door with your hands full. All you had to do was just raise up your knee and press down on the latch. The door would spring right open. Problem was, latches don't differentiate between users.

And all the bear had to do to gain entry was be interested enough in the food on the other side of the door to give it the old college try.

Shortly thereafter, my parents had the door handles changed. They switched them from the push-down latch variety to the grip-and-twist model that would exploit the bears' lack of opposable thumbs.

I tell you this story because even there, up in the mountains, surrounded by peace and nature, even my parents found themselves falling victim to the Safety Trap. Had they seen the bears before? Yes. Had the bears come up to the house? Yes. Had they witnessed the bears demonstrate an increased level of interest in the house? Yes. Did my parents make sure the access control features into the house would thwart their efforts of entry?

No, they did not.

PROTECTIVE TAKEAWAY

All those ways you know to break into your own home are exactly how the bad guys are going to break in too.

PROTECTIVE AWARENESS

In most places, in most times, in most environments, if I said to you, "What's the likelihood of you coming home to find a bear in your kitchen?" the obvious answer would be, "Low." But for my parents, given the totality of circumstance of all that had transpired before, that answer was completely different.

There were pre-incident indicators that went ignored. And while the takeaway of the incident had resulted in more hilarity than harm, it very easily could have gone the other way.

Which brings me back to our discussion surrounding residential security.

Redefining Safety in the Home

For many of us, our homes are our safe havens, our own personal and private sanctuaries where we feel most safe. Our homes are where we build our lives, raise our children, make our memories, and plan our futures.

To help ensure your certainty of safety and to reduce the likelihood of risk or violence ever impacting you or your loved ones at home, I wanted to discuss some of the overarching concepts that will help to frame your expectation for what safety in your home really means and how you can effectively achieve the level of security you both want and require.

Let me begin with a scenario and a question:

Let's say, assuming that you and I have never met, I come up to you some random day as you are walking out of your office, the gym, the grocery store, or wherever you happen to be, and I ask you a simple question: "Is your home secure?"

You are very likely going to answer me with an assertive and a definitive, "Yes!"

Now, here's the kicker.

What if I then asked you this: "If I drove you to your home right now, could you break into your own home and—without leaving any signs of forcible entry—make your way up to the master bedroom in less than ten minutes?"

Now your mind is racing, but you answer with the same near-immediate assertiveness: "Hell yes I could!"

So what changed? In the span of a few moments, how did your own home go from so soundly secure to so easily breach-able so quickly?

Well, for starters, your first response was twofold. It was half what you wanted to believe and half what you would want to convey to a complete stranger. This is perfectly acceptable and understandable.

But the second question also brought to the forefront of your mind all those deficiencies that you always knew about but never thought to correct.

Things like how the side patio door never closes quite right; how the window in the downstairs guest bathroom is always just a tiny bit cracked open; how your kids never remember to lock the basement door after they come home from soccer practice.

But here's the thing . . .

All those ways you would break into your own home are exactly how the bad guys are going to break in too.

As we have discussed before, the most effective approach to staying safe is to identify the inherent vulnerabilities in our everyday lives, to raise our awareness to the most realistic risks we are most likely to face, and then to implement the safeguards that will prevent those risks from ever becoming a reality.

And this is where the personal threat assessment questionnaire (PTA) comes in. As I keep saying, Awareness + Preparation = Safety. Doing the PTA for all areas of your life is going to help you avoid the Safety Trap and stay truly safe, rather than just having a false sense of security.

Staying safe starts at home. In this chapter, we will focus on accomplishing this task in our own homes.

Try to break into your own home! Make it a family activity. One member tries to break in; others listen and detect. You'll identify obvious vulnerabilities, dark spots that need light . . . Best part, your family will know what to listen and look for. Notify neighbors as needed!

PROTECTIVE PREPAREDNESS

Here are the top twenty-five residential security questions for you to include in your own home security assessment:

1. **How visible is your home from the street?**

    Why this is important: The more visible your home is from the street (including your house number), the easier it is for a police patrol car to notice if something is wrong. It can help the first responders to more easily identify your home. Ideally, your home is situated far back enough from the curb or sidewalk that it is noticeable but not so close that it can be reviewable. On the flip side, if your home is hidden behind large hedges, thick trees, and dense foliage, it may offer you privacy, but it also makes it more difficult for your home to be identified in an emergency or, worse, allows those with more nefarious intent the cover they need to commit a crime without worrying about the watchful eyes of nosy neighbors or routine patrols.

    If your home is hidden from the street, lighting and landscaping become more important. Make sure there is good lighting along the walkway and driveway from the street to your home. Make sure trees are pruned up at least six feet from the ground. You may even want to consider emplacing lights in the yard that light your home from ground level; ground lighting will not only give the impression that your home is illuminated in a high-end fashion but will also serve to cast a large and noticeable shadow of anyone who attempts to approach your home from the yard instead of the pathway.

    Here's what a bad guy is thinking: How exposed would I be if I were to target this house? What's the likelihood that someone would see me?

2. **Does your home have a fence? What kind?**

    Why this is important: The best kind of fence is one that is sturdy, well maintained, and serves as a clear demarcation line of where public property ends and your private property begins. The best fences for homes are also ones that offer some field of view from inside and outside the property. High, solid fences may offer you additional privacy, but they also offer good cover and concealment for criminal activity too.

    Here's what a bad guy is thinking: An empty home with a

privacy fence is the best kind of home to rob. Once I'm inside, I can take my time without worrying if anyone can see me from the street. All I have to worry about is the in and out, and that is the easiest part of all.

3. **Is your name on the mailbox?**

Why this is important: Vanity mailboxes are like vanity license plates—they look cool, but do you more harm than good. When it comes to where you live, those who need to know should know. Those who don't, don't. One of the simplest steps to reducing your vulnerability is to simply not promote private information that does not absolutely need to be shared. It's also a good idea to invest in a secure mailbox, one where a key is required to retrieve the contents and has built-in theft-deterrent features.

Here's what a bad guy is thinking: Wow! Nice house. Name on the mailbox says *Johnson*. I wonder if this is the same guy who is a partner at that big law firm downtown? Let me look him up on social media. Yup. That's him. Posted a pic of himself mowing the lawn just last week. Oh! And it looks like they are planning a vacation to Bermuda next month. Okay, cool. That gives me a few weeks to plan. Thanks, Mr. Johnson!

4. **Are there any items of value visible through your windows?**

Why this is important: Most home robberies are crimes of opportunity. Bad guys see something they want. They do their research, plan their attack, and then assess the risk. There are things you can do to help thwart their effort—like privacy blinds and window tinting. This isn't to say that having a nice TV will instantly make you a target, but a nice TV behind open blinds, on a quiet street, with a pile of mail collecting dust on the porch may lead you to become a target of opportunity for a would-be thief.

Here's what a bad guy is thinking: Sometimes I'll just drive to an affluent area when I know everyone is at work and just walk my dog around the neighborhood. I like looking through your windows. I'll come back a few different times, taking notes, looking for patterns of when you are not home. I'm also looking through your window for things I might want and for flat-screen TVs or gaming systems I can sell for quick cash. If I see something I like, I'll come back at night. See who's home. Who's closed the blinds. Do more research. I may even tape a food delivery menu to the handle of your front door to see how long it stays there.

5. **How strong of a protective posture does your home promote?**

    Why this is important: Does your home have motion lights? A sign that says PROTECTED BY ABC SECURITY COMPANY? Are there security cameras visible? Is your lawn well maintained? Are you flying a flag? Are there noticeable signs of a dog? Promoting a positive protective posture signals to the bad guys that you take your safety seriously. It lets them know they'll have a much higher likelihood of success by concentrating their efforts on someone else. Bad guys are as lazy as everyone else. If they can get the same reward for less work by targeting the house down the street, they will.

    Here's what a bad guy is thinking: Big dog + military flag + security camera = No, thank you.

6. **Do you have a dog?**

    Why this is important: Unlike the rest of us, dogs don't negotiate against their own instinct. Even if you don't have a naturally protective, well-trained dog, the presence of *any* dog will throw a wrench into the works of even the most well-planned attacks. Bad guys need anonymity to be successful, and the presence of a dog—any dog—will greatly reduce their likelihood of success.

    Here's what a bad guy is thinking: Two things I hate to see when conducting research for a robbery are any signs of a dog . . . or a nosy neighbor.

7. **Other than your family, who has recently been inside your house?**

    Why this is important: Insider threats cause more harm than outside actors. Those who have had access to the inside of your home now know a few things about you that could prove useful in their plan to harm you. They now know the layout of your home. They will likely know the location of any valuables. And they can ascertain with a high degree of accuracy just how seriously you take your security.

Here's what a bad guy is thinking: I appreciate you letting me use the guest bathroom when I delivered your new mattress last week. I hope you don't mind that I unlatched the window. I'll come back in that way when you're at church next weekend.

8. **Can you see your alarm control panel through the window?**

Why this is important: If your alarm control panel can be seen through the window, it will communicate one of two things to a potential robber. If the bad guy comes to your home, sees the alarm panel through the window, and can see that it's armed, they will know you take your security serious enough to transition their efforts to a different target. However, if the bad guys know you're not home, can see the control panel, and see that it's turned off, then you are very likely not taking your security very seriously, and they will then take the next steps in the research and planning of their robbery.

Here's what a bad guy is thinking: Okay. So they have an alarm system. Bigger question is, do they use it? Gentlemen, place your bets!

9. **Where do you store your valuables?**

Why this is important: As a general rule, you don't want to put all your eggs in one basket. Whenever possible, keep your valuables in separate, compartmentalized areas. No sense in helping the bad guys hit the jackpot in one simple score. If there are important documents that you want to keep but don't necessarily need to have on hand, consider a safe-deposit box. This way, you'll always know where they are, you'll always know they are protected, and should you have to leave your home in a hurry, they are one less thing to worry about as you go racing out the door.

Here's something else to consider: Unlike a safe, which is obvious and burdensome, a secret and secure hiding spot can be designed or even purchased online. Let's be honest, there is nothing more valuable than a human life, and the last thing you want to do is prolong an unfortunate encounter with a bad guy in your home. The problem with a safe is that even when homeowners are willing to part with their belongings, they sometimes find themselves unable to communicate the codes or call upon the fine-motor function required to open the safe. A secure hiding place will alleviate this concern. Even better, some of these hiding spaces are so clever, they hide in plain sight. This means the bad guy conducting research and planning on your home (or who asked to use the bathroom) will be none the wiser as to where your prized possessions are protected.

Here's what a bad guy is thinking: Oh. Wow. Shocking. You keep your expensive watch in the sock drawer and your emergency cash in the underwear drawer. So original. You almost had me fooled. And what do we have here? Is that a safe in the closet? Did you remember to bolt it down? No? Okay, cool. I'll just take it with me.

10. **Do you live in a gated neighborhood? Are there any access-control features into your neighborhood or into your home?**

Why this is important: Access control is important because it offers you some measure of management over who is allowed into your area (gated community), but it also helps to cut down on the availability of anonymity that bad guys need to be successful. Don't live in an area where this is available? Having some version of a scene camera like Ring or one of the other instant-alert cameras is a great way to document and monitor those who may be conducting research and planning around your home to see if you are a target that offers a high likelihood of success. Rather than physical keys, you can use electronic locks where everyone has their own unique access codes. The problem with keys is that keys work all the time. But with an electronic lock, you can program the landscaper to have access only during his limited window of work. The same for the pool cleaner. Or the intern. And even better, electric locks means never again having to worry about losing your keys.

Remember: just having these features isn't enough. You have to use them. So if you see an unexpected someone in a delivery uniform snooping around your home, you can share this infor mation with your local police department and your neighborhood Facebook group. The key takeaway of access control is *awareness*. Who is doing what, where, when, and why?

Here's what a bad guy is thinking: Okay. I had to sign in to the gate when I came in for work. They copied my driver's license, took my photo, and know exactly where I'm supposed to be and where I'm not. This is a target-rich environment, but it's not worth the risk.

11. **How good do the grounds look?**

Why this is important: Neglecting your yard and house exterior only goes to show that there's nobody home and leaves more opportunity for someone to hide, especially if the unkempt landscaping around doors and windows provides better concealment of criminal activity.

Here's what a bad guy is thinking: How someone does one thing is pretty much how they do everything. If you're not willing to keep your property looking nice, you're probably not going to bother protecting your property either. Unkempt lawns and neglected houses are prime targets for exploitation.

12. **How often do you lock your front door?**

Why this is important: Most break-ins don't actually involve a break-in. Statistics vary from town to town, but an acceptable average is that more than 25 percent of robbers simply knock on the front door, and then when no one answers, they walk in through an unlocked front door. Meanwhile, 23 percent of burglars climb in through an unlocked or otherwise open first-floor window, and 22 percent use the back door to gain entry. So even if you're leaving your home for a short period, make sure all the entry points to your home are secured.

Here's what a bad guy is thinking: One of the last things I do before breaking in is approach the house in an attempt to probe how effective the security defenses are. Do the motion lights work? Does an alarm sound? How close can I get to the house before I run the risk of being detected? If I'm able to get all the way up to the house and the coast seems clear, I'll knock. If you answer, I'll hand you one of the flyers I have with me and say I was just knocking before leaving it at your door. If you don't answer, I'll try the handle. If it opens, jackpot!

13. **Do you store your ladders and tools in a locked garage or shed?**

    Why this is important: Leaving your tools out on the deck or lying around your yard is the equivalent to leaving the lid off the trash can. It attracts the wrong kind of attention. Power tools, generators, coolers, and other home-maintenance machinery like lawn mowers, weed trimmers, and mulch machines are all sought-after commodities of the criminal trade. If you want to keep them, lock them up.

    Here's what a bad guy is thinking: They make it so much easier when I don't even have to break into the house to make my time worthwhile, but since you also left the ladder out here for me to steal, I'm going to use it to see if you left the second-floor window unlocked.

14. **Do you keep an inventory of your personal property?**

    Why this is important: Burglars are always looking for items that are quick to turn over and easy to resell, so it's a good idea to mark and record your property so places like pawnshops and secondhand shops know to notify the police if they suspect a stolen item is being offered for purchase. If you've been the unfortunate victim of a robbery, the first thing the police (and your homeowner's insurance) are going to ask for is a list of what is missing. Then they are going to ask for what documentation you can provide to prove you had these missing things in the first place. It's not that they don't trust you, but if the police storm a warehouse full of stolen goods and the owner of the warehouse contests that they are the legal owner of such goods and wares, arming the police with legally arguable information like photos of the belongings inside your house and corresponding serial numbers will go a long way to not only getting your belongings back but helping put the bad guys behind bars.

Here's what a bad guy is thinking: I'm really hoping that since you were dumb enough to leave these items where I could steal them, then you also weren't smart enough to record their identifying details.

15. **Do you have shatterproof film on your first-floor windows or secondary locks on sliding glass doors? Do you secure sliding doors with a dowel on the inside track?**

    Why this is important: Shatterproof film helps keep the glass from shattering into a million tiny pieces and actually helps keep the broken glass intact and inside the seal of the door. This protective film has the added value in that it not only helps keep your home protected from break-ins, but it will help keep your home protected during bad storms too.

    Here's what a bad guy is thinking: If your doors are locked, your alarm is off, and no one is home, I have no problem throwing a big rock through your back window. Your neighbors won't care. Human nature is pretty consistent. If they hear one crash, they'll stop and listen. If they don't hear anything else, they'll go back to what they are doing. But if I throw a rock at your window and it doesn't break through, now I've got to decide just how willing I am to expose myself by making an even bigger noise the second time. Might be best for me to just cut my losses and leave.

16. **Do you have motion sensor lights installed?**

    Why this is important: Motion sensor lights are one of the most used components of a home security system. If you don't have them, you'll be surprised by how helpful they are to have them. No more taking out the trash or going out to the garage in darkness. They are energy efficient in that they don't always have to be on, but they are also highly effective at serving as "go-away" lights to thwart those with nefarious intent from getting too close to your home.

    Here's what a bad guy is thinking: Motion lights are a pain in the ass. There's really no way to tell how far away I have to stay to keep them from going off. One wrong step and I'm lit up like a Christmas tree. If there is a way to get around them, I will, but if they are set up in equal intervals around your home and they are also supported by a surveillance camera, that's not really a risk I'm willing to take.

17. **Do you have your mail held at the post office when you travel? What about your Amazon deliveries?**

   Why this is important: Mail theft and package theft are more common than they should be—especially around gift-giving holidays. Some carriers will allow you to set up a delivery window time if you will not be at home, or you can ask them to hold it at the nearest office. Believe me when I tell you that bad guys notice when a package is left unattended and when your mail begins to pile up. If you know you're going to be out of town and unable to collect your mail and packages, reduce your likelihood of being targeted by making the appropriate arrangements to either have your deliveries held until you get back or picked up by a trusted friend or neighbor.

   Here's what a bad guy is thinking: I see mail piled up, and I see packages being delivered, but I don't see anyone coming to help you out. If your neighbors don't care enough about you to help protect your property when you're out of town, then they probably aren't going to care when they see me walk around the side of your house and pick the lock to your back door. But don't worry, just to make sure you're not being lazy, I'll have a food delivery guy knock on your door to see if you answer. If you don't, I'll act like I live there and take the food for myself. All these break-ins can really make a man hungry.

18. **Are you cross-shredding personal documents and other sensitive information?**

   Why this is important: It's absolutely astonishing how much about a person you can learn from their trash. Business dealings, credit card information, bank statements, phone records, personal correspondence. Each piece of trash is like another piece of a personality puzzle. Protect your privacy by cross-shredding *all* personal information before placing it in the trash. ATM receipts, credit card receipts, bills, and even used airline tickets. You should also immediately shred expired credit cards, visas, passports, and IDs. This isn't just good operational security, this is day one, lesson one of Vulnerability Reduction 101. Anything with your name or identifying information should be cross-shredded and disposed of across multiple receptacles. And if it's supersensitive: *burn it.*

Here's what a bad guy is thinking: If I notice a bunch of trash bags out by the curb full of shredded documents, I won't even bother looking at your house twice. If you're willing to take the extra step and shred your trash to keep guys like me from learning your secrets, then you've probably got a few security secrets waiting to catch me in the act. I'd rather not find out about those. So on to the next one.

19. **Does your home gym have a panic button?**

    Why this is important: A home-gym panic button serves two purposes. The first is that other than in the kitchen, a home gym is where an accidental injury is most likely to occur. If you're seriously injured and unable to get to help, a panic button may just save your life. If the panic button isn't going to be worn, the button should be hardwired at knee level somewhere along the wall. If you are having a heart attack or get thrown off the treadmill, you may not be able to stand up. By keeping the panic button low to the floor, you'll be able to reach it more easily.

    Here's what a bad guy is thinking: Not all home security considerations are designed for thwarting the efforts of bad guys. Sometimes the best safety features are intended to help you help yourself.

20. **What do you do with the packaging from big-purchase items?**

    Why this is important: If you purchase a new high-value item, try not to overpromote this fact to complete strangers. I'm sure you're going to love that new TV that you got just in time for the Super Bowl, but putting the box out by the curb will attract the wrong kind of attention. Instead, try breaking the box down into smaller pieces and then putting those pieces into a bag in the recycling bin. Or even better, discard the box somewhere else, like a recycling center.

Here's what a bad guy is thinking: Did someone have a birthday? I noticed a bunch of boxes by the curb on trash day. Looks like you got a new computer, some gaming equipment, and a surround-sound system. Can't wait to see them for myself!

21. **How much cash do you have on hand at home?**

Why this is important: Cash is basically impossible to trace. While it makes perfect sense to have some cash on hand for emergency situations, keeping too much around where it can be discovered could increase your odds of being targeted. If you are going to keep large sums of currency inside your home, *do not* keep it all in a single location. Be creative with your hiding places.

Here's what a bad guy is thinking: Cash is king. If I have any reason to believe there is a significant amount of cash lying around your house, you just moved yourself up to the top of my research-and-planning list.

22. **Where do you park your car?**

Why this is important: According to recent crime reports, cars are now being stolen in an average of just ten seconds—six times faster than ten years ago. In fact, your car may be the reason the bad guys are breaking into your home in the first place. With so many of today's new vehicles utilizing fobs and proximity keys to start the ignition, many car thieves now prefer to steal keys during a house break-in and then simply drive the car away.

Here's what a bad guy is thinking: I noticed when you come home from work you always have your hands full with kids and groceries. Sometimes it takes you two or three trips to get everything into the house. I also noticed that you have the proximity key to your new car attached to your purse, and that's the last thing you remember to bring into the house. One of these days, you're going to leave it in your car overnight, and when you do, I'll be ready.

23. **When was your last home cybersecurity checkup?**

Why this is important: A protected home network means you and your family can use the internet more safely and securely. Most homes now run networks of devices linked to the internet, including computers, gaming systems, TVs, tablets, smartphones, and wearable devices that access wireless networks. To protect your home network, the first step is to make sure all your internet-enabled devices have the latest operating systems, web browsers, and security software. This includes mobile devices that access your wireless network. Unless you secure your router, you're vulnerable to people accessing information on your computer, using your internet service for free, and potentially using your network to commit cybercrimes. When in doubt, be suspicious of emails bearing attachments, even from people you know. When it comes to getting hacked, everything starts with email.

Here's what a bad guy is thinking: Do I want to steal your computers or hack what's on them? Decisions . . . decisions.

24. **Do you conduct monthly inspections (e.g., smoke detectors, spare tires, jumper cables, fire extinguishers, carbon monoxide monitors)? Do you practice using those tools you'll want to call on in an emergency?**

Why this is important: One of the best ways to avoid the pitfalls of the Safety Trap is to, at regular intervals, inspect what you expect. Too many of us have burned a piece of toast, set off the smoke detector, and then whacked the battery loose with a broom handle to shut the damn thing off before it woke up the rest of the house. Too many of us have also never bothered to replace the battery like we said we would later on that day. Same thing goes for the fire extinguisher that's likely collecting dust under the sink as we speak. (In fact, stop what you're doing right now and please go move the extinguisher to a place that will promote a more practical purpose.) When moments matter most, like a kitchen fire, you don't want to have to be searching around for the tools you need to keep you and your family protected. As a general rule, fire extinguishers should be mounted on brackets or in wall cabinets with the carrying handle placed three and a half to five feet above the floor. This will not only make them easily retrievable when you need them but will also prevent them from being damaged or moved from where you expect to find them.

Speaking of fire extinguishers, how many of us have ever actually used one? The inherent risk of a kitchen fire is infinitely more likely than a home invasion. So now that you are *aware* of this risk, why not take some time to *prepare* yourself on how to put it to work? The wrong time to be reading the directions is when the grease fire is crawling up the wall. Practice makes perfect. Remember: no one fears that which they know well. So take an hour or two this weekend to teach yourself, your family, and even your neighbor the proper pull, aim, squeeze, and sweep technique (PASS) for how to best put out a fire. Same goes for how to use the jumper cables in your car. If you've never used them, search YouTube for how to use them and teach yourself how. Same for checking the spare tire to make sure it hasn't deflated after all that time sitting in your trunk. Same for the jack and the tire iron you'll have to employ to help you change it. Check the candles. Check the batteries in the flashlights. Whatever you may think you'll need to use in an emergency should be checked, inspected, and verified as being mission ready. Trust me, when moments matter most, you'll be glad you had.

Here's what a bad guy is thinking: Like I said before, not all home safety considerations are intended to thwart the efforts of bad guys. More often than not, the positive protective posture that will stem from you simply engaging in active participation of your own protection will promote to a would-be offender that they will have a higher likelihood of success transitioning to a more vulnerable target. Bad guys don't want to see you training to put out fires in your backyard. Bad guys don't want to see you changing your own tire. Bad guys don't want to see you returning from Home Depot carrying a brand-new fire extinguisher. Bad guys want their targets to promote absent-minded and self-doubting behavior. Bad guys don't want to go after the strongest among us. They want to exploit the vulnerabilities of the weak.

25. **Do you have a 9:00 p.m. routine?**

   Why this is important: Having an established time of day where you dedicate a few minutes to participating in your own safety helps to ensure you are doing your very best to ensure the certainty of safety. A 9:00 p.m. routine is a great time of night to make sure all doors and windows are locked, all the blinds are drawn, your outside lights are turned on, and the security alarm is armed and ready.

   Here's what a bad guy is thinking: Lots of nice things in that house. Too bad they couldn't make it easier on me, but this house is like clockwork with their security routine. Ah, well . . . better luck with the next one.

   Remember: Your home is your sanctuary, your safe haven. Treat it as such. The foundation of any effective security program begins and ends not only where we spend the most time but where we come together to support and defend one another. The home is where your heart lives. You don't need to live in a fortress. I wouldn't want you to. But I do want you to come home every day to a place you know is best suited to protect you and your family. And I want you to know how you can continually strive to implement and improve upon the most practical strategies to help you not only succeed in staying safe but also incorporate these foundations into all the other aspects of your everyday lives.

19

SCHOOL

What Happened

November 14, 2019

As I look up from my desk, I see the breaking news banner come across the television. There was another school shooting today. A fourteen-year-old boy and sixteen-year-old girl are dead and three other students were injured after a classmate opened fire at a high school in Southern California. Video footage from the school shows the gunman in the quad of Saugus High School in Santa Clarita where he took a gun from his backpack, shot five people, and then shot himself in the head. The entire incident took sixteen seconds.

It has only been a few hours since this tragedy took place, but the Safety Traps are already being revealed: complacency, shirking responsibility, avoidance, us versus them, effective response. So many others will certainly come to light. The students and parents being interviewed are giving the same responses we have heard so many times before. "Why does this keep happening?" "This kind of thing doesn't happen here."

Is safety possible? Yes, it is. But it's not a guarantee. Your safety is up to you.

PROTECTIVE TAKEAWAY

Until drastic, federally mandated changes are made, schools are simply not capable of keeping your children safe.

PROTECTIVE AWARENESS

This means the burden of responsibility for your child's safety is on you.

I want to be very clear about one thing. I don't care where your child goes to school. This next statement is 100 percent true: *your child's school is simply not capable of keeping your child protected.* I do not mean this to sound pejorative, but while our country's schools may have some of the best educators imaginable, these teachers are arguably the worst protectors on the planet. Don't get me wrong, I have the utmost respect for teachers. In fact, both of my parents were teachers. They are both top-notch educators, but neither of them have the mindset of a protector. The fact that a protective mindset is even now being discussed as a prerequisite of an educator is another conversation entirely.

If you honestly believe that your child's school will keep your child safe in the face of violence, please allow me to disillusion you of that belief. It is not true. It is false. It is a lie. If you continue to believe that your child's school is able to do anything more than make your child *feel* safe, then I don't know what to tell you. I really don't.

Maybe it will help if I explain it this way:

The Columbine High School massacre took place on April 20, 1999.

Since then, gun violence in schools has gone down, but mass shootings have gone up.

Tell me again about how good schools are at preventing threats.

Six mass shootings in the last twenty years: Columbine, Red Lake, West Nickel Mines, Sandy Hook, Parkland, Santa Fe, plus forty-two more where an armed assailant fired indiscriminately at teachers and students.

Well, schools may have a failing grade at prevention, but they get an A+ at response, right?

Wrong. Schools fail this class too; 2018 was the worst year on record for gun violence in the United States, hitting an all-time high of ninety-seven incidents.

(2018) 56 deaths

(1993) 40 deaths

(2012) 38 deaths

But the schools had no way of knowing, right? I'm sure these were just criminals targeting these poor schools . . .

Wrong again.

91 percent of shooters targeted the school they attended

87 percent exhibited clear signs of leakage prior to shooting

78 percent revealed their attack plans to others/shared on social media

All were male

Most were white

So are you saying these lockdown drills are a joke?

No. Absolutely not. But lockdown drills are not intended to protect against a threat that is already inside the building. Lockdown drills are meant to do just that . . . *lock down* the school to keep the bad guys *out*.

The following is a perfect example of how a lockdown/shelter-in-place strategy was intended to be employed.

Corning, California

On November 14, 2017, a forty-four-year-old man with a homemade AR-15-style rifle went on a lengthy shooting rampage in Northern California and, after arriving at the school, fired more than a hundred shots, wounding a six-year-old boy who was hiding inside a building. The following responses to a *Washington Post* survey were provided by Corning Union Elementary School District superintendent Richard Fitzpatrick.

Excerpts from Rancho Tehama Elementary School's Survey Responses

What did you learn from the shooting?

"We are largely powerless from determined shooters with high-capacity, high-velocity, semiautomatic assault rifles. Bullets from a 5.56 mm rifle easily penetrated sealed windows, doors, cabinets and walls. But lockdowns can save lives."

What type of drills, if any, had the school done before the shooting (classic lockdown, active-shooter, ALICE, or something else), and how often had they been practiced?

"Since Sandy Hook, the district has conducted lockdown drills regularly . . . It should be noted that these drills were done with consistent behaviors and language, regardless of the perceived threat. Crucial to the survival of our students in the shooting, any adult employee is empowered to trigger a lockdown."

What other types of safety measures, if any, did the school have in place before the shooting (metal detectors, SROs, special door locks, pepper spray, armed teachers, etc.)?

"All schools in the district were equipped with 'lock blocks.' These devices allow keyless locking from inside in less than a second. All playground aides and office staff also had walkie-talkies."

Did students and staff follow the drilling procedures they'd practiced?

"Flawlessly. The campus was completely locked down within 48 seconds of it being called."

What ultimately ended the shooting?

"After firing over a hundred rounds of 5.56 mm at the buildings, the shooter became frustrated by his inability to gain access to the school. He left and, some minutes later when confronted by law enforcement, took his own life."

Did any of the safety measures specifically work—meaning, they kept students safe from harm—and if so, which ones?

"Yes. Lockdown and lock blocks prevented any loss of life. One kindergarten student was shot through a building wall in the chest and foot. He recovered. There were no other injuries on campus."

In retrospect, what—if anything—do you believe could have been done to stop the shooting from happening at all?

"Sensible gun control. The shooter had an AR rifle which he purchased online in parts. He was prohibited by the courts from owning or possessing firearms."

What safety measures were put in place after the shooting?

"The shooter rammed a locked gate to gain entry to the school. His truck was stuck in the gate, delaying his ability to access the school quad. This allowed the valuable seconds to complete the process. A six-foot wrought iron fence was installed in the front of the school, which previously had a three-foot fence. An armed security guard is now present at the school during all school hours."

So are you saying we should give the teachers guns?

Absolutely not! More guns anywhere increases the risk of gun violence. Even those who are allowed to carry guns get themselves into trouble. (I'm specifically thinking about the teacher in Utah who shot herself in the leg.)

But the other real reason is this: people perform poorly under pressure.

Most people are completely incapable of completing even the most basic of tasks when they become even the slightest bit nervous, excited, or scared. This is something that takes a lifetime to overcome. It requires years of exposure to stress inoculation to not become susceptible to the physiological stressors of external stimuli. The one tool most of us are most comfortable and familiar with using is our phone. We can use them with ease. We can use them without looking. Our phones are all but a natural extension of our physical selves.

As anyone who has ever protected a public figure will tell you: the number-one argument against giving anyone a gun and then expecting them to perform under pressure is to observe the complete and total incompetence of someone trying to take an impromptu selfie with a celebrity.

What if teachers want to arm themselves?

I am a supporter of the Second Amendment, and if a teacher wants to arm themselves, has gone through their state's process for carrying a concealed weapon, and if that school has authorized the teacher to carry their weapon on school grounds, then I have no argument against that teacher having a weapon for the purposes of *self-defense*.

However, the one and only caveat for my advocacy of these specific teachers being armed would be that if it ever became understood that the teacher was armed or if the weapon in their possession was ever seen by a student, that teacher's concealed-carry privilege on school property should be immediately revoked.

Reason number one being that the professional carrying of a weapon is predicated on the fact that a weapon hides behind you but you never hide behind the weapon, and any professional breach of this core value would be a flagrant infraction of this recognized standard in practice.

Reason number two would be for the fact that not only would a would-be offender likely target that teacher first in their attack plan, but that teacher's weapon may be the very weapon the assailant attempts to seize to carry out their attack plan.

Well, why can't I just hire a security expert to tell my kid's school what to do?

If your child goes to a private school, they very likely have already had one done.

When it comes to public schools, the decision to conduct a security assessment is typically spearheaded by the superintendent and/or the school board.

The scope of the assessment is typically a district-wide endeavor.

Unlike booster programs or fundraising support for extracurricular programs—when it comes to the health, welfare, and safety of a student, what is done for one school must be done for all. (Think: school lunches.) Public schools also need to concern themselves with the liability they assume *after* the assessment is conducted. Once the assessment has been conducted, a school district would need to make sure they had the adequate budget set aside to then move forward with the recommendations gleaned from the assessment.

Can you imagine the criminal charges and the civil suits that would be filed against a school board should a tragic incident occur *after* the school had been made aware of a particular vulnerability but then chose to do nothing about it?

Every parent I have ever advised *wants* to have a security audit performed, but dollars only stretch so far. Budgets are determined by what matters most. The likelihood of sports and the arts having a favorable impact on the student body is very *high*. The likelihood of violent harm is very *low*. For this to change, school safety programs would have to be as mandatory for school boards as seat belts are for cars at Ford. Until then, the smartest steps for budget-constrained schools is to audit the safeguards they already have in place. Ensure they perform as expected.

So are you saying we are helpless?

No! *Absolutely not!* My entire reason for telling you this is so that you understand the responsibility of keeping your child protected at school is *not* something teachers are trained, equipped, or even supposed to handle. The responsibility for teaching your child the lifesaving strategies they will need to survive a real-world threat is *your* responsibility. All you as a parent can realistically expect the school to perform is accountability. Your child's survivability is up to you.

What have *you* done to help save your child's life in a crisis?

What are the nearby safe havens you want *your* child to run to? What is *your* family reunification plan? What have *you* done to empower *your* child to defy what everyone else is doing and trust *their* own inner voice of protection? If your answer is nothing, you are failing your child.

As we discussed in chapter 2, "False Authority," those who worked at the World Trade Center on 9/11—and lived—were the ones who *did not* return to their desks after building security told them everything was clear to return to work. They listened to their own survival instincts. They defied authority. They lived. Have you given your child this same permission?

The only real reason you want to ask the school any of the questions I pose is so you can have a better understanding of how they will answer these questions so you can educate and empower your child on what they should do, where they should go, and how they should get there.

If you have one takeaway from this entire section, please let it be this: the school will not be able to protect your child, but *you* can empower them to save themselves!

But surely there is something that can be done to keep these shootings from happening, right?

Yes, there is. We can help those who are hurting. School shootings will continue so long as we do nothing to address the emotional turmoil some students endure and the harmful ideation they fantasize as remedy to their grievance. We need to help those who are hurting. This isn't about the stigma of reporting. This is about a willingness to help those children in need. No student is ever harmed by someone providing them the resources they need to improve, to heal.

How do you feel about the whole run/hide/fight program?

The year 2018 had the highest level on record of gun violence and gun deaths. How do I feel about run/hide/fight? *It is a complete and total failure.*

As my clients will often hear me say, the first rule of safety is to get to somewhere safe. Life and death is not a game of hide-and-seek.

If you can run to your hiding spot, you can run away. So keep running. Put as much time and distance between you and the threat as possible. Run until you can't run anymore. Then catch your breath and keep running.

I am *not* a fan of this entire practicum of an immediate rush to cower in a corner at the first sense of danger, and I would certainly argue against the concept of any of these "red lines" of safety that schools have started putting in classrooms as the visual cutoff line for where you can see through the glass of the door.

The fact that the door even has glass is enough of a point to prove how ineffective it will be to save you.

I will say it again: *life and death is not a game of hide-and-seek.*

Which is harder for a would-be-shooter to hit? The student gaining time and distance with each step they take, or the one in the corner of a classroom?

Run/hide/fight was never intended as "Run to your hiding spot." Hiding—or temporarily being unseen—is not the same as being safe. Bullets travel through doors, windows, and walls. *Bullet resistant* means the product will likely stop the first bullet—not so much the second and third.

Sheltering in place was meant for high winds and falling trees. It was intended to keep the public safe inside their homes while the bank down the street was being robbed. It was never meant for an active-shooter scenario. Everyone watching a horror movie yells at the screen when the coed runs up the stairs instead of out the front door. Why are we teaching our children to make the same mistake?

Sheltering in place becomes even more absurd when we consider that the would-be offender already knows what the students and teachers are going to do. The majority of school shooters are students at their own schools. The reason students attack their own school is because that is where their grievance is first endured, where they first feel they can resolve their grievance with violence, where the research and planning of their attack can be disguised as everyday participation, where they can easily breach security safeguards as an inside actor, and where the success of their efforts is most likely to be achieved. The reason for this success is that they themselves have taken part in those very drills meant to thwart their efforts. They know the other team's playbook.

In fact, one could argue that active-shooter drills have the opposite effect of what they intend. Instead of making things better, they make things worse. They instill more fear into the students while empowering the offender to become more effective. Marjory Stoneman Douglas High School had recently conducted an active-shooter drill, yet seventeen lives were lost. The shooter was so successful in his efforts, he simply accomplished what he wanted and then left. He just walked away.

Regrettably, there is no single solution to such a critical concern—only a comprehensive one will do. Every school needs a restriction plan, a prevention plan, and a reaction plan. One plan to keep bad guys from getting in, one plan to keep the students from hurting each other, and one plan to get everyone as far away from harm as possible. Think of it like a three-legged stool: make one leg bigger than the others and everything becomes unstable and vulnerable for attack, but if all three legs are equal, balance is maintained, and a certainty of safety can be cultivated and grown.

PROTECTIVE PREPAREDNESS

These are the top five school safety questions every parent should ask—and every school should be able to answer:

1. **When was the last safety and security assessment conducted? Who conducted it? What were the findings? What enhancements were recommended? What actions were taken? When is the next assessment scheduled?** When it comes to the safety of your child's school, these are among the most important questions a parent can ask of the school board. Even though the state may mandate certain guidelines, each school board controls the purse strings for every contract that gets signed, and votes on each new policy before it gets put into place. If you really want to ensure your child is getting the best education they can in the best safety environment possible, look to your school board, and question with boldness.

2. **Who is the administrator responsible for handling the school's threat assessment and management program?** The Secret Ser-

vice urges every school in the United States to establish threat management teams to assess threats. They have published an operational guide to help. It offers guidance on spotting suspicious behavior and figuring out when and how to intervene. In almost every incident of school violence, warning signs were present, but too often, concerns slip through the cracks because too few people had too few pieces of important information. Ask about the methodology for how concerns are assessed and managed. Is there a central processor of all concerns? Are reports written on paper and filed away, or are they recorded electronically for follow-up later? Can concerns be reported anonymously? Can parents report concerns? What is the social media and bullying policy? Ask how you can help.

3. **What is the school's access control policy for visitors and student readmittance once classes are in session?** How is this policy enforced? In most cases, schools have a very well-written policy for granting entry into the school once classes are in session. In reality, those who are responsible for putting that policy into practice are often inundated with other responsibilities. The result is buzzer pressed = access granted. This means, for example, the gatekeepers may confirm the legitimacy of a visiting parent but may miss the ill-intended intruder "tailgating" behind them. One of the biggest risks facing many schools is the wide divide between policy and practice—between what they say is being done and the reality of what is accepted as the everyday practice.

4. **What are the determining factors for when to evacuate and when to shelter in place? Who is the decision-maker?** The difference between when to evacuate and when to shelter in place is pretty cut-and-dried. As a general rule, if the threat is external to the school (high winds, falling trees, severe storms), you stay inside and shelter in place where it is safe. Conversely, if the threat is internal to the school (fire, gas leak, active shooter), the best practice is to evacuate to put as much time and distance from the threat as possible.

5. **What nearby safe havens are in proximity (running distance) to the school where your child could go in the event of an emergency evacuation? What is the school's "family reunification" plan?** Safe havens are places that offer safety, support, and protection. Restaurants are great. They have food, water, bathrooms, and landlines for making phone calls. When in doubt, run to a restaurant. (Restaurants are great for family reunification too.) Most schools are designed as a series of interconnected and compartmentalized areas that offer their own pockets of protection in the form of dispersion and separation. Evacuation locations negate this protection by having everyone move from their respectively disjointed areas to a single, predesignated position. If someone really wanted to do the most harm, the evacuation point would offer the greatest "likelihood of success" because most evacuation points are outside of the secure perimeter and are easily researched on social media.

20

WORK

What Happened

In the early morning hours of August 26, 2015, news reporter Alison Parker and photojournalist Adam Ward with CBS affiliate WDBJ in Roanoke, Virginia, were shot and killed while conducting a live television interview at Bridgewater Plaza near Smith Mountain Lake. Also injured in the attack was Vicki Gardner, the executive director of the local chamber of commerce who was being interviewed by Parker at the time of the shooting. The gunman, who live-streamed the shooting via his Twitter feed, was a former colleague, Vester Lee Flanagan, who had been fired from WDBJ two years earlier for "volatile behavior." During his termination, Flanagan had lashed out at newsroom staffers. The police had to be called to escort Flanagan out of the building. As Flanagan was escorted out, Ward documented the incident with his TV camera. Flanagan would later file an EEOC complaint against WDBJ alleging racial discrimination. Alison Parker was named in the complaint.

For the next two years, on Facebook and Twitter, Flanagan continually repeated his claims of discrimination and specifically named both Parker and Ward as the genesis of his grievance. In his postings, Flanagan claimed that Parker had made racist remarks during her internship at WDBJ about one of Flanagan's friends and that Ward had filed a complaint against him to WDBJ's human resources department after working with him on one occasion.

Two hours later, at 8:26 a.m., ABC news received a twenty-three-page fax from Flanagan, titled "Suicide Note for Friend & Family," in which he described his grievance over what he believed to be racial discrimination and sexual harassment. He believed he was specifically being targeted because he himself was both black and homosexual. Flanagan also claimed to have been motivated by the Charleston church shooting that had occurred two months before. He described the shooting as a "tipping point" and that his anger had been "steadily building" ever since his termination from WDBJ. In the manifesto, he described himself as a "human powder keg . . . just waiting to go BOOM."

Later that morning, at 11:14 a.m., Flanagan uploaded a self-shot video of his attack on Parker and Ward. In the video, a point-of-view framing shows Flanagan walking toward the interview location while showing off his handgun for the camera. As he gets closer to Alison Parker, Flanagan can be heard saying, "Bitch," just before he takes aim and fires at Parker. Ward's camera drops down as Parker turns to run. Flanagan pulls the camera away and turns it off.

At 11:30 a.m., Flanagan shot himself while fleeing from a Virginia state trooper who recognized his car. The pursuit lasted only two miles. It ended when Flanagan's car hit an embankment and ran off the side of the road. As the state trooper approached the vehicle, Flanagan was found to have suffered a self-inflicted gunshot wound. Flanagan was airlifted to a hospital and was declared dead at 1:26 p.m.

PROTECTIVE TAKEAWAY

Most people who get fired won't be likely to harm you, but the people most likely to harm you are also almost always the ones who were already fired.

PROTECTIVE AWARENESS
Employee terminations are a difficult but sometimes necessary decision

When putting a termination plan into place, it is important to ensure the safety of those still hired is prioritized above the considerations given to those being fired.

Shortly after the WDBJ tragedy took place in Virginia, I started fielding a lot of calls—especially from law firms that had clients with HR concerns regarding their employee termination process. They wanted to know how they could make their process more effective—and safer—for everyone involved. The employment law attorneys who typically advised their clients in this area were much more experienced in dealing with severance packages and insurance guarantees than they were with threat management.

The employee termination process cannot exist in a vacuum

The decision to terminate an employee cannot be as cut-and-dried as hired or fired. To ensure the safety of everyone involved, a series of questions should be considered. For one, why are they being fired? Who made the decision to fire them? What factors influenced the decision? What's the relationship between the person being terminated and the person doing the firing? Are they friends? Enemies? Do they even know each other? Any history there that could complicate things? Was a threat assessment done? What does it say?

Why would a threat assessment be needed simply to fire someone?

Basically, because you want to know how the person in the room is going to respond. How likely are they to break bad? But it's more than that. What you really want to know is: What's the risk to the client? Is there money involved? A severance package? How is it structured? Lump-sum payout or in stages of cooperation? Do they have access to sensitive information? What's the plan to have locks changed? Access rescinded? How much do they know that can hurt you? How much damage can they do to your reputation? Your brand? Your sphere of influence?

In most cases, the decision to terminate an employee typically comes down to one of three tipping points: performance, cause, or budget.

Performance

These are those cases where the employee on the chopping block has been given every opportunity to improve their performance but just can't seem to get their act together. These are the ones who know it's coming and are just doing everything they can to prolong the inevitable. This can be a problem. If they know it's coming, if they can read the writing on the wall but don't make the necessary moves to circumvent an otherwise inevitable outcome, you have to ask yourself, why? What are they waiting for? It's a legitimate concern, because if someone is already somewhere along the pathway to violence, the most dangerous of advantages is time to plan.

Cause

These are the employees who have typically acted out. They've likely committed a fireable offense or done something that violates a code of conduct. These are the things like sexual harassment, racist remarks, theft, or even making threats. These are the actions where the employee knows that if they were to get turned in—or caught—it is going to get them fired. But for whatever reason, they do it anyway.

The biggest risk with this category of concern is for those who don't think they'll get caught. When they do, they have an overwhelming tendency to act out. They immediately go into self-preservation mode. Which begs the question, just how far will they go to defend themselves? How fervently will they fight? The concern here is that they've already displayed a willingness to act outside of appropriate behavioral norms. So the question becomes, once you have them in the room, what else might they do?

Budget

Budget is often the most emotionally disruptive to the employee, because it can feel like no matter what they do, the world is conspiring against them. The decision to let them go has nothing to do with how well they have been doing their job and has nothing to do with their attitude at work; the company simply cannot afford to keep them on payroll and has to let an employee go.

Employers like to come up with less impactful names for this kind of termination. Some call them *layoffs*, some may call them *letting you go*. But for the person who will soon find themselves without a job the next day, they only see it the one way.

Everyone handles stressors in their own unique way

Ninety-nine times out of one hundred, the moment you tell someone they are getting fired, it's a gut punch. Even if they walk into the room knowing it's coming, people will cling to avoidance of an issue until they no longer can deny the inevitable. Right up until you say the words, they'll think they have a way out. I've seen it a thousand times over. I've seen too many grown men break down crying in the corner of the room because they simply didn't have the courage to face the truth of what they knew all along.

Why do they take it so hard? If it's performance related, it's because they know they've been given every chance to improve, but for whatever reason, they just couldn't rise back up to the required standard of performance. If it's for cause, it's out of embarrassment and the realization they've just destroyed their reputation. It's going to be a while before they get hired again. If it's because of budget, they are likely already in some kind of financial bind, and this news only makes things worse.

The lower the degree of financial frustration, the lower the concern

Those who are living paycheck to paycheck are much more likely to feel like they are being targeted than those who are more financially secure. If they are already overleveraged and cash-strapped and feel like their job is all that stands between living on the street and going home to a bed, an unexpected termination may just be the catalyst of their grievance—especially if things don't turn around for them in the immediate future.

At the executive level, you are dealing with a more socially in-tune and financially well-off kind of colleague. Employees in the C-suite don't often "get fired," because they can see the writing on the wall. When something isn't working, they simply resign. Move on. Find something more fitting.

Should employers have security in the room during a termination?

It all depends. Totality of circumstance is everything. I will tell you this. The last thing you want is to have someone in the room who's acting like a heavy. Firing someone is already a confrontational act. An ex-cop in a cheap suit all but screams to the person being terminated, "I'm here because they are scared of you." There is zero benefit to making a volatile situation more so. What you do want is someone in the room who has a high degree of emotional intelligence and can de-escalate a tense situation, but who can also softly project that they are not likely to be intimidated by the threat of a physical altercation.

There have been a few times when I've been asked to be in the room during a termination. Only a few times have I ever had to interject myself into the dynamic. More often than not, my mere presence in the room prevented my need to participate. In those rarest of cases where someone was a bit ramped up because in their particular office "getting called up to HR" was known to mean "you're about to get fired," a few have entered the room with an oversize amount of bravado. They do this because they were mostly expecting to go one-on-one with someone they already knew. But once they see someone else is in the room, that desire to escalate quickly deflates. Sometimes seeing someone else in the room is enough to convince the person that the situation is serious. In most cases, I am introduced as a lawyer. I am *never* introduced as security. I smile. I nod. Nothing more.

In those very rare cases where emotions ran high, I was a sympathetic ear for them to share their story. Their boss or their human resources representative will leave the room to ease the tension. But I'll stay behind. Why? Because I'm an unknown. They have no emotional connection to me. If the mood of the room starts to boil over, I can ask the employer to leave. Ask to give us a minute. Just me and them. Console them. Cool things down. Assure them the next thing will be better. Reaffirm these things have a way of working themselves out. "This too shall pass."

Employee termination must maintain dignity

In the exact moment someone finally accepts the reality that they are being terminated, all anyone cares about is their pride, their dignity. If they can walk out of the office, the building, or the warehouse with their head held high, the likelihood of retaliation is very, *very* low.

In his presentation "Non-Violent Communication," Marshall Rosenberg talks about the importance of moving away from a right-versus-wrong confrontation. When someone is more invested in being right so they can receive the reward than they are being wrong because they don't want to endure the pain associated with being wrong, we lose sight of what we had originally set out to achieve—to be understood.

Ex-employees attack their coworkers and places of employment because that is often where the initial grievance is born, where the ideation that they can "do something about it" is first nurtured. But this pathway to violence is really only a last resort. What they really want is for the emotional truth of their own story to be understood by someone other than themselves. Not to judge but to listen. To help them express themselves in a way they are otherwise unable to convey. To help them interpret the raw angst into real words. These preventable acts of violence in our workplaces will continue so long as we do nothing to address the emotional turmoil some people endure and the harmful ideation they fantasize as remedy to their grievance.

Ten Proven Strategies for Enhancing Workplace Safety

Regardless of where you work, you expect to feel safe, and you deserve to be protected. Truth is, security decisions are often impacted by what matters most to the bottom line. When budgets are limited and hard choices must be made, it is important your voice is an informed part of the decision-making process.

It doesn't matter if you are a senior manager at your office or a recent graduate interviewing with a prospective employer. Your voice matters. It is never too early, or too late, to be informed about the security situation at your workplace.

1. Employee Safety Surveys Provide Key Insights into Concerns

A safety survey should be repeated at regular intervals and should cover everything from how staff feels about management's commitment to safety, to the effectiveness of safety training, to the ease of reporting concerns. The answers should provide employers with insights into favorable feedback, procedures in need of improvement, and priority areas of concern. Conduct an honest assessment to discover the most realistic risks you are most likely to face, and then ask what safeguards are in place to prevent those risks from becoming a reality. Here's a hint: In the wide divide between business policy and employee practice is where the risks of harm often hide. Inspect what you expect.

2. Take an Honest Look at Your Current Protective Measures

Most business leaders are aware of the risks associated with bringing their services into the marketplace, but what about those concerns inherent to their actual place of business? However unlikely it may be for a business to be directly targeted, the reality is that too few businesses have taken any proactive measures to effectively reduce their vulnerability. Today's owners have a responsibility to understand the limitations of antiquated and reactive security measures and learn as much as they can about more proactive practices that today's operating environment requires. The modern marketplace offers a host of consultative and technological advantages to help ensure the safety of all involved.

3. Conduct Routine Security Audits

There is often a very wide divide between policy and practice, between what an organization says they can do and what they can actually accomplish. However unlikely it may be for a business to be directly targeted, the reality is that too few businesses have taken any proactive measures to effectively reduce their vulnerability. Business leaders have a responsibility to understand the limitations of antiquated measures and learn as much as they can about the proactive practices required in today's operating environment.

4. Promote a Positive, Personal Interaction

Greeters, information providers, security guards, or a host who simply says hello to every person who comes near your venue is an effective yet noninvasive approach to promoting a positive protective posture. The everyday human interaction resulting in an unshared concern is arguably the greatest untapped source of protective intelligence available to any business of any size. The psychological deterrence of a simple inter-personal communication carries much more weight than the thought of "being watched." Human interaction offers an immediate notification of potential harm. If a personal interaction triggers something suspicious, immediate attention can be called to the situation. This human approach is a much more practical application than sole reliance on someone in a command center noticing something suspicious.

5. Maintain Positive Access Control

Access control saves lives. A venue's ability to predetermine where an initiation of violence must first take place allows for a venue's protective resources to be allocated where they will be most effective—at the point of entry!

It is perfectly possible for a place of business to have an open and welcoming environment, but there is no need whatsoever to give all who enter free rein throughout the entire facility. Banks do this well. While the lobby is relatively open to the public, few have access to get behind the teller desks, and even fewer have access to the vault.

6. Eliminate Evacuation Zones from Your Emergency Response Plans

Schools and office buildings are a matrix of interconnected and compartmentalized areas that offer their own pockets of protection in the form of dispersion and separation. Evacuation locations negate this protection by having everyone move from their respectively disjointed locations and instead come together at a single, predesignated position. If someone really wanted to do the most harm, the evacuation point would offer the most bang for the buck. You do not need an evacuation zone to serve as a clearinghouse to make sure everyone is accounted for. Mobile phones, social media, texting, and email are all perfectly appropriate ways to check in and make sure everyone is safe. If you say that Pete and Barb are sharing a photo on social media with a #HomeSafe hashtag, they are much safer than anyone still standing around waiting to be counted. Technology should never be counted on to help you escape a problem, but it is perfectly acceptable for your emergency response plan to leverage technology in a postcrisis campaign.

7. Incorporate Threat Management into Your Employee Termination Plan

The workplace environment is often where a grievance is first initiated, where the ideation of "something could be done" is first conceived, and where the research and planning of an attack plan can be easily concealed behind everyday action. Corporate responsibility may not always extend to those who were fired, but it is certainly indebted to those still hired. The risk of violence by disgruntled and recently terminated employees is a concern every business should take into consideration.

8. Initiate a Protective Intelligence Program/Clearinghouse of Concerns

Protective intelligence is the process for collecting and assessing information about persons who have interest, motivation, intention, and practical capability to do harm. When it comes to identifying and assessing those events that are most likely to be a concern, information is invaluable:

- The creepy, curly-haired guy you noticed going through the work trash out back, write it down.
- The flower delivery guy who, for whatever reason, made the hair on your neck stand up, write it down.
- The obsessive gym guy who won't take no for an answer driving by your office, write it down.

Someone may not see everything, but everything is seen by someone. The smallest things can be huge indicators when viewed through the prism of space and time. If you see something, say something, because chances are that others saw something too. Even if you talk about it with your coworkers in the break room, writing it down while it's still fresh in your mind will not only serve as confirmation of what you saw but will provide a time/date stamp to compare against similar reports.

Those wishing to act with violent intent must engage in some aspect of *research and planning* that makes their behaviors observable to the general public. Trespassing, surveillance, and attempting to breach security are all pre-incident indicators of violence.

Start a simple email address at work that can be universally used by all, like concern@BusinessName.com. The more puzzle pieces you provide, the more likely a potential hazard can be managed toward a peaceful resolution. After access control, an effective protective intelligence and threat assessment program is the next most important precaution for reducing risk and preventing violence.

9. Establish a Crisis Management Team

A crisis management team, or CMT, typically includes executive directors, department heads, staff representatives, threat management, and media advisers. The CMT's job is to ensure the certainty of safety by working together to detect the warning signs of concern, tabletop what-if scenarios, and prepare best practices for emergency situations.

10. Keys, Doors, and Locks

Keeping people out is easier than getting them out. Effectively controlling who's allowed through your front door is especially important if once someone is allowed inside there is nothing preventing them from having free rein throughout the rest of your establishment. The problem with keys is that they work all the time. Keys are cheap, frequently lost, and easy to copy. Keys don't validate their user the way card readers and key codes do. Consider dual-authentication options to limit and monitor access.

PROTECTIVE PREPAREDNESS

Here are the top thirty questions for you to include in your own Personal Threat Assessment for keeping yourself safe at work:

1. **What is the biggest threat to your workplace?**

    Why this is important: Awareness + Preparation = Safety.

    The biggest threat facing your workplace may change over the course of time. It is important to routinely make sure the threat you are expecting to confront is the threat most likely to be revealed.

2. **How well prepared is your workplace for the threat you outlined above?**

    Why this is important: To help prevent this threat from ever becoming a reality, it is important to be as prepared as possible.

What more can be done to reduce risk and prevent violence? What more can be done to ensure the certainty of safety for everyone involved?

3. **Do you feel safe at work?**

    Why this is important: If not, why not? What is it about work that makes you feel unsafe? Be specific. Identify your specific framework for what you fear and then work to resolve that concern. Do others within your workplace share this same concern? Who is the appropriate point person in the workplace who can best help to resolve this issue?

4. **What is the process at your workplace for reporting a concern?**

    Why this is important: It is important for your understanding of this process to be as informed as possible. What concerns are these systems intended to support? How easy is this system to use? Have you ever used it? If so, did you feel your concern was addressed in a timely fashion? How could this system be improved to help promote ease of use?

5. **Does your workplace encourage staff to report concerns?**

    Why this is important: What concerns is your workplace encouraging you to report? Are there any concerns you would want to report but were discouraged from doing so? Do you or any of your coworkers feel stigmatized for using this system? Is this reporting process anonymous? What can be done to help make this system more effective?

6. **Do delivery persons (food, mail, flowers, etc.) have to be approved and confirmed before being granted access to your workstation?**

    Why this is important: What is this process like? How often does it happen? Are they escorted, or can they just walk in? Do you have to go to them, or can they come to you? Access control is a key tenet of workplace safety. While the nature and public-facing openness may be different for each business, a best practice for ensuring safety is to create a document for the purposes of maintaining a historical record of the date, time, duration, and purpose of anyone who may come into your work space. This is especially important if the nature of your work is confidential or if your work space requires an additional level of access to be granted.

7. **If you forget your key fob, badge, ID, and so on, how likely is it for a friendly security guard to let you in because they know you— even though this is against policy?**

    Why this is important: Policy only works if it is followed every time. If they are willing to make an exception for you, how likely are they to make an exception for another? How easy would it be for you to go about your entire workday and never once use your key fob, badge, or ID? Simple or difficult? Is there a temporary policy? Does your workplace still use physical keys? How does that system differ? Better or worse?

    The important takeaway for this question is to understand how effective at becoming a barrier of entry the access control of your workplace really is versus how much of it is just for show. How easy is it to circumvent the system via social engineering or via insider insights (e.g., the back door leading down from the stairs to the loading dock that closes but never locks, which thus affords an additional—and unsecured—option for entry)?

8. **How often is your workplace in the news?**

    Why this is important: Sometimes? Always? Never? Does your workplace have a policy in place about speaking to the press? Do you feel as though this news coverage impacts the safety of your workplace? This question is important for understanding if the narrative of a news story—which may identify the location of your workplace—increases the likelihood of your workplace to be targeted by an outside actor.

9. **Is there a process in place for reporting employee concerns— including inappropriate messages received at work via email, voice mail, social media, and handwritten letters?**

    Why this is important: How are inappropriate communications assessed and managed? What are the parameters your workplace has in place for the identification and reporting of these communications? Does your workplace have a social media policy? Do you have a dedicated threat management team with whom you share concerns?

10. **How are accidents and incidents investigated? How timely?**

    Why this is important: Does your workplace take these concerns seriously? Are there plans in place? Is there someone who has the assumed role of safety manager? How instilled with confidence are you by the handling of historic concerns at your workplace? Highly confident? Moderately confident? Not confident? Why do you feel this way?

11. **How wide is the divide between corporate policy and employee practice?**

    Why this is important: Does your workplace have a dedicated policy and procedure in place, or is your workplace framework more unconventional? What are the pros and cons for how these disparities between patterns in practice are managed? What are the impacts of this management style on organizational security and your personal safety?

12. **How are bullying, verbal threats, and physical acts of violence defined, and how are any reported concerns handled by management?**

    Why this is important: How are these concerns defined, and how are they handled once reported and/or recognized? Are these concerns taken seriously in practice, or are they only referenced in the policy? What are the consequences of these actions? Does your workplace employ a zero-tolerance policy?

13. **How does your workplace inform you of an emergency? How is one emergency differentiated from the next?**

    Why this is important: Much like your phone has different tones to denote the difference between a text message, an email, and a phone call, how does your workplace inform you of a different emergency scenario? Are they using the same alert for all notifications regardless of priority? Why? How can this be improved?

14. **If you are seated at your desk when violence erupts, do you have a plan for what to do, where to go, and how to get there?**

    Why this is important: Do you have a plan? When was the last time you mapped it out in your mind? When was the last time you walked the routes to make sure your plan is foolproof?

15. **In the event of a workplace evacuation, what have you been instructed to do, and where have you been instructed to go? How likely are you to follow these guidelines?**

    Why this is important: Only *you* are in charge of your survival decisions. While an overarching corporate direction may be an option to consider, only you can tell you what to do. Never negotiate against your own survival instincts simply because everyone else is hell-bent on following the other lambs to the slaughter.

16. **How able is someone to roam freely throughout your workplace once they have gained entry inside?**

    Why this is important: How is access control restricted? Does one badge open everything, or are there zones of admittance? What about areas of critical infrastructure like a cash room, a vault, or a server room? How is access in and out of these places enforced and managed?

17. **Are you trained in first aid and/or CPR? Do you know how to apply a tourniquet?**

    Why this is important: You are your own first responder. Prepare yourself to save yourself whenever possible.

18. **Does your workplace offer first aid/CPR certification to anyone who wants it?**

    Why this is important: Same as above. If not, have you asked about it? What other options are available to you to become certified? How many others in your workplace do you know with a current first aid/CPR certification?

19. **Do you know where the fire extinguishers are located? Do you know how to use them?**

    Why this is important: You are your own first responder. Do you know where the fire extinguishers are located? Do you know how many are on hand? Are you intimately familiar with how to use them?

20. **Do you know what the most likely natural disaster to impact your workplace is?**

    Why this is important: When moments matter most, you will not want to find yourself wanting. What contingencies would you need to help you endure a natural disaster? Make a list. Formulate a plan. Put those necessities together, and then keep them on hand.

21. **Does your workplace have someone whose job it is to help keep your workplace safe?**

    Why this is important: If the responsibility of workplace safety is not a clearly defined role, everyone will assume it is the responsibility of someone else. So let me ask you: Who is responsible for the overarching safety and security concerns of your workplace? How confident are you in their performance? What are three things they are doing well, and what are three things they could improve?

22. **What was the scariest thing to ever happen at your workplace?**

    Why this is important: What happened? How did this impact you? Would you do anything differently if it were to happen again? How long ago did this incident take place?

23. **How likely is that scary thing to happen again?**

    Why this is important: What can you do to help reduce the likelihood of this happening again? What can others do? How likely are they to help? Knowing that this has already happened once before, what safeguards do you already have on hand?

24. **Does your workplace have security cameras, and are they monitored in real time?**

    Why this is important: How seriously does your workplace take their security? How positive of a protective posture does your workplace promote to outsiders?

25. **Does your workplace take cybersecurity seriously?**

    Why this is important: What is the biggest cybersecurity concern impacting your workplace? What is being done to help make this bad thing better? Do you have an internal IT team, or are they a contracted vendor? How can this issue be improved?

26. **If someone wanted to wreak havoc on your workplace, what is their likelihood of success?**

    Why this is important: This question goes directly to how effective an insider threat could be at causing harm through violence versus how impactful an outside actor could be at doing the same thing. How difficult would it be for *you* to do harm if you felt so inclined? Do you have access to the server room? Could you go inside that room right now and either upload a virus or simply start pulling plugs? Given the likelihood of someone who you believe to be good deciding to break bad, how much damage and destruction could they foreseeably accomplish before finally being stopped?

27. **What are the top three things your workplace does to ensure *your* safety?**

    Why this is important: Are you happy with these, or do you wish more (or less, or something different) was being done?

28. **Do you feel empowered to make your own decisions when it comes to your safety?**

    Why this is important: What might an example of this be? What would you do differently? Why does what they are instructing you to do not sound right?

29. **Does your workplace have a strict visitor policy?**

    Why this is important: What is this policy? How is it enforced? How is it put into practice? How can it be made better? Do you feel this policy helps to keep you and your office better protected, or does it put your workplace more at risk?

30. **What is one security policy you believe may be doing more harm than good?**

    Why this is important: Is there anything being done in the name of security that is more of an inconvenience than a safeguard? Sometimes a solution that is valuable as a short-term fix is a detriment as a longer-term solution. Just because there is a policy/practice under the banner of security and safety does not automatically disqualify it from being assessed for effectiveness as any other policy procedure would.

21

LIFE

What Happened

Almost dying is a great reminder of what makes life worth living. I will never know how this gift of ours works, but when I think of all the good I have been able to do since that day, when I think back to all the wonderful times I have enjoyed, the lives touched, the loves experienced, and the wines tasted, I am forever grateful not just for all those days that had come before but for every moment after.

There were several times in my life when I was more than certain my time on earth was at an imminent end.

One such time was in Jordan in 2012.

It was the end of May. I had just finished an assignment in Aqaba, and I was en route to the Dead Sea, with a local driver we'll call Moe.

Highway 65 is a paved yet poorly cared for road that serves as the predominant route for commercial transport between the two resort towns as well as the primary route for tourist buses and private travel.

Road maintenance is not a high priority in Jordan outside of Amman. Resources, manpower, and machinery are difficult to allocate in the barren stretches of desert, and where similar maintenance and upkeep projects may only take a few days or a week to complete in the United States, a similar project outside of Amman may take months if not years to finish.

Accidents along these routes are a common occurrence not just because of the poor road conditions but because of the poor judgment
of the drivers as well. There is also a rampant drug and alcohol problem inherent to the commercial truck drivers who make multiple daily
runs between the capital of Amman and the two southern resort towns.
Methamphetamine allows the drivers the ability to stay awake for long
hours spent on the road, and the alcohol helps them to remove the edge
to fall asleep for those randomly prescribed hours their schedules allow.

Driving north on Highway 65, there were long stretches of cutouts
in the road where road crews had removed the macadam surrounding
potholes and other road abnormalities in stretching sections hundreds
of feet on both sides of the road. Oftentimes, these cutouts would be in
sections no more than fifty feet from each other, forcing drivers to switch
from one side of the yellow line to the other, avoiding the deep cuts on
the road like a downhill skier negotiating the flags on a slalom course.

For a significant amount of time on the drive, we were the only vehicle on the road. About an hour south of the Dead Sea, the road signs indicated an S curve ahead, where a narrow overpass followed the contours
of the mountains.

It was on this narrow stretch I thought beyond a doubt it was all over.

As we approached the bottom of the S curve, a cutout in the road
forced us onto the opposite side of the road. What we did not know, and
what was impossible to see coming, was a tractor trailer approaching the
top of the S curve—the cutout on his opposite side keeping him tightly
in his own lane.

As we both entered the middle of the curve at the same time, the cuts
in the road changed into alternating patterns, forcing us into a collision
course. We both noticed each other within the length of a football field,
but as we were both on an overpass with a mountain on one side and a
guardrail protecting us from an abyss on the other, there was nowhere for
us to turn.

To make matters worse, as the margin between our small sedan and
the tractor trailer closed, the driver of the tractor trailer panicked and
began to swerve, which forced his trailer to jackknife across the center of
the road, leaving us nowhere to go.

I braced for impact as best I could. We were just feet away from the tractor trailer at this point, my view of the world out the dashboard window consumed by the grille of the Peterbilt truck moving in the direction of the guardrail and the deep ravine below.

Instinct forced my body into a modified parachute-land-fall, which had been ingrained in me from my army days. My feet and knees closed together, my chin tucked down to my chest, and my elbows and forearms came together up in front of my face.

I remember hearing the driver shout out in English, "Oh My God, I am so sorry!" I was about to die, and all I remember thinking was, *He's Jordanian. Why isn't he calling out to God in Arabic?*

In moments like these, everything slows down. I sensed the crash as we struck the truck, not so much hearing the loud collision but sensing the impact. I felt another impact through what I assumed was the guardrail, and I remember thinking, *This is it. This is how I die.*

My eyes were closed, and I imagined us falling through the air, picturing the car in my mind's eye, wondering if it would be sudden or if the car would crunch into a mangled mess. My body tightened and braced for the impact.

Something wasn't right. Too much time had passed, and we hadn't yet hit the bottom of the ravine. There was no way we were still falling. Had time slowed down that much?

I opened my eyes.

Through the passenger-side window, I saw nothing but sky.

Was I still alive?

My senses came flooding back to the present. The airbag on my side had only partially deployed, and there was a softball-size crack in the dashboard glass in front of me.

There was a lot of blood on the dashboard.

Moe's door was flung open, and his driver's-side window was smashed out. He had been thrown from the vehicle. I couldn't see him, but I could hear his screams—muffled at first but then clearer—the unmistakable combat screams of a grown man in unimaginable pain.

I ran through my self-assessment check. My toes wiggled, my hands made fists, I flexed all the muscles starting with my calves and working

THE SAFETY TRAP   321

my way up to my chest and shoulders. I wasn't in any pain, but I knew that could be from shock.

I tried to open my door, but we had been thrown at an upward angle, and my door was wedged against the guardrail. The door handle was operating as it should, but it wouldn't budge. I tried to unfasten my seat belt, but it wouldn't come undone. Reaching into my waistband, I pulled out my tactical folding knife and cut myself free as I swung my legs over the center console to lower myself out the driver's-side door. I caught my reflection in the rearview mirror and looked myself in the eyes. How was I still alive?

My feet hit the ground, and I looked around. The tractor trailer was hundreds of feet away, the cab smashed flat against the side of the mountain. Moe was lying in the middle of the road. He was conscious but in obvious pain. The left side of his body was covered in blood as he tried to move.

I reached into my pocket for my mobile phone to call for help, but it wasn't there. It had been in the middle console of the car so it could charge on the drive. We were in the middle of nowhere, and my mind clicked over to assessment protocol. There was no smell of gasoline from our vehicle, nothing was sparking or smelled of fire. Just the unmistakable nose twinge of singed rubber from the tire tracks burned across the empty road.

I remembered my go bag in the trunk had a trauma kit and a sat phone, and I walked to the trunk of the car to retrieve them, but the trunk would not open without a key. Searching the front seat of the vehicle, I was fortunate to find the keys still in the ignition.

The trunk now open, I grabbed my go bag and unzipped the top front compartment to retrieve the satellite phone. I turned it on, happy it had not been damaged in the crash.

As the phone powered up and searched for a signal, I removed the trauma kit and shouldered my go bag, making my way over to treat Moe.

Moe was in bad shape and was screaming for help.

The phone chirped as it connected with the satellites, and I made the call to base camp back in Aqaba. I gave them the brief rundown and our position. The road marking had us at 150 kilometers south of Amman. It would take a while for help to arrive, so I told them I would initiate basic first aid and try to stabilize Moe.

Moe did not look good. His face was cut and swelling from the smashed window, and his clothing was soaked in blood. Kneeling next to him, I laid out the trauma kit and donned the protective gloves before I proceeded to administer first aid. Moe was in obvious shock and kept repeating, "I'm sorry, I'm sorry," amid his pain-induced screams. I cut off Moe's shirt to see what we were working with and began rinsing and gauze-wiping his arms and torso of excess blood to see the wounds properly.

Moe's left shoulder was deeply bruised, likely shattered, and his left forearm had deep lacerations with minor lacerations to his left wrist and hand. The left side of his abdomen and upper thigh were bruised. It appeared as though his pelvis had been broken.

I comforted him as best I could and applied pressure dressings to the wounds and wrapped them in gauze.

As I was finishing, a military truck approached and stopped to help. One of the soldiers spoke English, and I explained to him as best I could what had happened. I pointed to the tractor trailer behind us, and a few of the soldiers jogged down to check on the driver. They turned back shortly after getting a closer look, gesturing with the universal swipe of a hand across the neck that the driver of the truck did not need any immediate attention. The soldiers made a few calls on their radio I could not understand and informed me that it would be better if they took Moe to the hospital immediately rather than wait for the ambulance.

I agreed with them. There was nothing more we could do for Moe there on the side of the road. The more immediate medical attention he received, the better off he would be. I made another call to base camp to inform them of Moe's status and informed them I would remain on-site for my own transport.

A short time later, police and paramedics arrived on scene. There was a significant language barrier, and they were very confused as to why I was covered in Moe's blood but had no apparent injury. The paramedics had me in the back of their truck, running numerous tests. A short time later, an Arabic-speaking member of base camp arrived with a few others and helped to clear up the misunderstanding. I was apparently very close to being arrested for questioning in the death of the truck driver.

With another base camp vehicle now on-site, we collected the rest of my gear from the back of the wrecked sedan and continued our journey to the Dead Sea. We got a call thirty minutes later that Moe was at a hospital not far from our location, and we decided to make a quick detour to check on him.

Moe was still in the same bandages I had dressed him in earlier, but had been administered some pain medicine that seemed to have him a bit more at ease. By all accounts, the doctors believed he would be okay after a long road of recovery.

Moe took my hand as I stood over him and apologized repeatedly for the accident. I felt guilty to have him apologize so profusely while lying there in a hospital bed while I stood above him unscathed.

We said our goodbyes, and we wished each other well.

I haven't seen Moe since, but I think of that accident more often than I would likely care to remember.

PROTECTIVE TAKEAWAY

Fortes fortuna juvat—fortune favors the brave.

PROTECTIVE AWARENESS

Life Is Stranger Than Fiction

I'm sure someone, somewhere, has a real-world story of a client pressing a panic button because they were really in trouble, but it has never once happened to me. In my professional experience, ninety-nine out of one hundred times, whenever the button was pressed, it was done so by accident. The other 1 percent of the time, it was because the client either wanted to see what would happen or they just wanted to show it off to their friends. In fact, false alarms happened to me so many times that I drew up a training practicum to make new agents aware of this reality. In the old days, if a panic button went off, an agent would come running in to save the day with their weapon drawn—expecting to engage a hostile intruder in an active-threat event—only to be met by a startled client whose only reason for pressing the button was to ask why the package they were expecting hadn't been delivered. As if their protector had a direct line to the FedEx carrier. Point is, no matter how many years of service you have, no matter how well you train, no matter how many contingency plans you have on hand, life has a way of throwing you a curveball you never saw coming.

What's ironic about the whole panic button situation is that there were times when my clients really were scared. There were times when they really were in immediate need. Maybe they cut themselves in the kitchen and needed first aid or broke an ankle on the treadmill, went flying across the room, and hit their head. Maybe they heard a noise in the middle of the night and froze in fear. The thing is, in those rare instances, where they really were in trouble or when they really were scared, the panic button was never used. In those moments of heightened stakes, they were always way too frightened to remember they had it available. Why? Because it wasn't second nature to them. It wasn't something they were expecting to have to do.

Which is why I always find it so absurd whenever someone tells me they have a gun or some other weapon for home or self-defense. Now don't get me wrong, if you are a trained shooter—meaning you have put at least ten thousand rounds of ammunition through the barrel of the very weapon system you are planning to use in a high-threat, one-on-one engagement of violence—then by all means, you have my full support. Unfortunately, most people do not invest this level of time, effort, and energy into their own protective strategy.

The Safety Traps being the pitfalls that they are, there is another key concept that everyday life needs to take into consideration: common sense.

Common Sense Is Not Common

There are a lot of reasons why common sense fails us. For one, we all come from different backgrounds. We all have different sets of experiences. We all have different vantage points from which we view the interactions of the world around us. Even our instincts differ from one person to the next.

This is one of the reasons why staying safe in our everyday lives is so much more challenging than, say, staying safe at work or staying safe at school. Life just has so many variables that it would be nearly impossible to provide any specific guidance around what would help *you* to stay safe.

Life's challenges are as individualized as we are, but having a better understanding of best practices can help us to pivot away from those initial decision-making assumptions that may lead us further down the rabbit hole of consequence. Just as stress inoculation helps to keep us from becoming overwhelmed in a crisis, having a solid foundation of an if-this-then-that decision-making matrix will help us to achieve a better outcome in whatever circumstance confronts us.

The better we hone these skills, the better we can course correct ourselves into better decision-making. After all, the more we can move ourselves away from the transactional decision-making of the checkerboard and onto the strategic decision-making required for the game of chess, the better trained we will become at seeing the bigger picture rather than our previously narrowed view.

Some examples:

How to Survive a Disaster

Preparing yourself both mentally and physically for the harsh reality of a natural disaster will help you to successfully survive the crisis and best handle the aftermath.

The following are essential tips to help in your own preparedness process.

1. **Have a positive attitude.** Your survival will often be the result of your own personal outlook. Doing your best to be proactive and maintaining a positive mindset, rather than embracing a victim mentality and simply waiting to be rescued, is often the biggest difference between those who survive a natural disaster and those who do not.

2. **Put a plan in place.** Every family should have their own emergency readiness plan. Your family may not be together when the disaster strikes, so it is important to plan ahead for how your loved ones will contact one another. Include in this plan known locations where your family can go to reunify. It is important these plans be communicated and discussed at regular intervals, as circumstances and scenarios may change throughout the year. For examples of emergency readiness plans, visit: http://www.ready.gov/make-a-plan.

3. **Keep emergency rations on hand.** Food and water may become difficult to acquire depending on the severity and duration of the disaster. Safeguard yourself from future stress, and stock up on reserves. Bottled water and shelf-stable food will keep your family properly nourished while handling the disaster at hand and will remove one additional factor of stress from the equation.

4. **Go bags should be prepacked and ready at all times.** A go bag is a prepacked and easily carried bag you take with you as you are running out the door in an emergency. The premise is such that your go bag is always packed, ready, and waiting with the essentials you will need to survive for two nights and three days in the outdoor terrain of your current location and climate. Your go bag should contain the necessities needed to survive but should also afford you the ability to remain mobile. Backpacks are ideal. Keep in mind that your packing list may change throughout the year, dependent upon the season, your physical location, medical requirements, and physical capability.

    Everyone who is physically able to carry a go bag should have one tailored to their own specific needs. Your own individual packing list may vary based on personal preference and necessity, but the contents serve as an excellent tutorial on what constitutes essentials. If you only do one thing to prepare beyond your in-home food and water storage, this is it. A go bag is what you need. Everyone should have one. Build or buy one today. Many pre-customized options are available online.

5. **Know where to go and know how to get there.** Safe havens should be identified as early and as often as possible. This means knowing where to go if you can't get home, as well as where you can safely go if your home is no longer an option.

6. **Decide today what's most important.** Have a discussion with your family today about what is most important to save should you have to leave your home. List them in order of priority in case time to prepare runs out. Important documents, photographs, and family heirlooms should be considered, but remember that nothing is more important than the lives of your family. If possible, make copies of the photos and documents most important to you. Print them out or save them to a thumb drive, and add them to your go bag packing list. Consider having this discussion with your family today. When moments matter most, you'll be glad you did.

7. **Prepare for power outages.** Today, all our communication devices require a charge, and your mobile devices will be critical to helping you negotiate your way to a better day. While a few commercial venues with backup generators may be able to facilitate the needs of the few, they most certainly will not be able to cater to the needs of the many. So skip the Starbucks cell phone charging line and invest in a solar-charging unit or generator. Goal Zero has a great selection available for every budget.

8. **Understand the importance of ice.** Keep some extra bags of ice in the freezer. King-size cubes will last longer than the ice-maker variety. The right amount of ice can help keep your refrigerator and freezer functional after the power goes out. Ice also has first aid application in the treatment of blister burns, splinter removal, oral numbness to treat tooth pain, and soft tissue injury, to name a few. Ice will also help keep essential medicine like insulin properly refrigerated. If a natural disaster is imminent, try to make as much ice as possible before the power goes out. Also, get yourself a high-end cooler like a Yeti that can keep food and ice fresh for days all on their own.

9. **Know the safe spots in your home.** These are the spaces in your home that offer you the most protection. Stairwells or spaces under large beams provide survival voids that rescue workers check first.

10. **Maximize insurance and fortify your home.** This will of course require the most foresight and preparation and will not aid you when the warning whistles blow, but looking out for things like dead trees that may blow over in strong winds or readily upgrading your home's doors, windows, and roof will provide significant vulnerability reduction in the face of a natural disaster.

It is important to keep in mind that while we cannot prevent natural disasters from happening, we can be best prepared for when they do. Plan ahead and you'll have the confidence in a crisis to know you are ready.

How to Keep Our Loved Ones Safe from Fraud

My dad is smart, capable, caring, fit, generous, and kind. He is also eighty-four. He freely admits it. He is old. For his generation—those who grew up in the heart of the Great Depression—technology peaked with color TV. He's never used a computer. He's never been online. The running family joke is from when I was off at college and my sisters tried to explain email. His first question was legendary: "Where do you put the stamp?" He is polite and courteous to everyone, especially strangers. He will do anything for anyone. He's the most selfless man I know. That's what makes him the ideal target for the guy who just called his cell phone.

It's 8:30 p.m. on a Wednesday night, and we've just been seated to dinner. The waitress finished taking our drink order when his phone rings. I can see by his puzzled expression that he doesn't recognize the number. Then he does what few under the age of sixty would do in a similar circumstance: he takes the call.

"This is who?" He can't make out the voice. "The IRS?!"

Clear confusion is on his face now.

"My accountant handles all of that." A longer pause. "Sure, it's 147-2—"

"*Dad!*" I wave my hands in front of me like I'm a referee miming an incomplete pass in football.

I motion for him to hand me his phone.

I don't even speak to the person on the line. I just end the call. The call log recorded the number. Google confirms what I already know. The number comes up as a fraud warning. Someone was just phishing for my old man's info.

He looks at me for answers. How do I explain this?

The simple fact is this: for those who wish to do harm, likelihood of success is the single most influential factor of target selection. Statistically speaking, the over-sixty population are most likely to own their own home, most likely to have modest savings, and most likely to have good credit. The "greatest generation" is also more likely to have been brought up to be nice, polite, and courteous to strangers. Elderly victims are less likely to report being a victim of fraud because they are fearful of family members believing they are incapable of handling their own affairs, and since financial crimes can be difficult to prosecute, elderly fraud is largely considered to be a low-risk crime for offenders. In other words, the elderly are ideal targets for those with nefarious intent.

Elderly adults (age sixty and up) who are targeted for fraud are 34 percent more likely to lose money than respondents in their forties.

Elderly fraud is a growing concern. The FBI has an entire web page dedicated to senior citizens and fraud protection. It covers everything from health care and insurance scams to telemarketing fraud and investment schemes. It is a must-read for anyone who has a loved one over the age of sixty.

Phishing Scams

Phishing scams like the one attempted against my dad are the most common. They often involve a phone call or an email message from someone claiming to be from a large national bank or a well-known government agency (like the IRS) asking their targets to update passwords or verify personal information under the guise of looking out for their safety.

I hand my dad back his phone and offer some advice as plainly as possible:

"If you don't recognize the number, you don't have to answer."

Today's home and mobile phones all come standard with caller ID. If you don't recognize the name and you don't recognize the number, there is nothing wrong with having them leave a message to see what they want. You can always call them back later. You're not being rude. You're being safe.

"If I call you, I have to prove myself to you. If you call me, you have to prove yourself to me."

No official organization or legitimate business will ever call you and then require you to verify who you are. The burden of proof is always on the caller. No matter who calls, never, ever, *ever* give out your complete social security number over the phone, to anyone, at any time, for any reason.

"Who are your favorite five?"

Every important decision is worthy of a second opinion. Any decision that has to deal with financial investment, medical decisions, legal concerns, family matters, or friendship endeavors should likely be discussed with another before making up your mind. As a general rule, you can trust your doctor, your lawyer, your accountant, your loyal family, and longtime friends.

"Strangers don't ask strangers for help. Strangers don't offer strangers large sums of money."

"Dad, when I was a kid, what did you tell me about strangers?"

He rolls his eyes at me.

"Let me ask you this: If you walked out of here tonight and happened to find a lot of money on the street, are you more likely to call someone you trust or to make an unbelievably generous offer to someone you never met?"

He nods in agreement.

Keep it simple: if it sounds too good to be true, it is.

"Unsolicited calls asking for donations should always be answered with a 'No, thank you.'"

No, thank you is a complete sentence. If you want to help support a great cause, do your own research and donate to the cause that looks best to you. Unfortunately, not all good deeds go toward good causes. Fraudulent charities always pop up around holidays and after tragedies. If you want to make a meaningful difference, a little extra effort is all it takes to make sure your money goes to where it will matter most.

Dad's phone rings again as dinner is being served. His head turns to the side as he shows me the number. Another unknown number.

"Voice mail?"

I nod.

He declines the call. Sips his beer. Looks down at his steak. Looks back up at me.

"I really hope that wasn't your mother."

How to Protect Yourself in the Parking Lot

Seven Steps for Self-Defense

Millions of shoppers use retail parking garages every year, but did you know that parking lots are among the most likely locations for would-be attackers to prey on unassuming victims? Recent findings show that more than 80 percent of reported crimes at retail and shopping establishments took place in the parking lot.

Why?

Perhaps the most significant factor is that in addition to shoppers having their hands full as they move to their cars, parking lots are a naturally reflective transition time. These are locations when our minds are often not in the now.

Moving to our vehicles is a time when the mind—however subconsciously—is most likely to either reflect back to whatever we were just doing or project forward to what we are about to do. This means we are less likely to be situationally aware of our immediate surroundings and more vulnerable to attack.

Be aware of this disadvantage. Make the following best practices part of your everyday parking process and help bring your mind back to the present. Increasing your situational awareness will drastically reduce your likelihood of being attacked.

1. **Whenever possible, choose a parking lot rather than a parking garage.** The natural visibility and surveillance of a parking lot is much better than inside a parking garage where line-of-sight safety is drastically reduced by support beams, ramps, elevator bays, and stairwells.

2. **Try to park in areas that are well lit and easily accessible.** Those closest to the main entrance or parking garage exits are best. If you have to call for help, you want to be found fast, so it's best to avoid dark, remote, and hard-to-describe locations. Ask yourself this question when you get out of your car. If you were to scream for help, would anyone see or hear you? If the answer is *no* or *not really,* park elsewhere.

3. **If you feel someone is following you or paying you the wrong kind of attention, look at them right in the face.** You may even choose to make some kind of out-loud, offhand comment describing them: "Red hat," "Blue shirt," "Brown hair." Saying something descriptive helps your mind to take a memory snapshot of what you're seeing. Criminals rely on anonymity to successfully carry out and get away with their crimes. Letting them know that you see them serves two purposes: it demonstrates to a would-be attacker that you are aware of their presence and have therefore taken away their element of surprise, but you also take away their anonymity. Now that you have seen their face, you could describe them to police and identify them in a lineup.

4. **Use the panic alarm.** If you sound the alarm well before you get to your car (like as you're leaving the store), the attention of everyone in the surrounding area will be brought to your car. Bad guys need anonymity to do their bidding. Your car alarm will bring the would-be attacker unwanted attention and drastically reduce their likelihood of success. Intentionally sounding the alarm raises your own awareness too.

5. **Attackers play your fear to their advantage.** Turn the tables and use it to yours. If someone is coming toward you, hold out your hands in front of you and yell, "No!" "Stop!" or "Stay back!" Most criminals interviewed after their crimes have repeatedly stated they would leave a woman alone if she yelled or showed that she would not be afraid to fight back. Criminals want easy prey. They prefer the weakest among us, not the strongest.

6. **If you have a baby, young children, or just a lot of stuff to carry, try to park so that the side of the car you use to load/unload faces the store's entrance.** You'll be safer where those entering and exiting the store can see and hear you.

7. **Keep in mind that how you park is just as important as where you park.** Parking so that your car faces out may make it easier when it's time to leave, but it also may make it easier for a would-be attacker to create a trap. If you see someone suspicious in the car next to you, especially if it's a van, exercise caution. Don't be afraid to go back inside and ask for an escort. *Trust your gut!* This is especially important if no one else is around. Remember that you can always use the passenger door to enter. Don't let yourself get boxed in. It's always better to be safe than sorry.

    Remember: effective self-defense begins long before a physical altercation. Awareness of your surroundings, awareness of your environment, and awareness of what looks out of place prepare you physically and mentally for what may come next. Being aware and engaged with your environment also promotes a confidence that is often your first line of defense in convincing a would-be attacker that they will have a greater chance of success targeting someone else.

What to Do the Day Before the World Doesn't End

When designing any emergency response plan, it is important to first identify the most realistic threat you are likely to face. Imaginations will always exceed budgets, so identifying and mounting a defense against the threat you are most likely to face will help manage your fear and your finances in equal measure.

Regardless of the crisis you may face, what all disaster scenarios have in common is the challenge to your safety and security after the event has occurred. When the dust has settled, the winds have died, and the waters calmed, you must survive until the return to normal, and my hope is this helps you find the best way to do so.

What should I do first?

You are right here . . . right now. Stop reading this chapter for a second and look around. One second from now, your world and your life will change forever. Are you ready?

SAFETY FIRST: Protect yourself and get to a safe and sustainable location. You will know your home and your neighborhood the best, so get there as quickly and as safely as you can.

CONTACT ANYONE AND EVERYONE WHILE/IF YOU STILL CAN: Let trusted people (friends and family) know where you are, where you are going, your physical condition, as well as anything you may need. If you haven't already done so, initiate your family emergency plan so that everyone knows where to go and what to do.

TAKE INVENTORY: Who is with you, and what do you have on hand? If you don't have what you need, decide immediately how important it is to have versus the risk of retrieval. This will obviously be a situational-dependent statement, but as a rule: anything less than the life of a loved one, and you should prepare yourself to be without.

TRIAGE: Is anyone hurt or injured? Require immediate medical attention? What do you need to do to ensure the health, welfare, and safety of those in your charge tonight? Are you safe where you are? Can you safely move to a better location? You will need to determine the most important tasks often as priorities may shift at any given moment. (Always be thinking: safety, food, and shelter.)

DELEGATE: If you are of good enough fortune to be with others, utilize them to their full advantage. There is strength in numbers. Do not try to do everything yourself.

If anything can be done 70 percent as well as you, delegate that tasking to another. They'll learn as they go, and getting something done is better than getting nothing done.

Where you live will determine what you need

Most of us surviving a crisis situation will be restricted to the immediate vicinity of our homes with little to no power or communication.

Where you live will determine the necessity of what is needed for your specific situation. If you live in an urban environment, where daily deliveries to markets and groceries are required, then your focus should be on food storage more so than if you live in a more rural environment where you could feasibly live off the land in a hunter-gatherer capacity.

Dependence on machine-generated climate control is another factor to consider. Understanding the susceptible changes to the natural climate of your location should be factored in when deciding where to bunker down.

What is a reasonable expectation of duration?

Four nights and five days of on-hand rations is a good rule of thumb. Emergency services are generally able to provide basic assistance within three days. However, having value-added goods on hand (cigarettes, ammunition, and alcohol) will afford you the ability to barter and exchange for necessities later on should the crisis continue longer than expected.

Who can I trust?

You already know the answer to this. If you're thinking, *I think so,* then the answer is no. If you can unequivocally say, "Yes," then the answer is yes. One may never know where loyalty is born, but the beginning of a crisis isn't when you want to find out.

ALLIANCES START NOW: Community counts. Find like-minded friends and neighbors who live in proximity, and start discussing the roles and functions of those who can provide varying and essential skills and services.

For example, if your neighbor has a generator and you have a giant freezer full of food in your garage, talk to each other now and work out a system to combine resources should the time come. If any of your neighbors are doctors, RNs, or police, invite them over for dinner. Start recruiting local support today. Tomorrow may be too late.

What should I have on hand?

As I stated before, your own needs will be conditional upon your situation. What's listed here is by no means the must-haves, but rather the should-haves for basic home defense and survival. I have listed them here in order of priority according to my own personal experience and practice.

1. Enough food, water, and prescription medication to last you five days. Assume your water won't be running or will be deemed unsafe. Buy one case of water for everyone in your family and stash it under the bed, in the basement, or in the closet (somewhere out of sight and out of mind so you won't use this cache as your go-to supply for car trips).

Water is the one thing you'll always wish you had in abundance. Some of it you'll drink, some of it you'll need to boil, some of it you'll use to bathe. You really can't have enough.

Your food on hand should be shelf stable and require no additional preparation. It's likely the power will be out, and if you're living in an apartment or similar enclosed location, building a fire won't always be possible. High-calorie, high-protein, and complex-carb meals will be the best. Watch some old-school cowboy movies for inspiration. Stock up on some cans of beans and beef stew, beef jerky, and trail mix. Look into Paleo kits too. Extreme athletes and CrossFit enthusiasts swear by them. I recommend you purchase at least one to see if you like them. On a budget, it's much cheaper to modify and make your own. Purchase the ingredients you like and vacuum-pack individually sealed single servings.

2. Have some extra bags of ice in the freezer. King-size cubes will last you longer than the ice-maker variety. Ice will help keep your refrigerator and freezer functional for a day or two after the power goes out. Fill up a few Tupperware containers with water and freeze overnight. Keep as many frozen bricks in your freezer as you can. Ice does more than chill your drinks; there are medical uses (blister burns, splinter removal, oral numbness to treat tooth pain, and soft tissue injury to name a few), so having some on hand will prove beneficial to your cause.

3. A go bag is, in layman's terms, the bag you grab when it's time to go, as in *right now*—when the time required to plan, prep, and pack will decrease your chance of survival. The premise is such that your go bag is always packed, ready, and waiting with the essentials you will need to survive for two nights and three days in the outdoor terrain of your approximate location and in current local climate. No creature comforts— just the necessities to survive, contained in a packaged weight, affording you the ability to remain mobile. Keep in mind that your packing list may change depending upon the time of year, the season, your location, your medical requirements, and your physical ability. You should be well versed in terms of your bag's content, knowledgeable of item location, and organized for ease of use.

Everyone who is physically able to carry a pack should have one. Your own individual packing list may vary based on personal preference and necessity. (See #8 below for individual ideas.) If you only do one thing to prepare beyond your in-home food and water storage, this is it. This is what you need. Everyone should have one. Build or buy one today. Many pre-customized options are available online.

4. A fully stocked first aid kit is a priority requirement for any emergency action plan. One should always strive to have as much medical and trauma training, resources, and equipment on hand as possible. Medical equipment can be cost prohibitive, but medical knowledge can be as cheap as a YouTube search. Being first aid and CPR certified (or at least capable) could literally save a life one day and could increase your own survival rate exponentially.

Staph infection is both silent and deadly, and if you find yourself unable to acquire professional medical attention or prescription medication, it is critical you possess, at the very least, the medical know-how and resources to clean, disinfect, and treat a cut, scrape, or sprain.

5. Man's best friend. Despite all the technological advances of the past century, the best home defense option available to you is still a mid- to full-size dog—especially one with specific (sentry) training tailored to your needs. In addition to being naturally defensive of their owner and territorial of their property, a dog can offer companionship in an otherwise lonesome scenario. (Think *I Am Legend* versus *Castaway*.) If you

already have a dog (even an untrained small dog), you're already ahead of the game. The yelp of a small pup directed toward an unwelcome visitor may be all that's required to bring attention to clandestine activities and thwart their evil intentions.

6. In every home, there should be an identified safe room, a last line of defense where you and your loved ones can safely barricade yourselves until help can arrive. There is no limit to the amount of money one can spend on the construction of such a sanctuary.

For the rest of us, we have door wedges. These specific door wedges were designed by EMS units to keep the heavy industrial doors propped open during their rescue operations. As good as they are at propping doors open, they are even better at wedging doors closed. Jam one of these under a closed door, and there is no way an intruder is pushing the door open. You gain additional security if you wedge one between the door and the frame too. (Just make sure you're on the side of the door that can see the hinges.)

For a few dollars more, some door wedges also come with an alarm feature, but if you can sleep through an intruder trying to kick down the door, I'm not sure the alarm of an AA battery will stir you from your slumber.

7. Today, all our communication devices require a charge. Assuming an EMP was not the cause of the crisis you're currently facing, your mobile devices will be critical to helping you negotiate your way to a better day. (Read *One Second After* by William Forstchen.) While a few commercial venues with backup generators may be able to facilitate the needs of the few, they most certainly will not be able to cater to the needs of the many. So skip the Starbucks iPhone-charging line and invest in a universal solar-charging unit.

8. Take the time to go through all the contents your go bag has available, and identify anything inside you think you may need to use in your home. Purchase in duplicate what's in the bag, but do your best to *not* use what's already provided. If you don't already have the basics of a lights-out scenario in your home, then you should most certainly acquire the necessary provisions of matches, candles, flashlights, and batteries. Other items of mention may also include a multi-tool, a home improvement

tool kit, survival literature, pocketknives, prepackaged meals such as MREs, or water purification tablets.

9. Promote a positive protective posture. Employ aspects of deterrence in hopes of promoting transference. The pros of a home security system far outweigh any cons. The innovation available on today's modern marketplace can match almost any imagination, and yet there are endless options available to work within the confines of even the tightest budget.

A good security system will alert, notify, and confirm the something/someone out of the ordinary with enough lead time for you to respond accordingly. More importantly, a positive security posture promotes one very important fact to the casual observer: you take your security seriously.

In times of crisis, necessity sometimes lends itself to immoral action. Social predators, looters, and criminals of opportunity will always reveal themselves when the social order is in chaos. Like lions stalking a herd of gazelle, they will evaluate the masses to identify the easy prey versus those who pose a challenge, a target drawn on the weakest and most vulnerable first.

However, criminals often act with childhood methodology in that hard work isn't warranted unless there's a guaranteed reward for their effort; otherwise, only the least bit of effort shall be asserted. So forget for a moment that in this crisis scenario you face, there is no power and your system doesn't work. The camera dome above your door and next to your window says something succinct about your home: "Another target will be easier."

10. Despite the fact that movies and television will have you convinced otherwise, a weapon will not be required or necessary for your survival in nearly every conceivable crisis you will realistically face. However, as a former soldier, I would be lying to you if I told you I didn't have a weapon as part of my own emergency action plan. If you decide to include a weapon in your inventory, please familiarize and train yourself to the fullest extent possible, and employ safety, rational thought, and sound moral guidance in all aspects of its use.

With all aspects considered, my final recommendation is the Mossberg

500 JIC. Mossberg took their understanding of emergency preparedness to heart when naming their Model 500 JIC, which stands for *Just in Case*. A shotgun such as this serves many masters. It not only acts as a psychological deterrent to the social predator when they hear the unmistakable *chuh-chink* of the slide chambering a round, and, being honest, you don't exactly have to be surgical when firing it either.

This weapon is equally effective at dropping the bad guy or the flock of ducks flying overhead for dinner. This weapon is lightweight, easy to use, and gets the job done. Just in case you really find yourself in need (or want) of a versatile and dependable weapon, having this on hand will serve you well. Cost: $479.

Every Day a School Day . . .

Your individual list of needs, wants, and desires may be completely different from mine, but what's most important is that you're forward thinking to a scenario you can help frame and manage before you find yourself whiplashed by the harsh reality of whatever unfortunate predicament life prescribes.

One advantage of advance preparation is that you afford yourself the extra time needed to get yourself ready both mentally and physically for whatever tomorrow may bring. Preparation requires forethought and action, and if you've read this far, you have already improved your odds for a successful outcome. Real life is different from T-ball. No participation trophies here. Big-boy rules are in effect. Expect the worst, and hope for the best. Know that problems will arise, and when life breaks bad, it often finds you when you are least expecting and most ill prepared.

Remember that survivors and winners have something in common: they both visualize victory, even when hope seems forsaken and the odds are stacked against you. Champion poker player Jack Straus embodies this philosophy with one of his key quotes after winning the World Series of Poker: "I had a chip, and a chair, so I knew I had a chance."

Hard work and sacrifice must be accepted as your reality. In the end, your commendation for action will not come in the form of applause, congratulations, and certainly not a trophy but rather in knowing that you and your loved ones will sleep in peace some future night because of your preparation today.

PROTECTIVE PREPAREDNESS

Here are the top twenty-five questions for you to include in your personal threat assessment checklist for staying safe in life:

1. **Do you have a family readiness plan?**

   Why this is important: A family readiness plan is your dedicated plan for what to do in an emergency. This plan may include challenge question-and-answer templates, which will help to serve as an extra level of authentication in an unsolicited digital communication but may also be useful in a proof-of-life scenario. A family readiness plan may also include a family reunification plan for how and where the family will get back together should family members not be together when a crisis becomes realized. A family readiness plan may also serve as a to-do list should the home need to be evacuated due to fire, earthquake, or some other form of a natural disaster. Anything and everything that may be important to your specific family dynamic in an emergency should be covered in your family readiness plan. Plenty of templates and additional insights are available online. Please do your part to prepare.

2. **Do you know what to do/what not to do when a cop pulls you over?**

   Why this is important: Despite what the local news and social media may lead you to believe, 99.9 percent of police officers are good, honest, hardworking people who have a very difficult job to do. In an effort of goodwill for the work they are doing and with respect for the very real danger they sometimes face, the following are considered best practices to follow when your vehicle is pulled over by a law enforcement officer:

   Turn off your engine.

   Turn off your radio.

   Roll down your window.

   Turn on the interior light.

Keep your hands on the steering wheel.

Answer all questions with *sir* or *ma'am*.

3. **Do you know CPR/first aid?**

    Why this is important: There is really no excuse for not being certified in first aid or CPR. Even if you're afraid of the sight of blood or you get faint at the sight of seeing someone injured, the practical takeaways of a blood-free and trauma-free first aid/CPR course are lifelong lessons that very well may help you to save someone's life someday and very well may help you to save your own.

4. **Have you taken a firearm familiarization course?**

    Why this is important: Even if you hate guns or have no interest in taking up shooting as a hobby, becoming familiar with a weapon is an excellent way to avoid making a deadly mistake with a handgun. Even if you yourself have zero interest in firearms, you never know when your children, the friends of your children, or some other acquaintance may willingly or unwillingly be forced to come face-to-face with a firearm.

5. **Have you ever taken a driving course?**

    Why this is important: So many deaths are due to road-related injury from accidents that it is truly surprising that more people are not flocking to offensive and defensive driving courses. Not only are they *a lot* of fun (ever do a J-turn at eighty miles per hour or an e-brake 180 on a sandy desert road?), but they are a dynamic skill set that will greatly improve your situational awareness and comfort level with the full range of your car's capability every time you get behind the wheel.

6. **Do you know how far back from a vehicle you should be when you are driving?**

    Why this is important: As a general rule, one car length for every ten miles per hour you are traveling will provide you with enough time and distance to come to a complete stop. Modern-day vehicles have a much shorter braking distance than older cars, but road conditions, climate, and the unpredictable maneuverings of other vehicles in your operating environment may also play a factor. When in doubt, the more time and distance between cars, the better. The faster you are going, the more separation is required, and *never tailgate.*

7. **Do you know how far back to stop from the car in front of you at a red light?**

   Why this is important: Whenever you are required to come to a complete stop and there is a car in front of you, you will want to make sure you are always able to see where the rear tires of the car in front of you touch the road. If you are any closer, you will not have the adequate amount of space you will need to make an emergency maneuver should you need to make a quick escape or have enough room to move out of the way of a vehicle that isn't slowing down and is about to barrel into you.

8. **Have you enabled dual authentication on all your devices and accounts?**

   Why this is important: Difficult as it may be to hack your bank account information, it is insanely easy to hack your fitness tracker. A novice can do it in a few minutes, and a professional can do it in a few seconds. And while it's true that hackers care less about your calorie count than they do your credit account, if you're using the same username and password for one as you are for the other, you are putting yourself at unnecessary risk. By turning on dual-authentication factors for all your accounts, you can not only rest assured that you are employing the necessary safeguards to protect your information, but you are also more likely to be made aware of illegitimate attempts to access your information.

9. **When was the last time you checked your credit score?**

   Why this is important: Not only is routinely monitoring your credit score considered good financial management, but it also helps to ensure that nothing illegitimate has been attached to your account. If you do find something wrong, your personal credit report will most often come with ways for you to make a dispute and correct whatever mistakes or oversights may have been made.

10. **When was the last time you field-tested a fire extinguisher?**

    Why this is important: If, at any time in your life, you plan to cook in the kitchen, barbecue on your grill, light a match, or light a candle, not only should you have a fire extinguisher in the home, but you should practice using one at least once a year. You do not want the first time using a fire extinguisher to be a literal trial by fire. So go buy two of them today. Practice with one, and save the other one for when it is needed most. Remember: PASS. Pull the pin. Aim the nozzle at the base of the fire. Squeeze the trigger. Sweep from side to side.

11. **Have you bought your own domain name?**

    Why this is important: If you don't buy your own domain name, someone else will. Today, more than ever, everyone should register, own, and use their own domain name. Once a domain name is claimed, it is almost impossible to reclaim, so stop what you are doing and claim your domain name now.

12. **When was the last time you googled yourself?**

    Why this is important: Googling yourself is the first step in vulnerability awareness. Most people are shocked to learn how much information about themselves is publicly available online. Did someone mention you in a blog post? Are those pictures of your kids at soccer practice? Did you know how much you paid for your home is on a local real estate website? Ignorance is more risk than bliss. I strongly recommend making a protective practice to conduct some opposition research on yourself on a routine basis. What you don't know *can* hurt you.

13. **How many different routes do you take between your daily routines and home?**

    Why this is important: Not only will taking different routes to and from home, work, the gym, and school make your everyday movements less predictable, but it also challenges your brain to be engaged in your activity and therefore avoid becoming complacent. The more things you can do to combat complacency, the more aware and mindful of your surroundings you will become, and the more likely you will be to identify the pre-incident indicators of harm.

14. **What did you do today to challenge yourself?**

    Why this is important: Every single time we do something challenging, we reinvest in the positive value we place in ourselves and in our purpose. The more comfortable we become with being uncomfortable, the more willingness we will display in confronting those concerns that warrant our attention, and the less likely we will be to engage in avoidance behaviors.

15. **How often do you let your gas tank get below half full?**

    Why this is important: How someone does something is how they do everything. Most people who allow for their fuel level to drop below half are equally likely to shirk their responsibility in other areas of their life as well. Take responsibility for your own safety by making sure that certain standards are met and managed—not most of the time but *all* the time.

16. **How often do you inspect what you expect?**

    Why this is important: We all like to think we are really good at spotting a liar and a fraud. Truth is, we are not. Our survival as a species is mostly based on trust. Throughout the history of human evolution, trusting genes beat out paranoid genes nearly 100 percent of the time. This default setting of trust is what makes the fraudsters and the con men so effective. They prey on this innate weakness, this intrinsic vulnerability. The only proven safeguard we have in our arsenal of protection is to do our own due diligence. The onus is on us to ensure that what is being measured is actually being met.

17. **Do you know where you are?**

    Why this is important: You may be confident about your exact location when you are in your own home or around your own town, but what about those times when you are anywhere else? Everyone knows to call 911 in an emergency. What everyone doesn't know is when you call 911 from your cell phone, the dispatcher does not see your actual location like they would if you are calling from a landline. On a mobile phone, your location information comes from a cell tower, which could put you miles away from where you actually are and could send help to the wrong location. To help correct this concern, always communicate your exact position so that first responders will know exactly where to find you. "I am at 281 Monroe Street in the back bedroom of the second floor."

18. **How regularly do you check the readiness of the spare tire in your car?**

   Why this is important: Too many of us assume the safeguards we have in place will perform perfectly when we need them the most. One of the more common roadside concerns occurs when getting a flat tire and then going to grab their spare tire, only to realize that they don't have one or that the one they have is inoperable. To help reduce this risk, make the first day of each month your dedicated day to make sure that everything from the spare tire in your trunk to the batteries in your flashlight are operational and ready for use.

19. **Do you have emergency supplies prepacked and ready to go?**

   Why this is important: Prepare for the unexpected by packing two easy-to-carry bags, and leave one in your car and one in your house. Ideally, these kits should contain items tailored to your personal needs. You can find prepacked options online, or you can make your own. A few basics to include are water, nonperishable food items, a first aid kit, a cell phone charger, a blanket, an extra jacket and pair of shoes, candles, matches, a flashlight and batteries, money, and (digital) copies of documents you might need in the event that your personal belongings are lost.

20. **What's your Starbucks name?**

   Why this is important: Coffeehouses use your name to keep drink orders straight, but then they call out your name for the world to hear and send you out the door with your name emblazoned on the side of the cup for all to see. Embrace your inner Carrie Mathison and try using a cover name.

21. **What's your plan when you're alone and unsure?**

    Why this is important: Always have a plan. When in doubt, call someone. Don't want to call someone? Use your phone's voice recorder or call your own phone line and leave yourself a message. Don't know what to say? Just look around and start describing what you're seeing. This serves a dual role of promoting both aspects of awareness and deterrence while at the same time adding the extra insurance of capturing it all on tape.

22. **Do you know the difference between a travel alert and a travel warning?**

    Why this is important: It can be easy to conflate the two, but they really are quite different. Travel alerts are always issued for a defined period of time, whereas travel warnings are in place until further notice. The State Department will issue travel warnings when they want U.S. citizens to consider very carefully whether they should travel to a country because of a chronic threat like disease or terrorism. Travel alerts are for short-term events, like local elections or planned protests, and are intended to raise the level of awareness to those who may be planning travel to a country.

23. **When was your last social media checkup?**

    Why this is important: All friends are not created equal, and what you share on social media is not always secure. It's important to take full advantage of the privacy settings your social media services have to offer. When it comes to protecting our privacy online, too many of us do the bare minimum. The privacy and security settings of your favorite social media applications are constantly being updated. You should be auditing these settings at regular intervals to make sure you have complete control over what is being shared.

24. **Where are you most vulnerable?**

    Why this is important: When was the last time you conducted a FOIL assessment of your own home? Everyone likes to believe that crime will happen to someone else. However low you may assess your own level of risk, always remember that none of us are risk-free. Identify those areas in your life that are most susceptible to exploitation, and then do whatever you can to help mitigate that risk.

25. **What are you doing to reduce risk and prevent violence?**

Why this is important: Everyday safety requires the participation of everyone. One hour of every day should be spent improving your knowledge, your skill set, and your outlook on not only your own life but of the world around you. The more aware you are of your own environment and the more mindful you become of the world around you, the more likely you will be able to identify the pre-incident indicators—the warning signs—of harm. And when moments matter most, those precious seconds may become the difference between safety and consequence.

Acknowledgments

I would like to take a moment to thank everyone who made this process possible:

To my friends Andre, Aneesh, Katie, and Kim; to my sisters, Kathryn, Monica, and Sara; and to countless colleagues who were always willing to entertain my all-hours texts, phone calls, and emails with their own answers and insights.

To my agent, Jenny Bent, my editor, Marc Resnick, and to my publisher, St. Martin's Press, whose equal parts of compassion and criticism made me a better writer, a better communicator, and a better storyteller.

To my father, Sam, who showed me what it meant to be a man.

To my mother, Suzanne, who never wavered in her belief of my ability to be the best at whatever I set out to do.

And to every single one of you who, knowingly or otherwise, helped me to help others.

To all of you, *thank you.*

I could not have done this without you.

Index